AF575144

THE WINNING EDGE IN BASKETBALL

How to Coach Special Situation Plays

THE WINNING EDGE IN BASKETBALL

How to Coach Special Situation Plays

William A. Healey
and
Joseph W. Hartley

Parker Publishing Company, Inc. West Nyack, New York

PARKER PUBLISHING COMPANY, INC.
West Nyack, N.Y.

Library of Congress Cataloging in Publication Data

Healey, William Albert.
The winning edge in basketball.

1. Basketball coaching. I. Hartley, Joseph W., joint author. II. Title.
GV885.3.H42 796.32'32 72-13044
ISBN 0-13-961334-X

Printed in the United States of America

DEDICATION

To the boys and young men who played on our teams, because they taught us so much more than we could give them.

How This Book Can Create a Winning Edge for You

Each coach owes it to his players to prepare them to meet the opposition on even terms. If he can give them an advantage by preparing them to meet any and all special situations, he is providing them with the *winning edge.*

These special situations can be categorized as out-of-bounds plays, jump balls, offensive and defensive foul line plays, overtime plays, overtime tip-off plays, last second shots, delayed offensive plays, special presses and other unique situations.

By anticipating and preparing for these situations ahead of time, the players will have a decided advantage. In many instances, a properly executed play or some specially worked-out strategy will result in securing or retaining possession of the ball, scoring a basket or preventing a score.

The coach cannot make plans to meet these situations as the occasion arises or on the spur of the moment, because the tension created by a close ball game is not conducive to rational and concrete thinking by either players or coaches. The noise and confusion which exist during a time-out period (at which time the coach is usually attempting to explain to the players the strategy to be used to meet the special situation) make it virtually impossible for everyone involved to understand clearly what is to be done. Consequently, many games are lost because the players have not been given instructions on how to meet these special situations.

A team must be prepared to deal with a change of play or strategy which might be employed by the opposition either offensively or defensively at any time during the game. While it may be true that all eventualities cannot be foreseen, the smart coach can anticipate many of them and prepare his team to meet them. By so doing, he is giving them the edge they may need to produce the win. Many games are won or lost by one or two points, and the inability of a team to cope with the special situation brought about by the opposition and the game situation may result in the opposition scoring these points.

The selection of a play or maneuver is the responsibility of the coach, and his selection should be based not only on the abilities of the players to execute the play, but also on whether the play will be the correct one to use for the special situation which exists at the time. It is with this in mind that numerous plays for these special situations will be shown and discussed. The coach can select the plays which fit his material and ones which his players will have the ability to learn and execute.

There are several basic principles which should be adhered to with regard to the use of any play or maneuver for special situations.

(1) The play or maneuver should be relatively simple to execute so that all the players are sure to make the correct moves and decisions which will result in a coordinated effort.

(2) The play or maneuver should be one that can be executed in a specific amount of time. For example, in the case of the last second shot, the play should be timed so that there will not be enough time left after the shot is taken for the other team to rebound and get away a shot of their own. On the other hand, the play should not take so long that time will run out before the shot is attempted.

(3) The play or maneuver should fit the personnel available. A play that requires a skill which is beyond the ability of any one player will result in failure. It is therefore important that the play or maneuver be one that will not result in failure. It is also important that the play or maneuver be one that will coincide with the individual and group abilities of all personnel. A play that is too intricate and complex may fool the opposition, but it may also fool the ones that are using it, because of their inability to perform the skills necessary for the play to be executed successfully.

(4) There should be an alternate play or option, should it appear that the play or maneuver will be unsuccessful before it is completed. The play should allow for some opportunity for individual initiative, which could result in a free-lance maneuver by any one player should the occasion arise or conditions warrant such a move.

(5) The play or maneuver should provide an opportunity to guard against the fact that the opposition could take advantage of the maneuver or play if it is not successful.

(6) The play or maneuver which is used should fit the situation. The play selected should be one that will, because of existing

circumstances, be successful if conditions remain the same and there is no change in strategy by the opposition which would tend to diminish the effectiveness of such a play.

(7) The number of such plays which are included in a team's repertoire should be limited, and those that are used should be well rehearsed. It is better to have only a few maneuvers and execute them well than to have many and execute them poorly.

(8) All special plays or maneuvers should be those which the players have confidence in and believe will produce the desired results in a given situation. The players should have faith in them to the extent that they are willing to accept them.

It is the intent of this book to present plays and maneuvers for special situations which might arise during a game, with the supposition that many of these plays can be prepared for in advance, thereby enhancing the possibility of completing the play or maneuver successfully. The coach can select the play that will best serve his team in a given situation, and this selection will be based on the team personnel and the adaptability of the maneuver or play to the situation. A team's increased ability to cope with special situations by using predetermined plays, strategy and maneuvers will provide a distinct advantage which can result in the winning edge that is needed to win the game.

Every practice session and every scrimmage held should be interrupted and placed in a special situation at various intervals. This can help the team become more adept at the less frequently occurring special situations. For example, the coach can interrupt the scrimmage and give the situation. It might be team A's ball at this spot; score is 67 to 69 with team B leading–and three seconds are left on the clock. Any of the special situations can be rehearsed in this manner, and they should be, until mastered to perfection. This also adds variety and spice to practice and scrimmage sessions. It helps make the practices challenging and interesting. It gives the players interesting discussion topics for locker-room lawyer antics and adds to team morale.

Bill Healey

Joe Hartley

ACKNOWLEDGMENTS

To make acknowledgments by name to everyone who has contributed to this book or books that the authors have written would be impossible. Certainly the authors owe a debt of gratitude to all their former high school and college coaches. The players who played for both authors throughout the years each contributed something in their own way. Many of these players have gone into successful careers as coaches, teachers, businessmen, professional athletes and professional men, and one such former player has made two trips to the moon. To have been a small part of their lives is greatly appreciated by the authors, and their contributions have made this book possible.

We are also indebted to all the coaches with whom we have come in contact throughout our careers. These contacts have been as colleagues in the profession of basketball coaching, as opponents, as fellow clinicians in the many coaching schools and professional meetings, all of which have contributed some additional fact to our basketball knowledge.

Any book, any effort, any production or manuscript that is worthwhile always requires the cooperation and teamwork of many people. To every such person involved, we express appreciation. Then last, but certainly not least, there are the "two coaches," our wives, Ruth and Beryl, who have patiently "coached the two coaches" who wrote this book throughout their careers.

CONTENTS

KEY TO DIAGRAMS

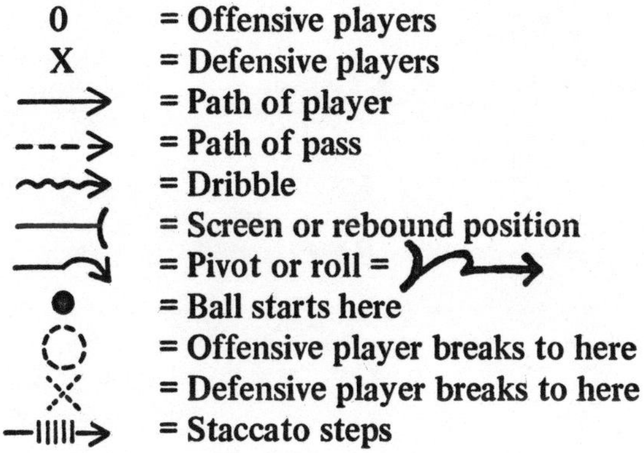

0	= Offensive players
X	= Defensive players
⟶	= Path of player
- - ->	= Path of pass
~~>	= Dribble
—(	= Screen or rebound position
—↘	= Pivot or roll =)↗⟶
●	= Ball starts here
◌	= Offensive player breaks to here
X (dotted)	= Defensive player breaks to here
—|||||→	= Staccato steps

THE WINNING EDGE IN BASKETBALL

How to Coach Special Situation Plays

ONE

OUT-OF-BOUNDS PLAYS FOR THE OFFENSIVE END LINE (Box Formations, Line Formations, Triangle Formations, Plays Against Zones)

Out-of bounds plays should be part of every basketball team's repertoire.

Purpose of Out-of-Bounds Plays

The primary purpose of any out-of-bounds play is first of all to gain possession of the ball after the pass-in, and not necessarily to score a basket. Although gaining possession of the ball is of extreme importance, it is also possible at times to score a quick basket by using a predetermined play, because the offensive team is placed in an advantageous position during an out-of-bounds situation. This situation or advantage is especially true under the offensive basket. For example, usually a team will have the ball out-of-bounds under the offensive basket from five to ten times per game. Therefore, if a team is able to score on half of these opportunities, it is well worth the time and effort spent in learning and practicing these out-of-bounds plays. Properly executed out-of-bounds plays can provide "the winning edge" in the close games and will more than compensate for the time spent in drilling on them.

Reasons for Use of Out-of-Bounds Plays

The reasons for the use of out-of-bounds plays may be listed as follows:

1. A good out-of-bounds play will not only have several options but will also have a safety value, so that ball possession can be a certainty should the scoring play not materialize.

2. A specific out-of-bounds play will assure every player a certain basic assignment which he is required to perform. He cannot free-lance because the success of the play depends upon a specific predetermined move on his part, which in turn will determine the moves of his teammates. No one can shirk his duty, but everyone must contribute to not only the success of the play but also toward obtaining possession of the ball.

3. A successful out-of-bounds play which results in a basket will tend to upset the opponents, shake their confidence and generally cause them to lose their poise. Several such scoring plays will have a demoralizing effect upon the opponents.

4. All out-of-bounds plays, if they are executed correctly, require teamwork which is in keeping with what is being attempted in the offensive pattern of the well-disciplined team. The out-of-bounds play gives the players a feeling of team play and a realization of the necessity of working together for a common goal.

5. If the out-of-bounds play is used correctly, it is possible to place the players so that they are in those areas where they can function most efficiently. The best shooters can be maneuvered into a position where they will be attempting the shot; therefore, a high percentage on all the shots taken will be obtained.

6. The use of the out-of-bounds play makes it possible to position the players in such a way that advantage may be taken of any defensive weakness on the part of the opponent.

7. The out-of-bounds play makes it possible to utilize the services of the team's best passer, as the same player is able to make the pass-in from out-of-bounds every time the opportunity presents itself.

8. The out-of-bounds play is conducive to team unity in the execution of a play. This is a deciding factor in the ultimate success

of the play, and is brought about by the fact that the players start the play only upon the signal given by the player who has the ball out-of-bounds and makes the pass-in.

Factors to Consider in the Use of the Out-of-Bounds Play

An out-of-bounds play is worthless unless it accomplishes its purpose; therefore there are several factors to consider when planning any out-of-bounds play.

1. Every precaution should be made to prevent the interception of the pass during all stages of play.
2. An attempt should be made to make as few passes as possible before the shot is attempted.
3. The player should get as close to the basket as possible before the shot is taken.
4. The pass-in from out-of-bounds is most important, and as in nearly all out-of-bounds plays, the only pass which is made, before the shot is taken, so it should be as accurate and as safe as possible. If there is any question of interception, the passer should turn down the scoring opportunity in favor of just gaining possession of the ball.
5. The shooter is a very important player in the execution of out-of-bounds plays and should be given every protection and every opportunity to obtain the best shot possible. This means that the other players must perform their tasks well by screening, cutting and faking, so that as much pressure as possible is taken off of the shooter, enabling him to obtain the high percentage shot.
6. Good floor balance should be maintained during the time the out-of-bounds play is being executed and also after it has been completed.
7. Good rebounding position should be a part of the out-of-bounds play.
8. The unsuccessful out-of-bounds play should not enable the defensive team to capitalize on a mistake.
9. A good secondary move should be part of the play in case the shot does not materialize.
10. The out-of-bounds play should always allow for good defensive coverage in case the pass is intercepted.

Learning the Out-of-Bounds Plays

The out-of-bounds plays should be easy to learn and simple enough so that an interchange of positions is possible. As a result of this situation, the same players will not need to play the same positions each time the play is used.

Selection of Out-of-Bounds Plays

There are, of course, many types of out-of-bounds plays. These plays, as is true with the offense, should be selected on a team's ability and the strong points of the players. Each play should have options or several scoring possibilities, as well as a safety valve, so that ball possession is assured if the scoring part of the play is not successful.

Success of Out-of-Bounds Plays

While it is true that there are many formations from which out-of-bounds plays may be started, all of them involve and utilize screens, fakes and cuts. Through the use of these components, opportunities are provided for the defense to become confused, enabling the screens, cuts and fakes to result in a successful out-of-bounds play.

The success of any out-of-bounds play will be determined to a large degree by the position of the players on the court. As soon as the official indicates which team has possession of the ball out-of-bounds, the players should take their positions immediately. Every player must be in the correct position and be ready to initiate the execution of the play when the signal to begin is given. It must be a coordinated effort, and the play's success will depend to a large extent on all players moving as a unit, with each player performing his specific task.

Putting the Ball in Play

There are various ways in which the ball may be put into play on all out-of-bounds situations. Many coaches have the same individual player handle the ball on every out-of-bounds situation no matter where the play originates. This is probably the simplest and easiest way. Whenever possible, the player who has the best peripheral vision, and who is the most adept at selecting the best option and passing the ball in to the proper receiver at the proper time, should take the ball at the out-of-bounds position. Some players have a knack for this type of pass selection, and if such a player exists on the team, his talent should be used at every opportunity. This practice consumes a certain amount of time, and, as a result, allows the offensive players to situate themselves in the desired positions on the floor.

The signal to start the movement of the players can begin in various ways, the most popular being when the player who has the ball out-of-bounds slaps the ball or fakes a pass-in. Other signals could be dropping the ball in a quick dribble, calling a number, a color, a formation or the name of a player. Signals have to be adapted to the players and what each squad responds to best. This is a technique that will differ from squad to squad, and each year from team to team.

Offensive End Line Out-of-Bounds Plays

This chapter deals primarily with out-of-bounds plays for the offensive end line or the front court base line.

The offensive end line out-of-bounds plays can be placed into the following categories: vertical line formations, horizontal line formations, box formations, diamond formations and miscellaneous formations, which include the triangle and the oblique formations. Plays against both the zone and man-to-man defenses must be available from all formations. There is an added advantage if several of the out-of-bounds plays originate from the same formation, as this will further confuse the defense.

VERTICAL LINE FORMATIONS

There are many coaches who will remember the vertical line formation plays as the first out-of-bounds plays they learned in their basketball schooling and playing days. These plays are still used, and are just as good as they ever were. These plays are most effective against the teams that play the man-to-man defense; however, they can also be very effective against shifting man-to-man and zone defenses. Perfect execution, correct timing and expert faking are the ingredients for the successful use of this type of out-of-bounds play.

The vertical line formation is a stacking of four players in-bounds in a line which extends from near the base line and toward the mid-court line or the free throw line. Present day rules give two advantages to this formation. The first advantage is the result of a rule which states that a ball out-of-bounds under the basket and in the 12-foot free throw lane area, should be taken out-of-bounds at the point to the right or left of where the free throw lane intersects the base line, whichever is nearer. This requirement places the vertical formation out to either side of the basket and on a line parallel to the free throw lane lines. This gives the players more operational space, and prevents the "thrower-in" from being hindered by obstructed vision, which he would encounter if he were to throw the ball in-bounds from directly underneath the basket. The second advantage results from a rule which states that offensive players in a vertical line or stacked position are not required to allow a defensive player a position between them if requested. This means the players may stack the formation as tight as they want, or they may spread it if they find it advantageous to do so.

Diagram 1-1. Here the players line up in a vertical line position to the right side of the free throw lane and in a straight line with the player who has the ball out-of-bounds. It is important that the players not be crowded. They should space themselves so there is approximately one full stride between them, yet not enough room to allow a defensive player a position in this space. The first player in-bounds—in this case No. 4—takes his position about two or two-and-one-half strides in-bounds from the end line and directly in front of the player with the ball. No. 3 takes the ball out-of-bounds. Players No. 5, 1 and 2 line up behind No. 4 at the designated distance, as previously mentioned. Usually the last player in the line will not be stationed any farther toward the mid-court lines than the top of the free throw circle. No attempt to obtain a screen or a rub-off is made on this play. Its effectiveness is dependent upon quick and perfect execution, exact timing and expert faking by all the players.

Diagram 1-1

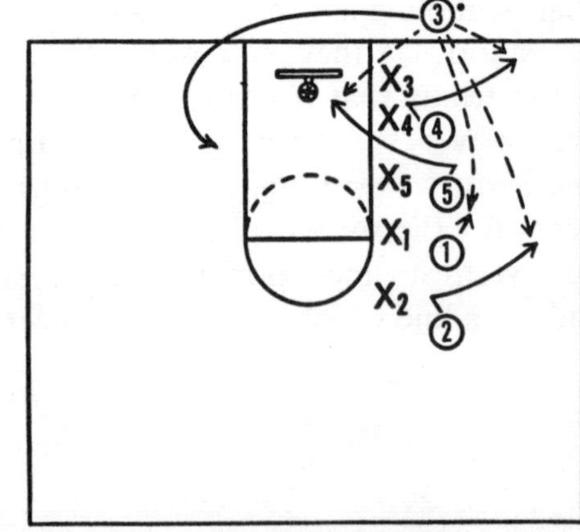

At the instant the team knows they have the ball at this particular out-of-bounds position, the players quickly line up in the vertical line formation. No. 3 takes the ball out-of-bounds and gives the prearranged starting signal (a slap of the ball, a fake, a drop dribble or an audible signal). No. 4 keys the play by his fake and move. He may indicate what his real move will be by a prearranged signal. His ultimate move determines the moves of Nos. 5, 1 and 2. For example if No. 4 fakes to the left and breaks to the right, then No. 5 should fake to the right and break to his left, as shown in the diagram. If either No. 4 or 5 are open, No. 3 can pass either one the ball. Usually, No. 1 will fake and break in the opposite direction of No. 5, and No. 2 would reverse the action of No. 1. However, experience and time have shown that it is best to have No. 2 reverse the actions of No. 5, with No. 1 remaining motionless until the other players have cleared the area and moved away from their starting positions. No. 1 should then move wherever necessary to receive the pass from No. 3. The surprising thing about this play is that No. 1 is usually wide open. He needs only to take one or two steps toward the ball, and be open for an easy pass-in from No. 3 and an easy lay-up shot. The option possibilities for No. 3's pass-in are shown. It is advisable to have No. 3 move in-bounds immediately after making the pass-in, so that he may also become involved in the progress of the play. For example, the diagram also shows No. 3 breaking from out-of-bounds and to the left of the basket for a possible return pass. He could be in a very advantageous position to accept this return pass, which could result in a scoring opportunity if the ball has been passed in to Nos. 1, 2 or 5. If a shot is taken as a result of any one of these opportunities, note that Nos. 4, 5, 1 and 2 can all move immediately into strategic rebound positions for follow-up shot possibilities. There are many variations and scoring opportunities from this formation, and the following diagrams will show some of them. The effectiveness of the play will depend to a great extent on proper timing, faking and the quickness with which the players move. Scoring opportunities will be available to Nos. 4 and 5, but the player in the No. 1 position will be free for the high percentage shot more often than any of the other players in the line. This play is shown on the right side of the free-throw lane. The same formation can be used from the left side of the lane, and should be practiced and rehearsed from that side as often as from the right side.

Diagram 1-2. Here the play is executed in an orthodox manner. No. 3 takes the ball out-of-bounds as the players quickly assume their vertical line positions about two strides apart. Using a prearranged signal, Nos. 4 and 1 fake to the left, and then break to the right. Nos. 5 and 2 fake to the right and break to the left. No. 3 passes in to whichever player is open and then moves in-bounds immediately, as shown in the diagram. Again, No. 1 is more likely to be the open receiver, especially if the defense plays the straight man-to-man defense and attempts to line up the defensive man between the offensive man and the basket. The confusion experienced by the defense as a result of these offensive moves, always seems to present the player playing the No. 1 position, as shown in the diagram, with the best chance of being free for the pass, and as a result the best scoring opportunity.

Diagram 1-3. In this diagram, the players line up in the vertical line formation quickly, and by prearranged signal. This signal may be given by No. 4. When No. 3 gives the signal to start the play, Nos. 4 and 1 fake to the right and break to the left. At the same time, Nos. 5 and 2 fake to the left and break to the right. No. 3 passes the ball in-bounds to the player who is free for the pass, and then moves in-bounds as shown in the diagram. In this situation, No. 1 will sometimes not be able to free himself, and in fact may find himself being very closely guarded. If this is true, he will usually find it to his advantage to stand still, or delay his move until he sees what commitment the defense has made. If No. 1 does break to the left after making the fake to his right, this usually leaves No. 5 with the best opening–although, at times, No. 4 will have a quick scoring opportunity.

Diagram 1-4. The movement that No. 3 makes after passing the ball in-bounds is important. He can move in-bounds after making the pass, as shown in Diagrams 1-1, 1-2 and 1-3. This move, as shown in these previous diagrams, was to the opposite side of the basket. However, he can change the pattern and break in the same direction as his pass with the intention of receiving a return pass which could result in a possible scoring opportunity. In this diagram, No. 3 has passed the ball in to No. 4, and followed the pass as described. By

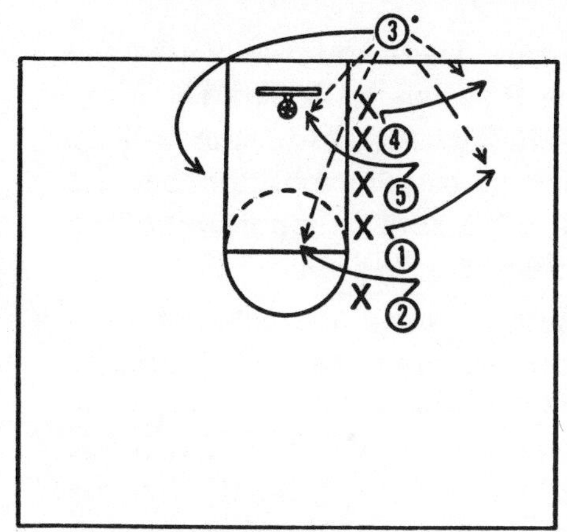

Diagram 1-2

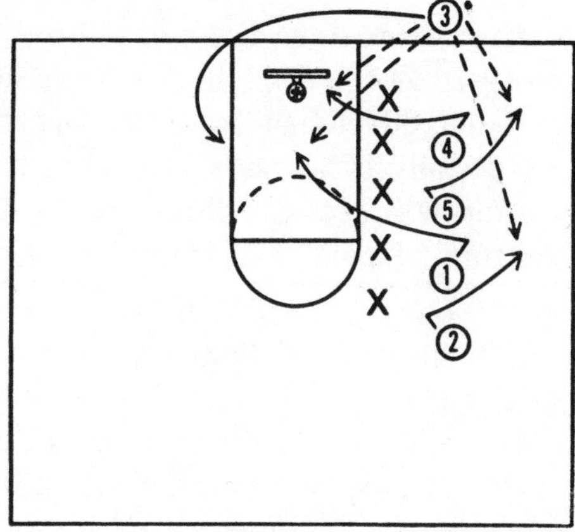

Diagram 1-3

cutting around behind No. 4, he can receive a return pass from behind a screen made possible by his cut. He then can obtain a shot from behind a good screen set up by No. 4. If No. 3 had passed the ball to No. 5, the same option could have been available to him and he could have obtained the shot from a more advantageous position. The thrower-in, No. 3, really has two main options after passing the ball in-bounds. He can pass the ball in-bounds and move in the opposite direction to which the pass was made or he can pass the ball in-bounds and follow the pass, cutting in behind the receiver for a screen and a possible return pass which could result in a scoring opportunity.

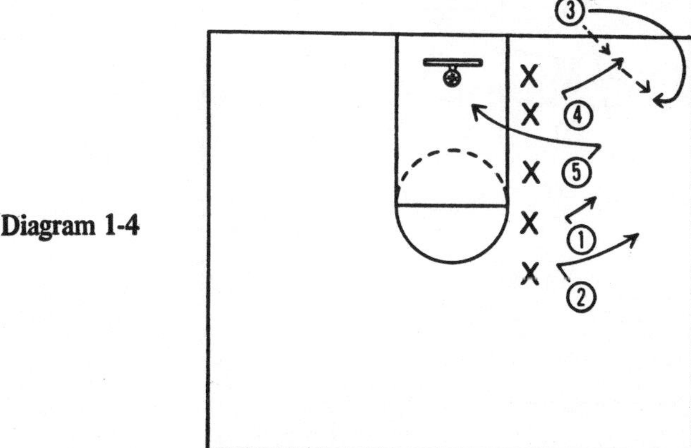

Diagram 1-4

In these diagrams, the forwards are usually numbered 3 and 4, the pivot post player is usually No. 5, while the guards are Nos. 1 and 2. It is not necessary to have a forward or No. 3, as indicated in the diagram, to take the ball out-of-bounds. The thrower-in can be any player on the team, and in plays such as shown in Diagram 1-4, it can be an advantage to have one of the guards throw the ball in, especially if he has a good shot from the base-line position, because after he makes the throw-in, he will often have an opportunity for a return pass and shot from this area after he moves in-bounds.

Diagram 1-5. Many defensive subtleties will be tried in order to stop the vertical line play. The more common one used, especially after playing the men tight and having been scored on, is to place the defensive players on both sides of the line as shown in Diagram 1-5. The defensive formation resembles a box zone, with the defense positioning two men on each side of the line, which enables them to pick up the cutters as they break out of the line. Usually, in this situation, X3 will still be aligned defensively on No. 3 who has the ball out-of-bounds. When the defense uses this tactic, the offense should use a signal to indicate the change. As a result of this defensive maneuver, the offensive players should vary their moves so as to offset this change in the defensive pattern. After the signal is given, Nos. 4 and 5 should both fake and break in the same direction. The diagram shows both breaking to the right after a strong fake to the left. No. 1 fakes, but does not break until the other players have cleared the immediate area.

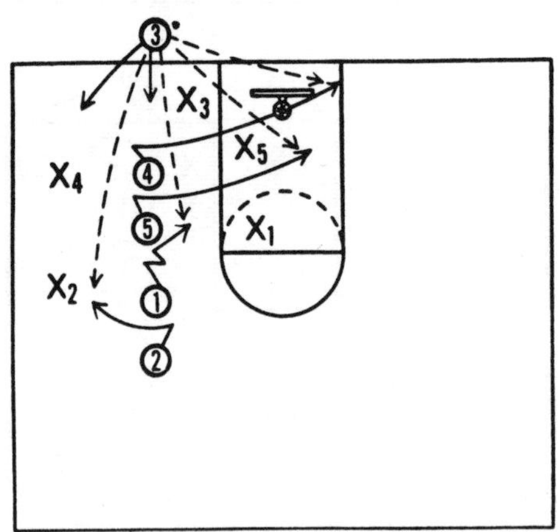

Diagram 1-5

No. 1 then, after a quick analysis of the defense, breaks to wherever he can be open. No. 2 fakes and breaks in the opposite direction of Nos. 4 and 5. This pattern of movement by the players should result in an overload in the area where Nos. 4 and 5 have moved. This could possibly pull the defense into positions that will provide better openings for Nos. 2 and 1. If the defensive player guarding No. 3 should shift to No. 4 or 5, then No. 3 can quickly pass the ball in-bounds and step inside for a possible quick scoring opportunity after receiving a return pass.

Diagram 1-6. This diagram further clarifies the different options for the vertical line formation out-of-bounds plays when the defense is using the box formation. Nos. 4 and 5 fake to the left and break to the right toward the middle of the floor and the right sideline. No. 1 holds his position after faking in both directions. No. 2 fakes to the right and breaks to the left side for an outlet pass from No. 3. Defensive player X1 must shift to help his teammate, X5. This maneuver will enable X3 to cover No. 4 and X5 to cover No. 5, as shown in the diagram. No. 1 moves forward behind No. 5, and, if he is open, No. 3 passes him the ball. No. 1 may either shoot from his present position, or, if he is able to do so, take a dribble toward the basket for a lay-up. Meanwhile, No. 3 quickly steps in-bounds for a return pass from No. 1 if No. 1 is unable to shoot. No. 3 may be in a position for a possible quick scoring opportunity. Defensive players X4 and X1 must make quick decisions and shifts to cover either No. 3 or No. 1. No. 2 may also present a defensive problem to X2 and X4. If he does, then this will leave No. 1 open for the outlet pass and the same options are now possible.

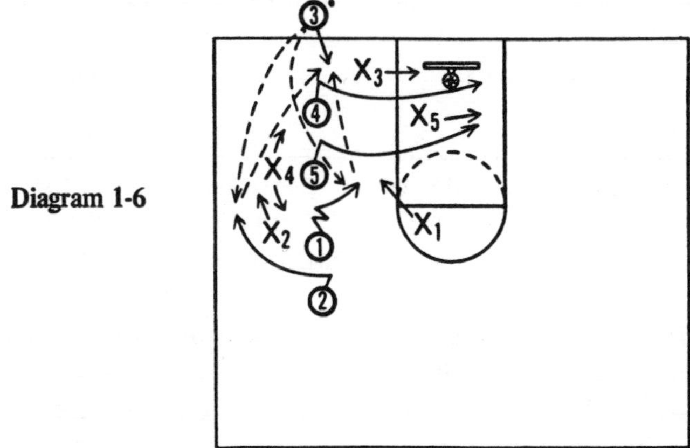

Diagram 1-6

Diagram 1-7. The possibilities from this formation become more apparent when Diagram 1-7 is closely analyzed. In this diagram, Nos. 4 and 5 fake to the right, and break to the left away from the center of the floor. The overload opportunities made possible by Nos. 4 and

5's cuts are obvious. If X3 does not shift to guard No. 4, No. 4 will be open. If X4 shifts to guard No. 4, No. 5 will be open. If X3 and X4 shift to cover Nos. 4 and 5, No. 1 should have a good middle opening, and No. 3 could pass the ball to him. No. 2 could also be open, especially if X1 has shifted. The diagram shows No. 3 passing the ball to No. 1, and then cutting to the opposite side of the floor. X5 will now have to make a decision as to whether he should guard either No. 1 or No. 3. One of them will be open for a good shot. Here the scoring opportunity could be available to any one of the five players.

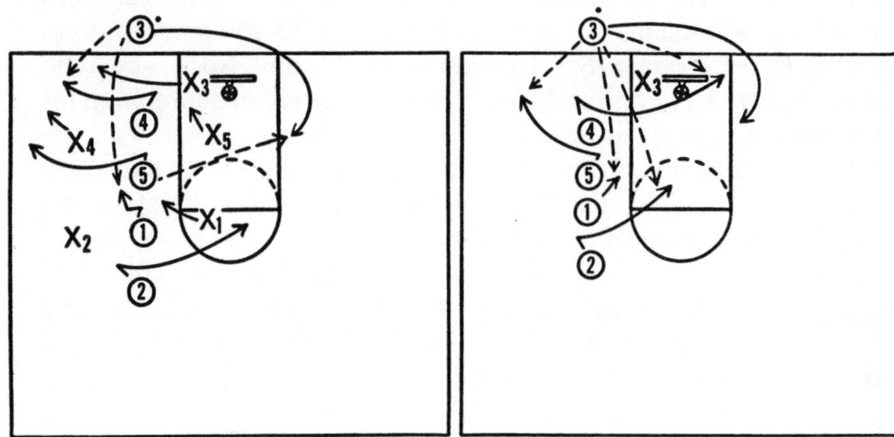

Diagram 1-7

Diagram 1-8

Diagram 1-8. The other possibility from the vertical line formation is the tightly stacked formation with the players lined up as close as possible and about one-and-one-half or two strides in-bounds from the thrower-in. A rule advantage given to the players in this situation is that the players can line up as tight as possible, without having to surrender a position between them to the opponents. The pattern of cuts, fakes and breaks are about the same as in the previous vertical line formations. The players line up quickly, and, on a given signal, Nos. 4 and 5 break in the opposite directions. No. 2 breaks opposite No. 5 and No. 1 will find that his best move is straight in toward No. 3. He will be open for a quick score, if none has been possible for either Nos. 4 or 5. No. 3 can follow his pass or break in the opposite direction, and, by so doing, create a possible scoring situation for himself.

Diagram 1-9. This play is devised to take advantage of or exploit the extreme height of any one player. The players line up in the vertical line formation as shown in the diagram and as close as they possibly can to No. 3, the thrower-in. No. 5 is the tallest player, and if he is extremely tall, his height can be exploited to a good advantage. On the signal to begin the play, No. 4 fakes to the left and then breaks to the right to pull a defensive man out. No. 5 remains stationary, and No. 1 fakes to the right and breaks to the left. No. 2 pulls out to the area near the top of the circle. No. 3 tosses a high lob pass to No. 5, who, taking advantage of his height near the basket, jumps high to receive the pass, and, while still in the air, simultaneously makes a semi-catch of the ball and a shot at the basket. Remember that Nos. 4 and 1 are not always committed to these same breaks. They may reverse their cuts, with No. 4 breaking left and No. 1 breaking right.

Diagram 1-10. The players line up in a tight vertical line position as shown in the diagram. No. 4 remains in place. No. 5 keys the break and signals a fake to the right, but breaks sharply to his left. No. 1 reverses the action of No. 5, and fakes to the left, but breaks to his right. No. 2 fakes to the right but tails out to the top of the circle for a possible outlet pass. If No. 5 is not open for a pass from No. 3, he reverses his direction quickly, and sets a screen on the defensive man of No. 4. No. 4, timing his move, fakes to his right to run the defensive man into the screen set by No. 5, and then cuts sharply behind No. 5 for a quick opening and a pass from No. 3. On this play, if No. 5 should signal a reverse of directions, then No. 1 would break to the left, and, if not open, he would set the screen for No. 4. It should work equally well either way.

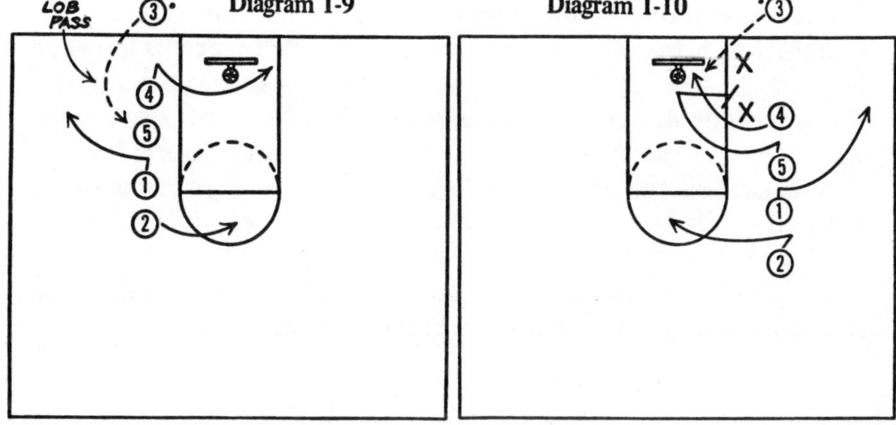

Diagram 1-9 Diagram 1-10

Diagram 1-11. This is a variation of the vertical line formation. When the ball is declared out-of-bounds, No. 3, the thrower-in, goes to the throw-in spot. Nos. 4, 5 and 2 line up in tight vertical formation as shown. No. 1 goes to the top of the circle as shown in the diagram to spread the defense and force it to loosen up. When No. 3 gives the signal, No. 4 remains stationary, and No. 2 screens the defensive man guarding No. 5. No. 5 makes a good fake to the left to run the defensive man into the screen, and then breaks two or three steps to his right. He should be open for a pass and a good shot from the position shown in the diagram. No. 4 moves straight in for the rebound. No. 3 breaks for the left side of the basket, and with No. 5 following the shot and No. 2 covering the long rebound, scoring and rebound possibilities are excellent.

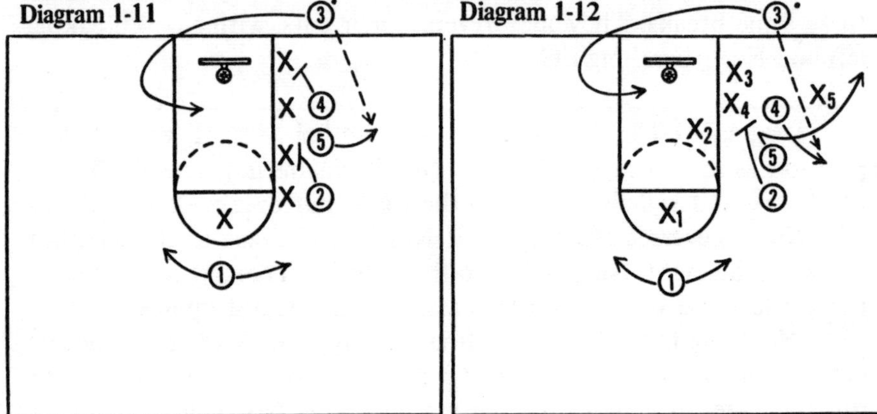

Diagram 1-12. Sometimes the defense will try to stop the special situation play shown in the previous diagrams by aligning themselves in a position as shown in Diagram 1-12. X5 is stationed as shown and will cover any offensive player breaking to the right out of the formation. If this should happen, there are several good options which the offense may use, and one of the best is shown in Diagram 1-12. After the prearranged signal to start the play is given, No. 4 remains stationary for a moment while No. 5 fakes to the left and breaks to the right as before. No. 2 screens as before, but this time he screens the player guarding No. 4. No. 4, after faking to the right or left or both, now steps back two or three steps. No. 3 passes the ball to No. 4, who should have a good shot from this position. Rebound assignments and follow-up shots are basically the same as in the previous diagram (Diagram 1-11) shown directly above.

HORIZONTAL LINE FORMATIONS

The use of the horizontal line formations in out-of-bounds situations has been extensive. Such formations are generally utilized for screening purposes against man-to-man defenses and usually result in a player being freed for a shot from a particular spot or area. The screening which is done in this type of situation is for the purpose of exploiting or taking advantage of the special talents, or, in many cases, the shooting ability of specific players.

This particular formation requires that the players line up facing the thrower-in. They are usually stationed in a tight shoulder-to-shoulder formation and parallel to the end line. The distance the first player in the formation is stationed from the end line can and does vary anywhere from the free throw line to the end line. One disadvantage to this formation is that when the players line up shoulder-to-shoulder in this manner, the opposition or defense can ask the officials for a position between the players, and, according to the rules, should be granted such a position. Usually, in the haste and confusion of such situations, this request is never made. If, however, the request is made, it must be made before the official places the ball at the disposal of the thrower-in. If the request is made after this, the official should ignore it and the play can continue.

Diagram 1-13. The players line up at the free throw line as shown in Diagram 1-13. If the ball is taken out-of-bounds to the right of the basket, the line can be shifted more to the right, and, if it is taken out on the left side, it can be shifted in that direction as needed. When the signal to start the play is given, players No. 2, 4 and 5 screen the defensive players guarding Nos. 1, 2 and 4, respectively, thereby forming a tight triple shoulder-to-shoulder screen for No. 1. No. 1, who should be the best shot from this position, fakes a deep cut, then steps back behind the screen, where he takes a pass from No. 3 from out-of-bounds. He should be able to obtain a high percentage shot from this position. Nos. 4, 5 and 3 rebound hard. If the defense scrambles to prevent the shot, then No. 1 should have some good option passes to the players who are freed as a result of the scramble, and who in turn should have good scoring opportunities.

Diagram 1-14. On the signal given by No. 3, the players who have lined up at the free throw line, as shown in Diagram 1-14, move into action. Nos. 2 and 4 both break toward the ball and then veer to the right and stop shoulder-to-shoulder to set a double screen for No. 5. As Nos. 2 and 4 break toward the ball, No. 5 fakes toward the base line and basket, and then cuts sharply to his left and behind the double screen set by Nos. 2 and 4. No. 5 should be open for a good shot as a result of this maneuver. If the defense switches from No. 2 to 5, then No. 2 can roll out of the screen and be in a good position to receive a pass and a good scoring opportunity. Another possibility is for No. 1 to fake toward the ball, and then step in behind the screen set by Nos. 2 and 4, for a possible pass from No. 3, and perhaps an unmolested shot from this position. The play has many possibilities and scoring opportunities which will present themselves as the play develops.

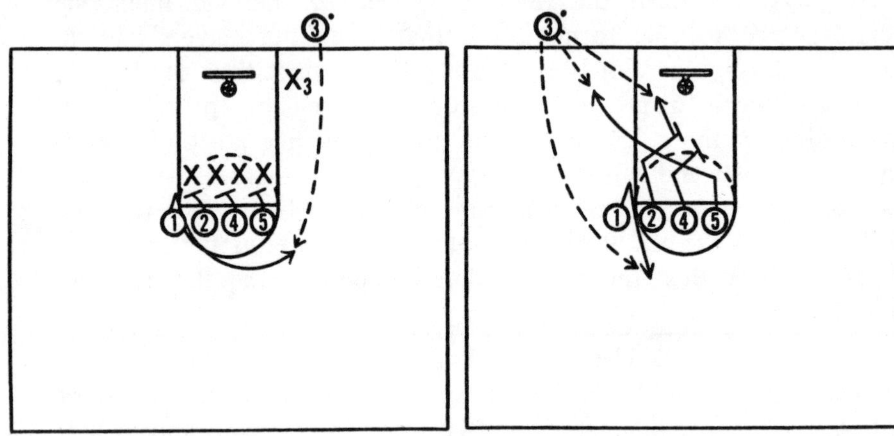

Diagram 1-13

Diagram 1-14

Diagram 1-15. Here the players line up about one-and-one-half to two strides from the end line on the opposite side of the free throw lane from where the ball is out-of-bounds. On the signal to begin the play, No. 1 fakes away from the end line and then cuts around No. 2 on the base-line side, with the expectation of receiving a pass from No. 3 and a possible shot from near the basket. If the defense switches, then No. 1 moves out toward mid-court, and, as a result of the switch, No. 2 could be free to receive a pass which could result in a fine scoring opportunity. No. 4 holds his position until such time as he is sure that neither No. 1 nor 2 will receive the pass from No. 3. He then fakes to the base line and cuts to the left side or the court side of No. 5. No. 5 sets a screen for No. 4 enabling him to move into the area where he can receive the pass from No. 3, as shown in the diagram. No. 4 now is presented with the possibility of obtaining a high percentage shot. No. 5 should execute a roll-off toward the basket after executing the screen for No. 4, with the expectation of clearing himself for a pass should the defense switch. This will place him in an excellent position for rebounding.

Diagram 1-16. The imagination and talents of the players are the only limiting factors that will determine the use of the screens and picks made possible by this formation and their effect on the team's success. All of the previously diagrammed screening combinations can be used. All the horizontal formation plays should be started in the same manner so that the beginning of each play will appear to be similar to every other one. Diagram 1-16 shows No. 3 giving the signal, with No. 5 faking to the base line. No. 5 then steps back and to the outside of the formation so that he may receive a pass from No. 3. No. 3 now breaks sharply in and around Nos. 1 and 2, thereby rubbing his defensive guard off. This enables him to receive a pass from No. 5, which will place him in a position for a good shot from behind the screen provided by players No. 2, 1 and 4.

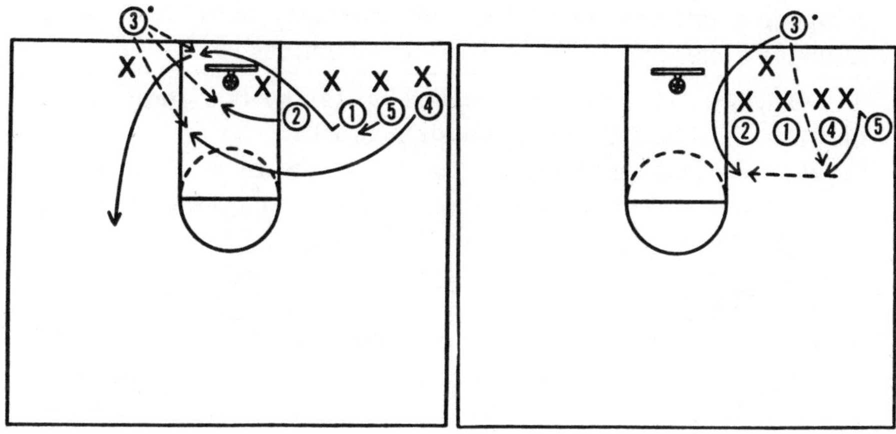

Diagram 1-15 Diagram 1-16

THE BOX FORMATION

The box formation for out-of-bounds plays along the end line in the front court is probably used more than any other formation. There is good reason for this because it has many possibilities for variations and options and can provide the necessary deception. The players are positioned in the box formation so that floor balance is good, and the formation is more easily adjusted to different defensive alignments, such as man-to-man, zones, and combination efforts made to stop a quick basket. The formation, as the name implies, places four men in-bounds in a box-like arrangement, all of them facing the thrower-in and the basket. Key players can be placed in key positions, dependent upon the type of play to be used. It should be remembered that positioning of the players in the box formation, and for that matter any of the formations described, can vary dependent upon many factors, such as the ability of the players both offensively and defensively under a particular situation, the use of a specific play and the necessity of using certain players to perform different skills.

The box formation has almost unlimited possibilities and options which can result in scoring opportunities. In analyzing the following diagrams, it should be remembered that any play shown to the left side of the basket can also be used on the opposite side. The diagrams presented here, however, will not show the same play being executed from both sides. Plays from both sides will be shown, but the movements of the players will be different and it will be a completely different play. The following diagrams give the basic formations and some of the more common options.

Diagram 1-17. The players line up in the box formation as shown in the diagram. The big question is: Where to screen and how? Usually the best procedure is to station the two tallest players nearest the basket. The tallest player should be stationed nearest the ball. This player should screen away from the ball, and then, if a defensive switch occurs, the screener can roll toward the basket for a quick opening. Diagram 1-17 shows that No. 3 has the ball out-of-bounds on the left side of the free throw lane. Nos. 4 and 5 line up about three strides in front of the basket, as shown in the diagram. No. 5 is the tallest player. Nos. 2 and 1 line up about even with the top of the circle, as shown in the diagram. When the signal to start the play is given by No. 3, No. 5 fakes left and then screens X4, the man guarding No. 4. To execute this screen, he should come in to the side and slightly behind X4. No. 4 holds his cut, then fakes a move to his right to move X4 into No. 5's screen, and then breaks sharply behind the screen toward the ball. No. 4 may be open, and if he is, then No. 3 passes him the ball. If the defense switches to stop the play, and if No. 5 has executed his screen properly, then there will be a moment when the defense will be split, and No. 5 should roll toward the basket before X4 can switch onto him. He should be wide open for an unmolested shot. In the meantime, while this maneuver is being executed, Nos. 1 and 2 should cut in a "cross," with No. 1 cutting off No. 2 to obtain a screen. If No. 4 or 5 are not open, then it is possible that No. 1 or 2 will be free to receive an outlet pass and a possible shot. No. 2 might be able to execute a roll-off down the middle and be free for a pass and a possible shot. But one of these players, either No. 1 or 2, should roll back outside to maintain defensive floor balance.

Diagram 1-18. As was mentioned in Diagram 1-17, one of the questions arising as a result of this play is whether to screen for the players stationed closest to the ball or for the players stationed farthest away from the ball. It has been found that the best offensive maneuver for this particular situation against switching defenses can be obtained by having the players lined up nearest the ball screen for the players farthest away from the ball, as shown in Diagram 1-18. However, it is possible to obtain the effect of both screening maneuvers by having the players closest to the ball screen away from it, and the players near the top of the circle screen toward the ball, as shown in this diagram. Here No. 5 screens on X4, just as shown in the previous diagram, 1-17. However, Nos. 2 and 1, the players in the top part of the box formation, reverse this procedure, with No. 2 screening toward the ball on X1 and No. 1 cutting off the screen for possible openings. If No. 2 executes his screen properly and the defense switches, then during the brief moment of the defensive "split," No. 2 could roll toward the ball and basket for a pass and possible shot, or roll out for an outlet pass if no other openings have occurred.

Diagram 1-17 Diagram 1-18

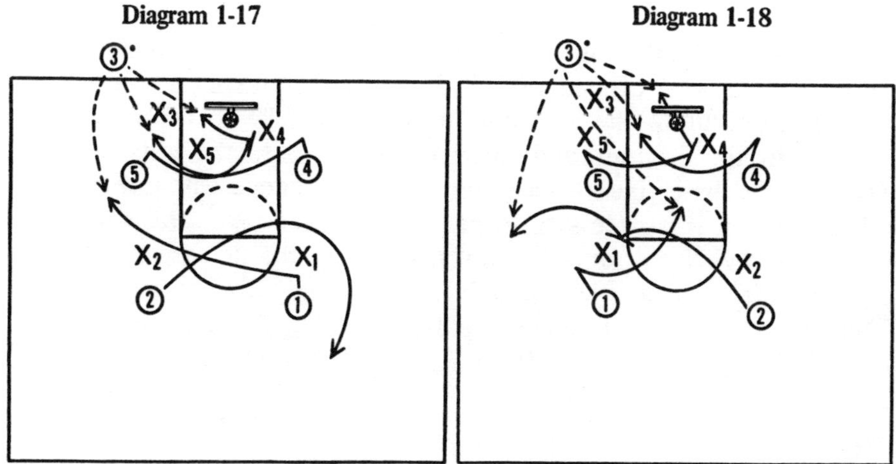

Diagram 1-19. This diagram shows how screening toward the ball can be done and how this type of screen can be used as a variation from the previously shown plays. When the players farthest from the ball screen toward it, and the defense switches, there is more likely to be a crowding of players near the ball. As a result, X3 who is guarding No. 3, can easily shift onto No. 4 to prevent a quick opening from the roll-out by No. 4.

Diagram 1-20. After the box formation screening play has been used a few times, the defense will anticipate the screen and execute the defensive switch early. When this happens, Nos. 5 and 4 should start their moves as usual, but No. 5 should fake his screen on X4, and, as X5 loosens up to switch to No. 4, No. 5 should break straight in toward the basket for an unmolested shot, as shown in the diagram. Nos. 1 and 2 execute their usual cross or screening moves.

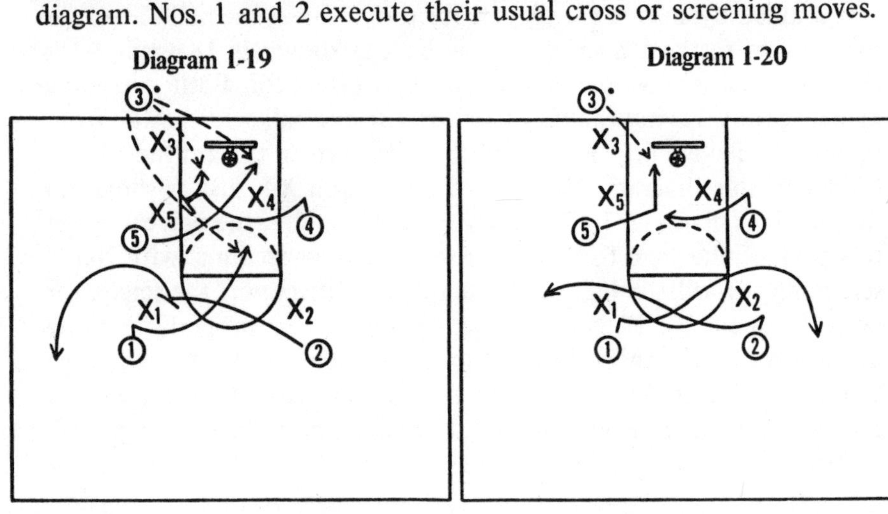

Diagram 1-21. This diagram shows an option to the play in the previous diagram. Instead of No. 5 or 4 either faking a screen, or actually executing the screening move, both fake to the inside as shown in the diagram, and then cut wide and to the outside and toward the base line to clear the area. This move will furnish an outlet pass if it is necessary to provide one. The fake screen is now executed by No. 1 or 2, in an area where the defense has been performing an aggressive switch. No. 1 fakes and moves to screen X2. No. 2 moves as in the regular pattern. Seeing the usual defensive switch being made, and before it is fully completed, No. 1 cuts

straight in toward the basket to receive the pass from No. 3 and an easy shot. If this shot does not materialize, No. 3 can pass to either No. 5 or 4. He then follows his pass with the expectation of receiving a possible return pass and hopefully a shot from behind a screen performed by either No. 5 or 4, depending upon which player he passed to. Nos. 4, 5 and 3 rebound. No. 1 can play for the long rebound, and No. 2 moves to the back court to provide defensive balance.

Diagram 1-22. The play shown in Diagram 1-22 can provide a quick opener for No. 1 off a double screen, or an opening for No. 4 if the defense shifts on the double pick. The usual maneuver from this play is to have the players closest to the ball screen away from it, and the outside players move toward the ball on the screen. This play shows a switch in maneuvers, with No. 5 faking his screen away from the ball but pulling wide to the outside, as shown in the diagram. No. 2 screens on X1, who is on the same side of the free throw lane as the ball. No. 4 now fakes a move in toward the basket, and then moves out to set a screen on X2, who has followed No. 2 in this maneuver. No. 1 now cuts sharply off the double screen set by Nos. 2 and 4. He could be open, but if the defense switches to stop No. 1 (X4 switching to No. 1), then the split leaves No. 4 wide open for a roll-in to the basket before the scrambled defense can guard him. He should be wide open for a shot. If none of these moves develop, then No. 3 can possibly pass to No. 5 or 2, either of whom may be free for a pass.

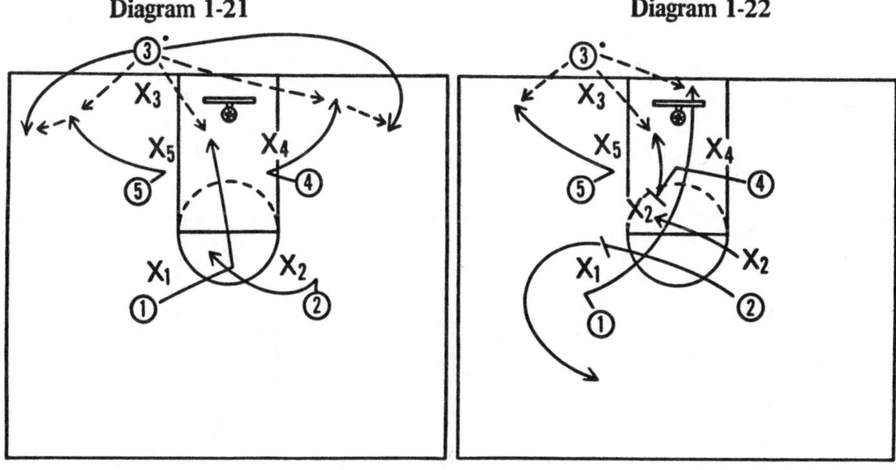

Diagram 1-23. This diagram shows the players nearest the ball, Nos. 5 and 4, setting blind screens on the defensive men guarding Nos. 1 and 2. When the signal is given to begin the play, No. 5 fakes as if to screen No. 4's guard, but instead he moves up to screen X1, No. 1's defensive player. He should be careful to set the screen one step from X1, since it is a screen from the rear and will be illegal if not properly executed. No. 4 performs the same type of screen on X2. Nos. 1 and 2 break to the outside of the screens. If the defense switches, No. 5 executes a reverse pivot and rolls in toward the basket off the defensive split for a possible pass from No. 3. No. 4 moves to the back court after the screen to provide defensive balance. No. 1, 2 or 5 could be free for a pass from No. 3 and a high percentage shot.

Diagram 1-24. This play is an old ruse that could be used from any formation, but is included here to add to the versatility of this formation. The trick or ruse could be worked by any one of the four players in-bounds. After No. 3 takes the ball in the out-of-bounds position, No. 1 (could be any of the other players) starts yelling to No. 3, saying, "Hey Joe, the coach told me to take the ball out-of-bounds on this play." He starts towards No. 3 as he is calling this out, as if to relieve No. 3 of the ball. The defense momentarily relaxes, No. 3 flips No. 1 the ball in-bounds and he puts it in the basket for two points. The defense could be aware of the fact that the rules state that once No. 3 has been handed the ball out-of-bounds, he is the thrower-in designated by the official, and he cannot legally exchange positions with No. 1 or anyone else on the team. The ruse is an old one, and it has been worked many times for an easy score.

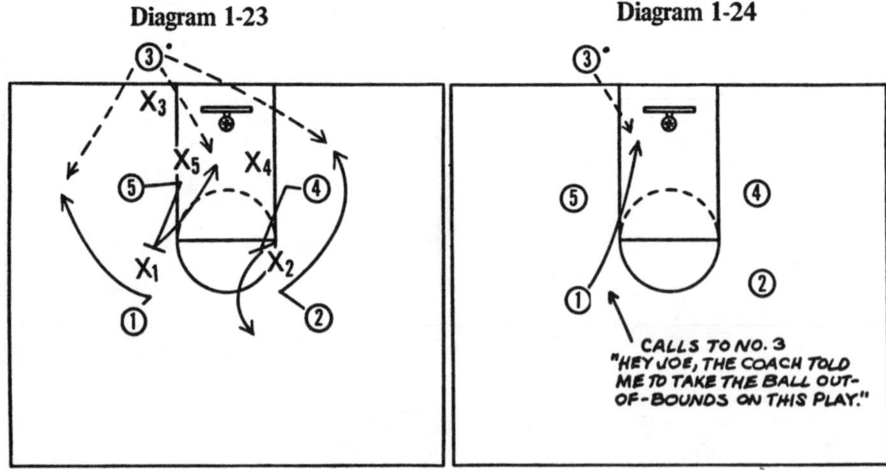

Diagram 1-25. This diagram shows a cross screening movement by Nos. 4 and 5. Nos. 4 and 5 line up in the box formation, and in the usual manner. However, Nos. 1 and 2 crowd in somewhat closer to Nos. 4 and 5, just above the free throw line and inside the circle. Nos. 4 and 5 fake their usual box formation screening moves, but then No. 4 sets a rear screen on X1 (guarding No. 1) and No. 5 sets a rear screen on X2 (guarding No. 2). After the screens, Nos. 1 and 2 cross and break sharp and close to the screens which have been executed for them. Either one may be open, but if the defense switches to guard the player who has been freed by the screen, then Nos. 4 and 5 both execute a reverse pivot and roll off the screens toward the ball and the basket for possible openings. No. 5 will roll off first, followed by No. 4. Either one or both may be open for a pass and shot. If Nos. 1 and 2 are not open on the first break, they fan out to the side and back toward mid-court to maintain floor balance and receive possible outlet passes from No. 3, in case the ball cannot be passed to either No. 4 or 5. Good faking by Nos. 4 and 5 on their original moves can be instrumental in setting up good scoring possibilities for the entire play.

Diagram 1-25

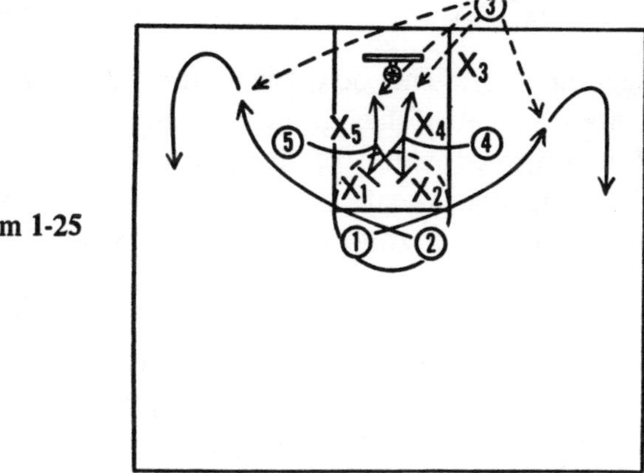

Diagram 1-26. A slight variation in the box formation can give good results, as shown in Diagram 1-26. Nos. 1 and 2 line up as usual, except that Nos. 4 and 5 spread wider, and farther back toward the mid-court area. They should be stationed just inside the free throw line extended area. On the starting signal, Nos. 5 and 2 break toward the ball, and then change direction to set a double shoulder-to-shoulder screen just inside and slightly to the rear of No. 4. No. 4, after faking to the base-line side of the screen to tie the defensive

man in, breaks over the top side toward the ball. If the double pick is effective, he will be open for a pass and a good shot. If there is a defensive shift onto No. 4, then either No. 5 or 2 will be able to take advantage of the defensive split and roll inward toward the basket for a short shot. No. 5 or 2 can roll outward, taking advantage of whatever opening the defense will allow as a result of the defensive scramble.

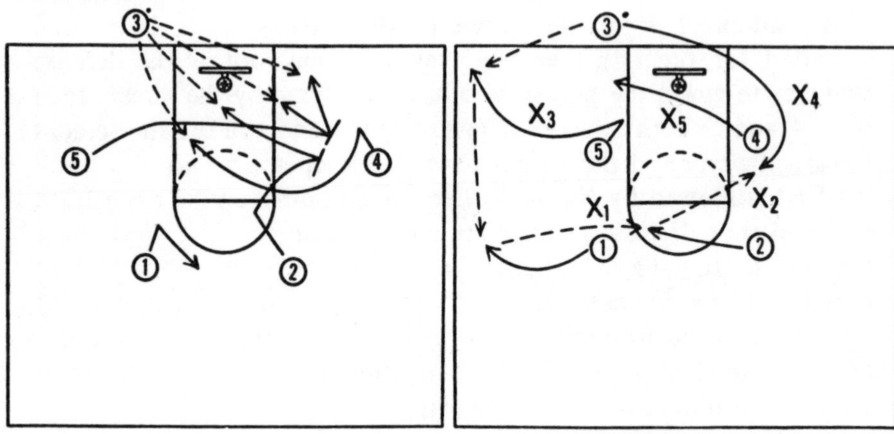

Diagram 1-26

Diagram 1-27

Diagram 1-27. The box formation has another advantage, in that it not only furnishes good deployment of players for screen plays, but it also provides for the positioning of the players so that when these players execute the proper moves, it can easily cope with the teams that use a zone defense against all out-of-bounds plays along the base line in the front court. Many teams have a standard practice of zoning all out-of-bounds situations along the base line. When this happens, the offense must be ready with a play that will result in a shot. In this diagram, the players line up in the box formation as usual. The one difference here is to be sure before the play begins that No. 3, the thrower-in, is the best situation shooter, or shot, from along the base line, or from spots 12 to 15 feet out from the basket to either the right or left side. This play is devised to get an open shot for No. 3, the thrower-in, from these spots. After lining up, and the starting signal is given by No. 3, No. 5 fakes a screening move toward No. 4 and breaks wide to the left to be sure to be open for a pass from No. 3. No. 4, after a good fake to the right, cuts to the left and under the basket. No. 1 may fake right, but breaks to his left and toward the side of the court to be sure he can be free to receive a pass. No. 2 breaks to his left to about the left side of the top of the circle, but should stay as much as possible to the middle of the court, so that he is able to pass the ball to the right side of the court when necessary. No. 3 passes the ball to No. 5. The defense will now shift to the left side of the floor to cover the players with the ball in this area. No. 5 quickly relays the ball to No. 1, after receiving the pass from No. 3 from out-of-bounds. No. 1, in turn, quickly passes it to No. 2, who has cut across the top of the free throw circle to the position shown in the diagram. No. 3, after passing the ball to No. 5, quickly breaks to his left and to the right side of the basket. He should be open at this position for a pass from No. 2. His position where he may be free to receive a pass may be anywhere from along the base line to the right of the basket, to an area 10 or 12 feet from the basket towards the free throw line. With the defense shifting to the left side to cover the ball on the throw-in, and with a quick relay of the ball by quick, fast passing, the ball can always be gotten to No. 3 in the area shown for a good position shot. Nos. 5 and 4 are in good rebounding position, and should take advantage of this important phase of the game on this particular play. The same play, of course, can be executed to the right or left side of the floor. The play does not have to follow the exact pattern as shown here, because when the defense shifts to cover the pass pattern and the shooter, it will leave holes or openings elsewhere in the defense that can be exploited by a change in player movement. The following diagrams will show some of the options.

Diagram 1-28. Several scoring opportunities can result from the play shown in this diagram which is a continuation of Diagram 1-27. No. 4 might be open as he moves into the area just to the left of the basket and underneath it. If so, the ball should be passed to him. If the defense sinks deep very quickly, No. 1 may bypass No. 2 and pass the ball to No. 3 in the area indicated. At times, the defense may sink deeply and flatten out to prevent the shot by No. 3. If this happens, No. 2 is the best candidate for the shot, as he may be open near the top of the circle or free throw area for a fine position, high percentage shot. If the defense shifts quickly back to the right side to cover No. 3's shooting area, at approximately the same time the ball reaches No. 2, the direction of the ball can be reversed and passed back to the left side again. If this happens, oftentimes No. 5 will be in a good position for a high percentage shot in his area. If the defense guards No. 4 closely in his move to the under-basket area, at

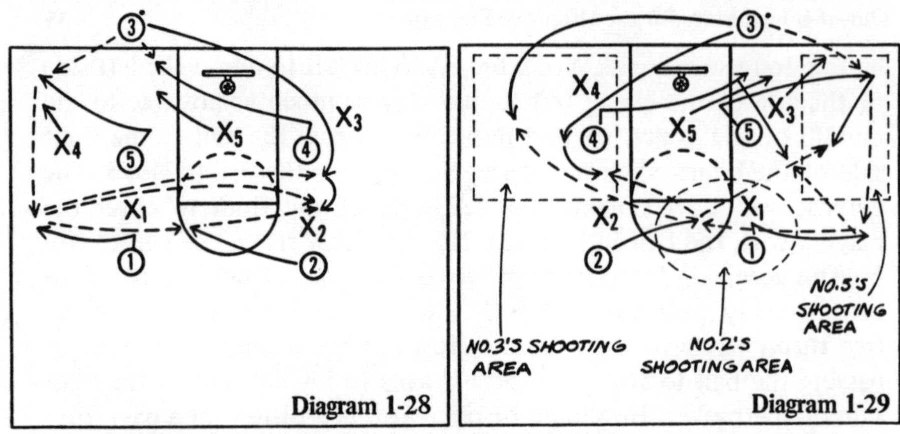

a time when the ball is being passed around the perimeter area, he can reverse his direction and move back toward the free throw line, which will enable him to be open frequently for a pass when holes or openings are left in the defense. Diagram 1-29 will give other options.

Diagram 1-29. This diagram shows the play as originating from the right side of the basket, and presents the many possibilities that can develop from this type of play. A good shot can nearly always be obtained by No. 3 on the side of the floor opposite from where the ball is out-of-bounds, if the passing pattern is executed quickly and with precision. This is why No. 3 should be the best shot from these positions. The second best shooter should be No. 2, as a good shot is often obtained from this position. No. 4 may also be free for a pass as he moves and cuts near the basket area, or he reverses his direction and maneuvers into the openings in the defense caused by the players shifting and the ball being passed around the perimeter of the defense. If the defense attempts to overshift and play to stop the shot at the No. 3 and 2 positions, the direction of the ball should be reversed and the pass should be made to No. 5, who will have a fine opening and an opportunity for a shot from his position. No. 5 will have to reverse his direction off the base-line position from the position where he received the pass from No. 3. He then must break out toward the ball in an adjustment maneuver so that he is in a good position to receive the ball and get a good shot.

THE DIAMOND FORMATION

In the diamond formation, as the name implies, the players line up in a formation shaped like a diamond in front of the thrower-in, who has the ball out-of-bounds along the base line in the front court.

This formation may have advantages over the box formation, in that the "point" player stationed nearest the thrower-in can give the direction of the play to either the right or left, and two teammates can be utilized, with quick striking force combined with fakes, screens and double screens, to give good scoring punch to the play. It can be easily adjusted to the zone defenses to secure position shots. The following diagrams show the explosive possibilities of plays from the formation.

Diagram 1-30. No. 3 takes the ball out-of-bounds on the left side of the free throw lane. The same play can also be run if No. 3 should have the ball out-of-bounds on the right side of the floor. The other players line up in the formation as shown in the diagram. No. 5, the point man in the diamond, starts the play with a fake which is timed with the beginning signal given by No. 3. He may screen to either the left or right, but it is usually best to screen "away from the ball" in order to avoid crowding, a maneuver that could be brought about by breaking into the area covered by defensive X3. Therefore, with this problem in mind, No. 5 screens away from the ball, to the right side, and screens X2, the defensive player guarding No. 2. No. 2 fakes to his right and breaks sharply off the screen set by No. 5. While this is happening, No. 4 fakes right and then breaks wide to his left to pull his defensive man out of the crowded scoring area. No. 3 will have passing possibilities to Nos. 4 and 2, who may be wide open for a shot, if the defense fails to switch. If the defense switches on the screen set by No. 5, No. 5 can break in slightly to the right of the basket off the split caused by the defensive switch. He could be open for an unmolested, easy shot near the basket, and this is the best possibility for two easy points. No. 1 can break right or left and always be open for an outlet pass if none of the other options materialize.

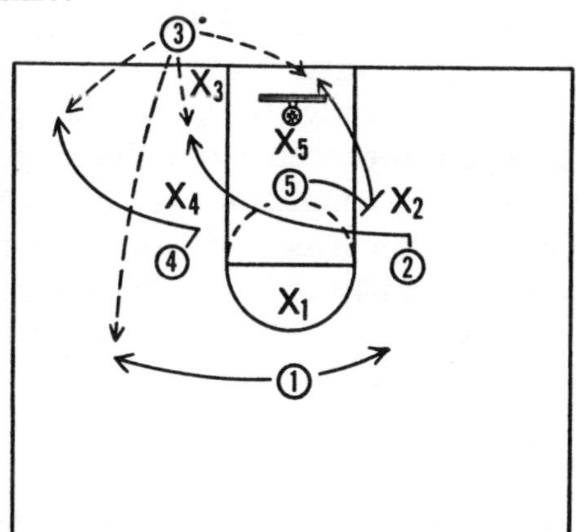

Diagram 1-30

Diagram 1-31. Variations in the preceding play can be made to meet defensive adjustments. In Diagram 1-31, No. 5 screens No. 2's defensive man, and then breaks in toward the basket off the split when the defense switches. No. 2 breaks to his left off the screen and across the free throw lane, knowing that the switch will cut off his scoring opportunity, and sets a screen on No. 4's defensive man. By prearranged signal, No. 4, instead of pulling his defensive man out of the area to the left, remains motionless until the screen is set by No. 2, then he moves his defensive man into the screen by a fake to his left. He then cuts sharply off the screen to his right and drives toward the basket. Nos. 5 and 4 could both be open. After No. 4 cuts past No. 2's screen, No. 2 rolls out to the left side for a possible outlet pass, and perhaps a scoring opportunity. No. 1 can be the receiver of the outlet pass to the far outside if no openings result from any of these maneuvers.

Diagram 1-32. If the ball is out-of-bounds farther to the right or left of the free throw lane than shown in the previous diagrams, the players should shift the formation to line up on the ball as close as possible, as shown in Diagram 1-32. The same play can be executed either to the right side or the left side of the free throw lane. The formation shown here is to the left side. No. 5, the point man, fakes to his left and then drives to the free throw lane area, where he screens the defensive man guarding No. 2. This move is a screen away from the ball. No. 2 fakes to his right, and then cuts sharply to the left off the screen set by No. 5. If he is not open, No. 2 continues his drive to the left and sets a screen on X4, the defensive player guarding No. 4. No. 4 fakes to the left, and cuts sharply off the screen set by No. 2 toward the free throw lane and the basket. He could be open for a pass and an easy shot. Nos. 5 and 2, after setting their screens, roll off the screens toward the basket to cause a possible "split" in the defense when switches are made. If they are successful in timing these moves correctly, they could be open for easy shots, especially No. 5, who can execute a roll-off to a position just in front of the basket. Possible openings are available to Nos. 2, 4 and 5. No. 1 is used for the outlet pass, and No. 3 can always follow his passes for a possible return pass and a scoring opportunity. Players No. 4, 5, 2 and 3 are always in good follow-up positions for rebounds.

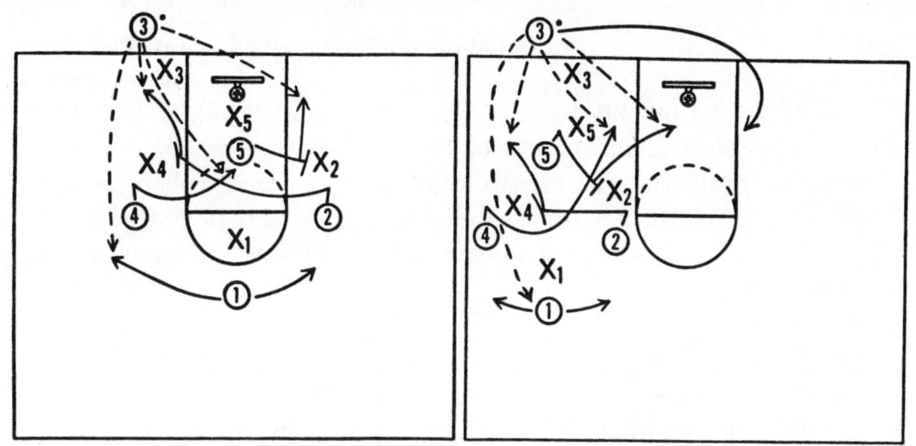

Diagram 1-31

Diagram 1-32

Diagram 1-33. If the defense should use a zone defense against the out-of-bounds play when the diamond formation is used, the offense can easily adjust to secure a position shot. Diagram 1-33 shows a 2-3 zone defense being used against the diamond offensive formation. This same type of zone defense was shown in previous diagrams against the box formation. No. 3, the thrower-in, should be the best position shooter and should take the ball out-of-bounds in both formations. On the starting signal, No. 5 moves toward the ball, and, in this particular diagram, cuts to the left of the basket. No. 4 fakes toward the basket and then pulls wide and deep near the base line to take the pass-in from No. 3. No. 1 sweeps to his left, and to just the outer fringes of the defense. No. 2 adjusts to a position to the left outer half of the free throw circle. The ball is quickly relayed from No. 4, to No. 1, to No. 2, who passes it quickly to No. 3. No. 3, after passing the ball in to No. 4, breaks to the right side of the basket area to receive the pass from No. 2. By quickly relaying the ball around the perimeter of the defense, No. 3, as a result, should be open for a good shot in the area shown in the diagram. When No. 5 moves into the basket area, he may be open, and if this is true, he then should get the ball, although his move here usually will draw the defense to this area. They must cover him. If the defense spreads wide and attempts to play the position shot by No. 3, they will often leave other holes or openings in the defense that can be exploited. The ball could possibly be relayed to No. 5 from No. 3, if No. 3 is guarded closely. No. 2 can possibly have an opportunity for a good position shot, and he also can relay the ball to No. 5 at times if the defense is guarding No. 3 very closely. The ball may be faked to No.

3, and reversed quickly back to No. 4 for a position shot, or No. 4 may relay the ball in quickly to No. 5 if the defense tightens the perimeter positions. The offense must be taught and drilled to take advantage of all these various situations. Also note that Nos. 4, 5 and 3, and even 2, are always in good rebound follow-up positions on all of these shots.

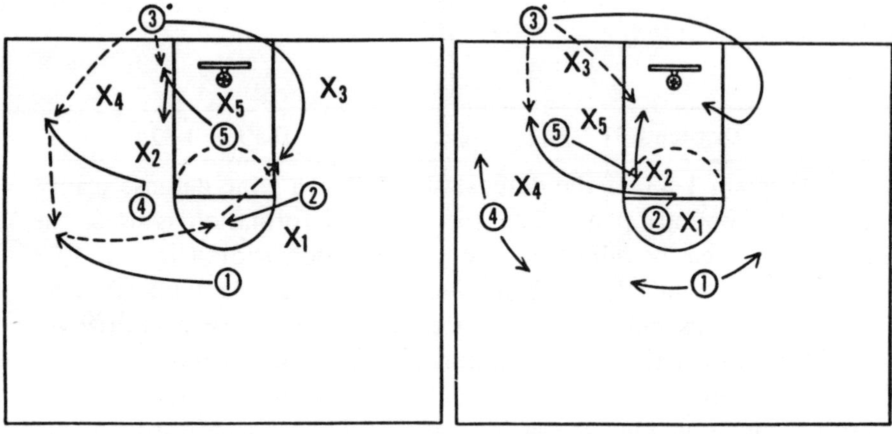

Diagram 1-33 Diagram 1-34

MISCELLANEOUS FORMATIONS—THE TRIANGLE

Diagram 1-34. The triangle formation is made for a quick, explosive opening for No. 5 or 2. Nos. 5, 4 and 2 line up in the triangle as shown in Diagram 1-34. No. 5 quickly sets a screen on X2, the defensive player guarding No. 2. No. 2 cuts sharply off the screen to his left and toward the ball. If the defense switches, No. 5 times his roll-off and cut toward the basket to be ahead of X2 before he can make the shift on defense to guard No. 5. If timed properly, No. 5 should have a quick opening. If the defense does not switch or doesn't switch quickly enough, No. 2 will be open for the pass from No. 3, and a possible shot. No. 4 breaks wherever he can best be free for a pass, if the quick maneuver between No. 5 and No. 2 does not produce an opening. No. 1 serves as an outlet pass man, and No. 3, after passing the ball in, will usually find it best to break to the opposite side of the basket for a possible rebound position, or a possible return pass and scoring opportunity.

MISCELLANEOUS FORMATIONS—THE OBLIQUE

Diagram 1-35. The oblique formation is unique in that it is neither a vertical nor horizontal line. Three of the players, on the signal for the out-of-bounds play, line up immediately in what may be termed an oblique line, or a slanting position, as shown in Diagram 1-35. It furnishes several scoring possibilities. In this formation, No. 3 should be the best passer, the best faker and the player who can definitely get the ball in-bounds. No. 4 should definitely be the best jump shooter. No. 2 can also be used for position and jump shots on this play. When the signal to start the play is given, No. 5 steps in to screen X4, the defensive player guarding No. 4. No. 4 steps back one or two steps, or enough so that No. 2 can clear in front of him. When No. 4 steps back, No. 3 immediately passes him the ball. A high lob pass might be preferred; however, the pass should be executed in such a manner that No. 4 can catch the ball while still in the air and execute a jump shot. As No. 4 steps back, No. 2 cuts directly in front of him and sharply off the back of No. 5. This provides a double screening possibility for No. 2, and also helps in the screening move to get No. 4 open. If No. 4 is not open, No. 3 should look to No. 2 as a possible pass receiver, should he be open. If No. 4 is not open for a shot after receiving a pass, and if the defense overplays or crowds through the screens to stop the jump shot by No. 4, he can have good passing possibilities to No. 2. Also No. 3, after passing the ball in to No. 4, always breaks in to the opposite side of the basket for possible openings and for good rebound positioning.

Diagram 1-35

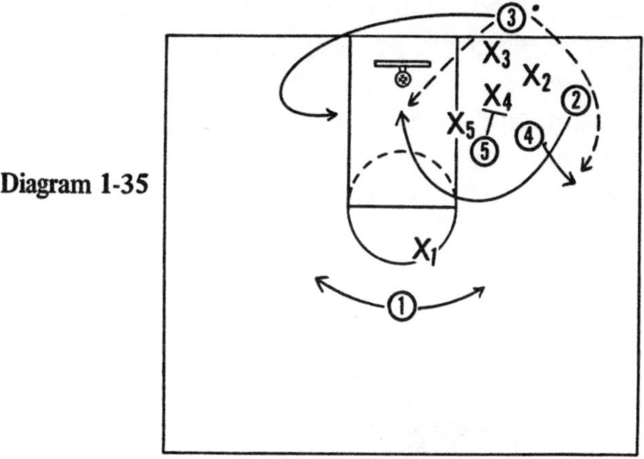

Diagram 1-36. If No. 4 does not have a shot, he may pass off to No. 2 or 3 as shown in Diagram 1-36. If the defense rushes him strongly, he may drive to the basket himself, since No. 3 has moved to the opposite side of the basket and pulled the defensive man away from the possible path of a drive by No. 4. No. 1 always serves as the long and safe outlet pass for No. 3, if none of the passes in options previously described develop. No. 5, or whoever plays this position, should be the best rebounder, as his move leaves him in excellent rebound position. The moves by Nos. 3, 2, 5 and 4 leave them all in excellent rebound positions.

Diagram 1-37. If the defense starts playing the play, or if they station a defensive player in the area near where No. 4 ordinarily would execute his jump shot, then the option described in Diagram 1-37 can be worked, with good success and excellent results. This play will usually result in a good position or jump shot for No. 2. No. 4 gives the prearranged signal, and this time, instead of stepping back to receive the pass for the jump shot, he cuts behind the screen set by No. 5. No. 2 at this moment fakes his usual move, but then reverses his direction and steps out into the open area created by the offensive and defensive moves. The surprise created by the move will usually give No. 2 an opportunity for a good position shot. If he is not open, he could possibly pass to No. 4 or No. 3, or perhaps drive the base line if the defense crowds him enough. This oblique formation and these maneuvers will produce many openings and variations, and the team should be coached to exploit all the possibilities that may develop from this play.

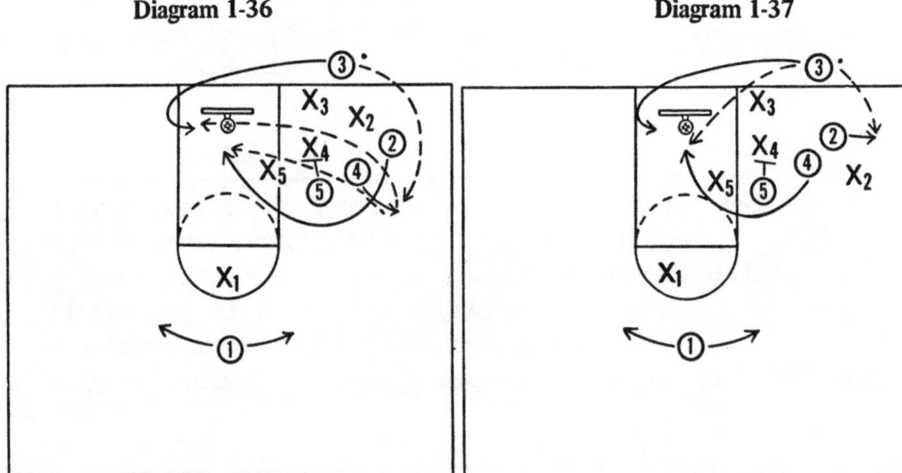

TWO

OUT-OF-BOUNDS—FRONT COURT SIDELINE PLAYS— MID-COURT PLAYS

Many basketball teams are not satisfied to use out-of-bounds plays, with the exception of those from the offensive base line, because they wish to assure themselves possession of the ball after the pass-in and are not concerned about scoring from the play. After gaining ball possession, they then go into their regular offensive pattern of play. The reasoning behind this action is usually motivated or determined by the philosophy or belief that the regular offensive pattern of play will result in or produce more scoring opportunities than an out-of-bounds play, other than those from the offensive end line.

Importance and Use of the Out-of-Bounds Play

It is important and necessary in basketball to use the out-of-bounds play from any out-of-bounds position, regardless of its origin, in attempting to gain "the winning edge." In such situations, when the play is well-executed, and even though a basket is not scored, ball possession can still be maintained. The threat of a well-executed out-of-bounds play puts constant pressure on the defense, and this pressure can many times cause a partial or, in extreme instances, a complete breakdown of the defense.

Opportunities for the Use of the Out-of-Bounds Play

While opportunities for the use of the out-of-bounds play from the front court and mid-court sidelines will not be nearly as numerous as the out-of-bounds situations along the front court end line or base line, they do occur frequently enough so that it is not difficult to realize their importance. Every coach should prepare his players to cope with this situation by giving them a fine repertoire of out-of-bounds plays that will bring about opportunities to score and help them gain a winning edge.

Factors Determining the Success of the Out-of-Bounds Play

The success of any out-of-bounds play depends upon the following factors:

1. The selection of the proper play. The proper selection of the play is the first determining factor in its success. The decision as to the selection of the play cannot always be determined by the coach, because the element of time in which the decision must be made to select the play must be considered. It is necessary that many of the decisions concerning the plays that will be attempted will need to be made by the players themselves. It is good planning, therefore, to have out-of-bounds plays ready for instant use from any out-of-bounds position.
2. The aggressiveness and tightness of the defense at the time of its execution. Whether a team is using a tight man-to-man or a loose fall-back zone type of defense.
3. The out-of-bounds spot from where the ball is being thrown in.
4. Other minor determining factors, such as alertness, or lack of it, by the defensive players; alertness and good organization by the offense; the clearness of decision and awarding of the ball out-of-bounds by the officials, etc.

Any one of these could be a factor in determining the success of an out-of-bounds play. Many officials are not decisive and clear in their calls and decision making. Any time the ball is out-of-bounds, the players should be coached to be there "on the spot" to get the ball, and to act as if it belongs to them–not to the point of being obnoxious, but to the point of perhaps helping an official make a decision in their favor where the decision may be doubtful, or there may be indecisiveness.

Types of Out-of-Bounds Plays

The out-of-bounds plays shown and discussed in this chapter include front court sideline plays, and mid-court out-of-bounds plays to be used against man-to-man and zone type defenses. Each will be successful in direct proportion to the type of defense used against it, the player personnel of the team executing the play and the climate of the game at the time the play is to be used. These factors in themselves may or may not furnish a situation that can make the play productive.

THE DRIVE, HOOK, SCREEN AND SLIDE SERIES

This series is a sequence of out-of-bounds plays which can be executed from the front court sideline. The use of these plays gives the team utilizing them an advantage over one that just throws the ball in for the purpose of obtaining possession, and then depends upon the regular offense for scoring rather than employing out-of-bounds plays. This advantage exists because in reality these out-of-bounds plays can be used to trigger the regular offense. They can therefore be used as a part of, or as a continuation of, the regular offense, with the play beginning from the out-of-bounds throw-in spot.

With minor adjustments these plays can be used against the man-to-man and zone defenses, both of which will be shown. There is an added advantage because they may be used as the beginning of the offense from out-of-bounds situations. They can also be used as a teaching device for drilling the defensive players in the "techniques of guarding the man without the ball." These situations arise many times during the game, and the development and improvement of defensive ability is a very important aspect of the game of basketball.

Diagram 2-1. Assuming the opposition is playing a man-to-man defense and the ball is awarded to the offense out-of-bounds on the sideline, somewhere between the mid-court area and the end line, the offense would line up as shown in this diagram. The play shows that the ball has been awarded out-of-bounds on the left side of the court. Any plays which are executed from the left side of the floor can also be executed from the right side. Actually, the team is set up in a regular offensive formation, with No. 3 in possession of the ball out-of-bounds. All the team is required to do in this situation is get the ball in-bounds and put the offense in motion. However the *drive, hook, screen* and *slide* series are special plays designed for doing this, and, as a result, will bring about a better opportunity to score. The diagram shows that the only defensive player guarding the player with the ball is X3. The other defensive players are stationed in weak-side defensive coverage positions. This will make it more difficult for the offense on these out-of-bounds situations; however, it will help them take advantage of all the opportunities that will come from defensive mistakes as they are made. The offensive formation shown here is one that can be used from a single pivot-post offense, or a weak-side cutter offensive series. Other offensive formations can easily be woven into this series of plays.

In this series, the guard in the No. 1 position, as shown in Diagram 2-1, will always signal or call the play that is to be used. If the ball is awarded out-of-bounds on the right side of the floor, then the guard in the No. 2 position will call the play. The play that is to be used can be indicated by utilizing various signaling systems, or it can be called out verbally. Experience has proven the verbal or oral signal to be the best to use in this particular situation. For instance, the guard in the No. 1 position will call out the word "Drive," "Hook," "Screen" or "Slide," as the team lines up in formation at about the time the official hands the ball to No. 3 out-of-bounds. The spoken word indicates the play to be used. No. 1 triggers the play, and this will be shown in later diagrams.

Diagram 2-2. Drive–No. 3 takes the ball out-of-bounds on the side of the court and gives the signal for the players to begin the play. Prior to this, No. 1 should call or signal the play that is to be used by calling "Drive" loud enough for all the players to hear him. This play is used with the assumption that the defense is playing a tight man-to-man style of play and that No. 1 can overpower his defensive opponent with speed and drive. When the play starts, No. 1, after a possible fake to the right or left, drives straight in toward the basket with all the speed and power he can muster in an attempt to beat his guard. If he is open, No. 3 passes him the ball and follows the play. If No. 1 does not get open, he then cuts on through under the basket to the opposite side of the floor, providing he is playing

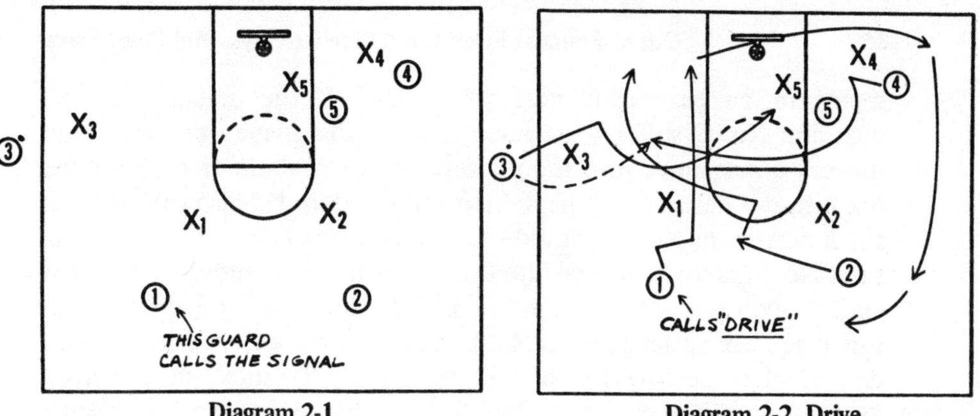

Diagram 2-1

Diagram 2-2. Drive.

against a man-to-man defense. No. 4 now jockeys his defensive man in such a way as to bump him into No. 5 as he cuts either over or behind No. 5. No. 4 then breaks into the pivot-post area just cleared by No. 1. If No. 4 is open, No. 3 passes him the ball. No. 2, who has moved to the left side of the floor at the time No. 1 made his drive, does a "split the post" move over No. 4 with No. 3. No. 4 may pass the ball to either No. 2 or 3. He may also maneuver for other options himself, or he may return the ball to the back court to No. 1, who has circled back to the guard position to be ready for the start of the regular offense. In this diagram, No. 4 is shown cutting over the top of No. 5, but, with proper maneuvering, it will be to No. 4's advantage to break behind No. 5 about 80% or 90% of the time. The reasons for this particular maneuver will be shown in later diagrams. At this point, note that actually the moves are little more than the execution of what might be a part of the regular offense. First there was a power drive by No. 1, followed by a weak-side move by No. 4, in an effort to clear his defensive player and obtain an opening so that he could receive the pass. This maneuver was followed by a "split-the-post" move by Nos. 3 and 2 after the ball was passed to No. 4 in the pivot-post area. Scoring opportunities can come from any of these moves.

Diagram 2-3. Drive—This diagram shows some option possibilities from the drive play. Again No. 1 calls "Drive" and then cuts through in an effort to get open. If he is not open, he clears to the opposite side and returns to the guard area. No. 2 moves to the left to cover the position left vacant by No. 1. No. 4 fakes a cut over the top of No. 5, but, after getting a declaration from his defensive man, reverses and cuts behind No. 5. As a result of this move, he could be open for an easy shot near the basket. If the defensive player guarding No. 5 shifts to cover No. 4 on this maneuver, No. 5 can make a quick move into the pivot-post area near the free throw line because the defense will be split on the switch. He also can be open for a pass from No. 3. Should the pass be made from No. 3 to No. 5, then Nos. 2 and 3 can execute the "split-the-post" move using No. 5 as the pivot-post player. If none of these moves are possible, No. 3 can make an outlet pass to No. 2, who can relay the ball to No. 5. No. 3, after passing the ball in to No. 2, can move in and do a "split-the-post" move with No. 2 over the top of No. 5. Scoring possibilities can result from any of these moves.

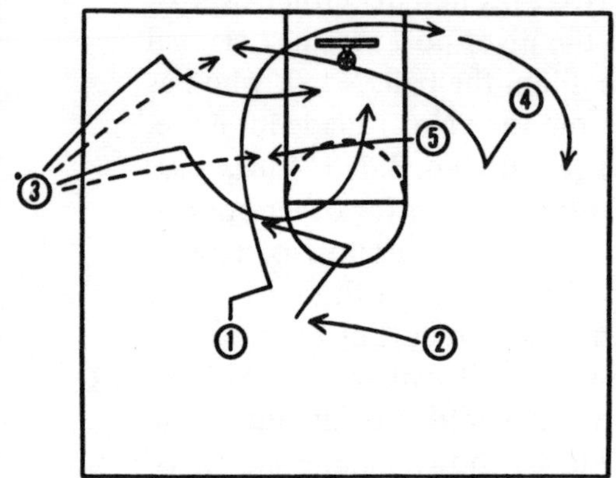

Diagram 2-3. Drive.

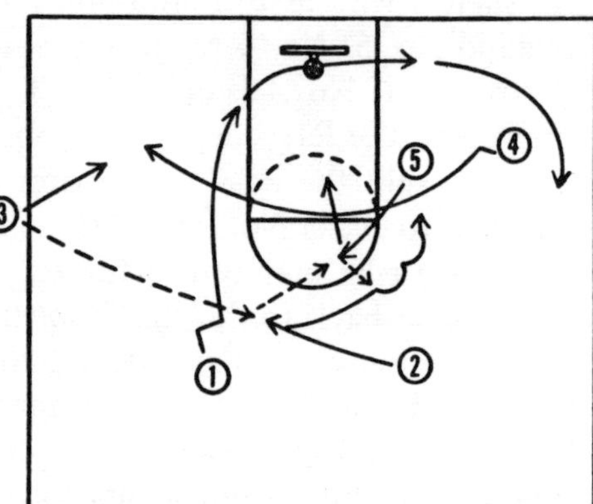

Diagram 2-4. Drive.

Diagram 2-4. Drive–Here the continuation of the offensive idea is carried further. If No. 1 is not open on the drive, he clears the side, moves under the basket and returns to the back-court area. If No. 4 is not open on the weak-side screening move, No. 3 passes the ball to No. 2 as No. 2 moves over to maintain floor balance and cover the area vacated by No. 1. As this maneuver takes place, No. 5 moves into a high post position near the free throw circle on the right side of the free throw lane. No. 2 may pass No. 5 the ball and follow for a return pass and a drive, or he may start a driving dribble past No. 5, using him in a post screening move. Scoring opportunities can result from this "pinched-post" move.

Diagram 2-5. Drive–With a slight adjustment, this play can be used to obtain a good position shot against a zone defense, should the opposition decide to use the zone in this situation. No. 1 again calls "Drive," but, as he cuts through, he realizes that the defense is using the zone, so he pulls up and moves into the left corner along the base line for an outlet pass instead of clearing to the opposite side, as shown in the previous diagrams. No. 3 (who in this case should be the best position shooter from along the base line, or from out 10 to 15 feet from the side of the basket) passes the ball to No. 1 as he pulls wide to the corner. No. 3 then drives hard straight through and to the opposite side of the floor near the basket. No. 3 then adjusts his position outside the perimeter of the defense as it shifts to meet the ball on the left side of the floor. No. 4 makes his usual weak-side move into the pivot-post area, and could be open for a pass or shot. Since No. 1 has informed his teammates by his swing to the side of the court that they are playing against a zone, No. 2 adjusts his position wide so as to receive a pass from No. 1. No. 5 then moves up to the top of the circle so that he is in a position to receive a pass from No. 2, and also to be able to relay the ball on to No. 3. The ball is quickly passed from No. 1, to No. 2, to No. 5, who in turn passes to No. 3 on the opposite side for a possible position shot. If the defense permits, the ball might be relayed to No. 4, to No. 5 and then to No. 3. If No. 5 is a better pivot-post position player, he can exchange moves with No. 4, and move across the free throw lane into the pivot-post area. No. 4 could then move out to the top of the free throw circle to receive the pass from No. 2. This would also be the best move if No. 4 is a better position shooter from the free throw circle area than No. 5, or if he is a better passer and could pass the ball across to No. 3. Many times a good position shot will be possible from the top of the circle, and should be taken, since it is a high percentage shot.

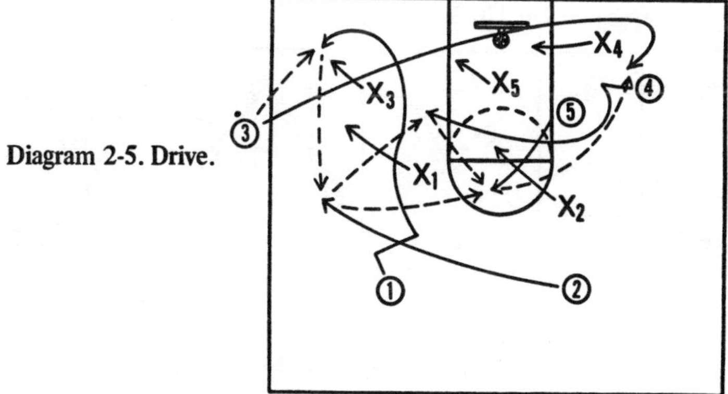

Diagram 2-5. Drive.

Diagram 2-6. Hook–When No. 1 calls "Hook," this play should be used. No. 1 starts his power drive through, but his defensive player plays him tight so that he is not able to free himself. After driving deep into the pivot-post area, No. 1 suddenly plants both feet, stops and does a button hook reversal movement, coming back to meet the ball just to the left of the free throw lane. This should free him for a pass. No. 3 passes him the ball, and cuts past him with the expectation of receiving a return pass. No. 2 may drive past No. 1 also in a "split-the-post" move. No. 4 cuts behind No. 5 in near the basket and could be open for an easy shot also. If not open, No. 4 pulls wide to the corner for a possible outlet pass. No. 3 should follow his pass-in and cut through hard for possible openings.

Diagram 2-7. Hook–If a zone defense is employed against the hook play, then the pattern shown in this diagram should be used. No. 1 makes his usual drive and hook movement, but he is smothered by the zone defense. No. 4 makes his usual move, but this time pulls wide to the corner, enabling him to receive the outlet pass. No. 3, after passing the ball in, drives hard to the opposite side of the floor, as shown in the diagram. No. 2 moves to the left, far enough to receive the ball from No. 4. No. 5 moves into the top of the circle area to receive the ball from No. 2. The ball is passed quickly from No. 4, to No. 2, to No. 5, who in turn relays it quickly to No. 3. No. 3 is now stationed on the opposite side of the floor ready for a position shot. Fast, quick and accurate passing of the ball can assure a good shot for No. 3. A reversal in the direction of the passes will sometimes find No. 4 or 5 open for a shot, or possibly a good scoring opportunity will present itself for No. 1 from the pivot-post area.

Diagram 2-6. Hook.

Diagram 2-7. Hook.

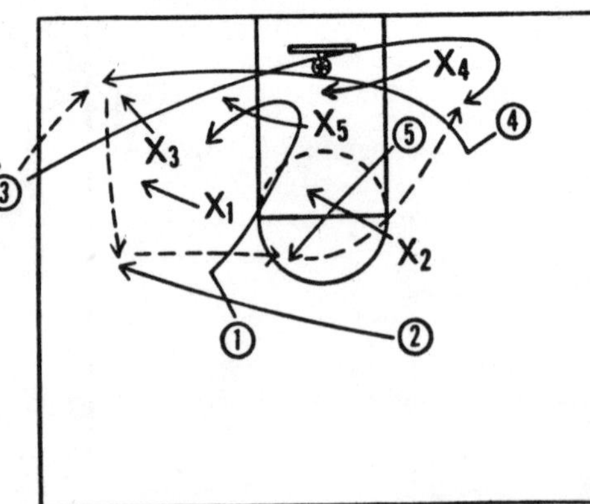

Diagram 2-8. Screen–When the guard, No. 1, calls for the "screen," this play is used. Here the opposition is using a tight man-to-man defense. However if the opposition should switch to the zone defense, the same pattern with slight adjustments, can be used to obtain good position shots. When No. 3 gives the signal to begin the play, No. 1, after faking a move toward the ball, breaks to the right in a diagonal move across the free throw lane and sets a screen on X5, the defensive man guarding No. 5. No. 4, seeing this move coming, fakes a move behind No. 5, and then breaks out over the top of No. 5. This move, in effect, results in a double screen and presents a fine opportunity for a shot if No. 3 is able to pass the ball to No. 4. If No. 4 is not immediately open, he continues across the lane and into a pivot-post area just below the free throw line. If No. 4 is open, No. 3 passes to him, and then follows the pass for a possible "split-the-post" move with No. 2, who has adjusted his floor position to his left as No. 1 cuts in to set the screen. No. 4 can pass to either player who might be open. As soon as No. 4 clears the screen set by No. 1, and continues across the lane, No. 5 cuts sharply off the screen and deep toward the left side of the basket. He could be open for an easy two points here, and No. 3 should pass him the ball if he is open. If No. 5 is not open, he continues on toward the corner of the court for a possible outlet pass. If the other options are exhausted, No. 3 could pass to No. 5 on this wide flare-out and break hard for the basket for a return pass using a "pass-and-go" move. Outlet passes can also be made to No. 2 if necessary. After Nos. 4 and 5 have cleared the screen, No. 1 flares back out to the guard position for defensive balance. Nos. 4 and 5 can also reverse their moves for good change-of-pace openings. With this reverse move, No. 4 fakes over the top of No. 5, and then cuts behind him and low to the basket for a possible opening. If he is not open, he can flare out wide. No. 5, seeing No. 4 make this move, will then break across the lane into the pivot-post area for a possible opening and a pass from No. 3.

Diagram 2-9. Screen–If the defense should zone the play, slight adjustments can be made and a good position shot can still be obtained. No. 1 starts the play as usual by driving across the free throw lane and setting a screen for No. 5. No. 4 fakes over the top of No. 5, then cuts behind him and low to the left side of the basket.

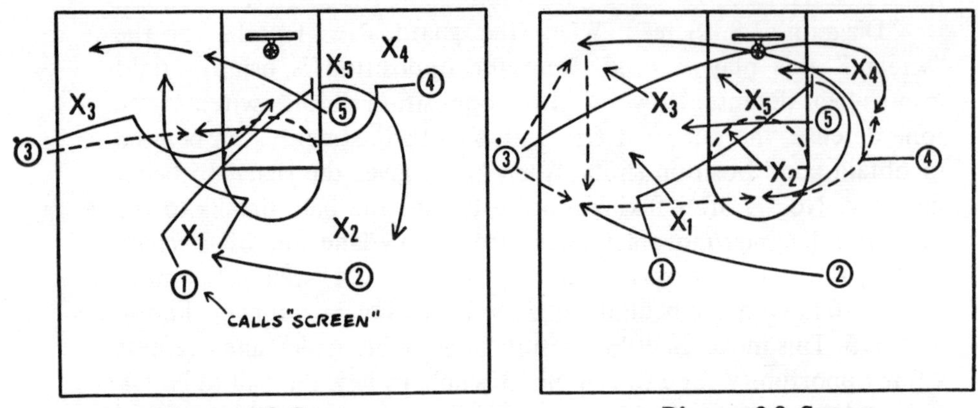

Diagram 2-8. Screen.

Diagram 2-9. Screen.

He could be open here for a pass and as a result a quick two points. If he is open, No. 3 should pass the ball to him. If he is not open, and the opposition is using a zone defense, this move is usually cut off. No. 4 continues on out wide along the base line and toward the corner of the court. No. 5 quickly breaks into the pivot-post area for a possible pass. No. 2 moves over to the left side of the court. No. 3 now passes to either No. 4 or 2, and then cuts through to the opposite side of the floor and into the area shown in the diagram. No. 1 flares quickly back to the top of the circle area. There can be an exchange of passes between Nos. 4 and 2, but the ball must be moved quickly from No. 4, to No. 2, to No. 1, to No. 3. Either No. 1 or 3 might have good position shots. Openings might be available for a pass to No. 5 also.

Diagram 2-10. Slide–If the guard, No. 1, calls "Slide," he fakes to set the screen on X5, but instead, just before he gets into the screening area, he breaks quickly to the left and deep toward the left side of the basket. He could be open here for an easy two points, but if he is not open, he flares on out toward the corner of the court for an outlet pass. No. 4 cuts across the top of No. 5 and into the pivot-post area. He could receive the ball in this position and set the stage for "split-the-post" plays which could result in scoring opportunities. If none of these pass opportunities are possible, No. 3 can pass the ball to No. 2, who is stationed in the outlet position. No. 5 then moves into a "pinched-post" position to the right side and into the outer half of the free throw circle. No. 2 can pass to No. 5 at this position and cut off him for a return pass, or he can dribble hard over the top of No. 5 for a rear pick-and-roll play. Diagram 2-10 shows the variables that could develop from the "slide" move. The *drive, hook, screen* and *slide* series furnishes a good set of scoring plays with many options available against both the man-to-man and zone defenses.

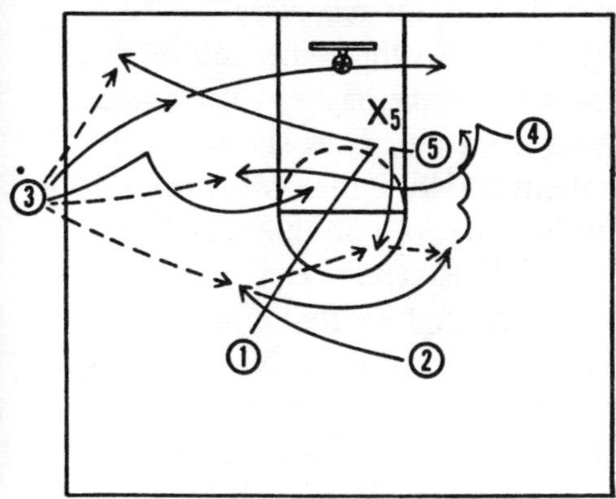

Diagram 2-10. Slide.

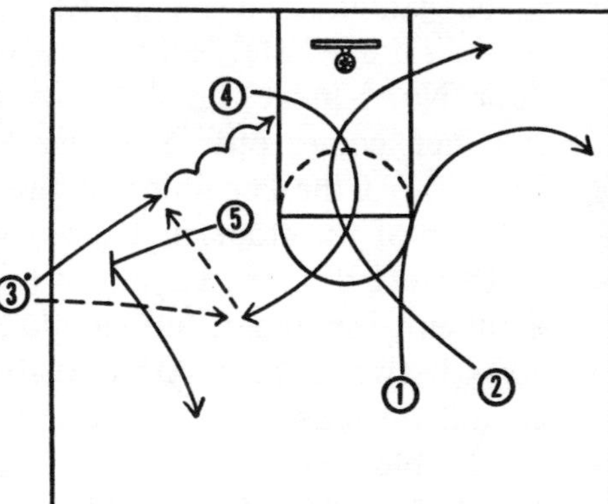

Diagram 2-11

QUICK OPENING PLAYS

In the quick opening plays which will be shown, it is assumed that the defense is tight, aggressive and mostly man-to-man. Some of the plays could be used for even more special situations where a quick shot or score is needed.

Diagram 2-11. In Diagram 2-11, No. 3 passes to No. 4, who has stationed himself near the basket area. At the signal given by No. 3 to start the play, No. 1 cuts toward the basket and veers to the right as he reaches the top of the free throw circle area. This takes his guard away from the basket area. No. 2 waits for No. 1's cut and then makes his break directly behind him. As No. 2 nears the free throw line area, No. 4 breaks toward the free throw line from his position near the basket. No. 4 cuts to the right side of No. 2 (his own left) so that he can use No. 2 as a moving screen. This maneuver will enable No. 4 to break clear for the pass from No. 3. No. 2 cuts in the same direction as No. 1 as he nears the basket area, in order to take his guard away from this area. After No. 3 makes the pass to No. 4, he breaks toward the basket with the expectation of a return pass from No. 4, as shown in the diagram. As No. 3 makes the pass to No. 4, No. 5 moves up to screen for No. 3, enabling him to clear himself for the pass from No. 4. No. 5 then moves out to a guard position for defensive balance.

Diagram 2-12. No. 3 takes the ball out-of-bounds and Nos. 4, 5, 1 and 2 line up in the box formation, as shown in the diagram. On the signal to begin the play, No. 1 shakes loose from his guard, enabling him to receive a pass from No. 3. After receiving the pass, he then immediately starts a driving dribble to the right side of the floor. No. 5 moves his defensive man toward the basket with a fake, and then comes out to receive a pass from No. 1, as shown in the diagram. At the beginning of the maneuver, No. 2 moves toward the left side of the floor, and, along with No. 4, sets a double screen just to the left of the free throw line area. This screen can be almost shoulder-to-shoulder, but should be wide enough so that a player can break between them. After passing the ball in to No. 1, No. 3 moves in, and then, as No. 1 passes the ball to No. 5, No. 3 breaks between the double screen set by Nos. 2 and 4, as shown in the diagram. This maneuver will enable No. 3 to break into the clear so that he can receive a pass from No. 5 and obtain an unmolested shot. Note that Nos. 3, 4 and 5 will be in good rebound and follow-up positions. If the defense aggressively switches, Nos. 4 and 2 could be in excellent break-in positions from the defensive split.

Diagram 2-13. In Diagram 2-13, No. 3 takes the ball out-of-bounds. When the signal is given by No. 3 to start the play, No. 1 moves toward the center of the floor and screens for No. 2. This should be a moving type of screen, as No. 2 should break toward the ball as soon as No. 3 gives the signal to start the play. No. 3 passes the ball to No. 2, who in turn passes to No. 4 at the top and left of the free throw circle. No. 5 moves across the free throw circle from his position, as shown in the diagram, so that he may screen for No.

Diagram 2-12

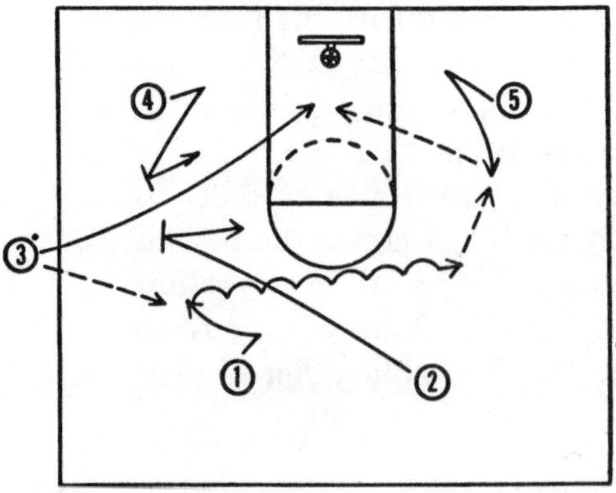

Diagram 2-13

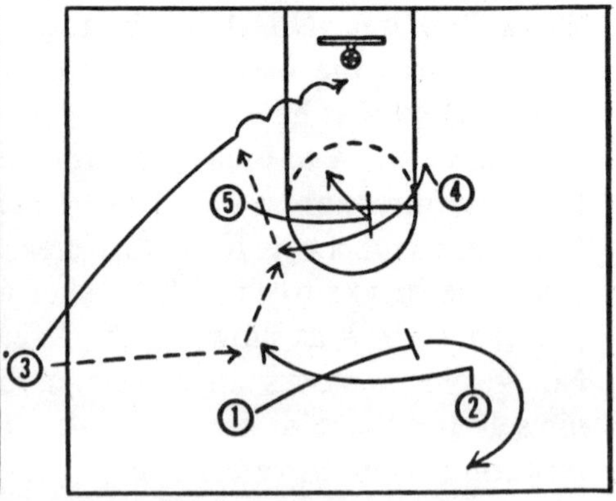

4. No. 4 jabs toward the basket to move his defensive man into No. 5's screen, then breaks over No. 5 and across the free throw circle, as shown in the diagram, to receive the pass from No. 2. There must be good timing between these two players in order that No. 4 will be ready to receive the pass as he is breaking across to meet it at the time No. 2 is ready to pass to him. After No. 4 receives the pass, he is now in a position to pass to No. 3, who has cut for the basket after he made the pass-in to No. 2. No. 1 rolls out to take the guard position, and for defensive balance.

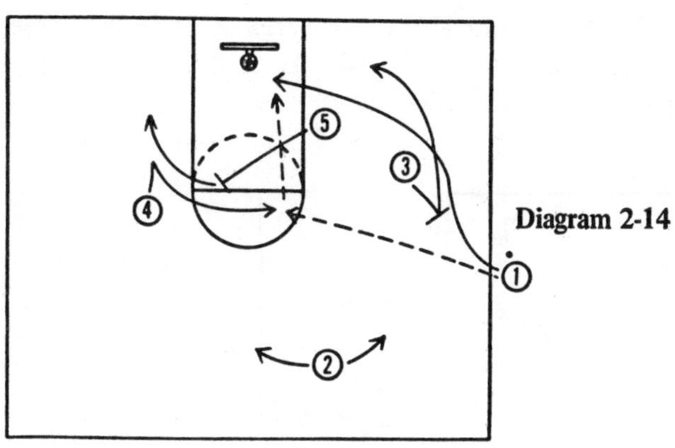

Diagram 2-14

Diagram 2-14. In Diagram 2-14, No. 1 passes to No. 4, who cuts toward the ball. No. 5 screens for No. 4 as he breaks across the top of the free throw circle, enabling No. 4 to free himself for the pass-in. After making the pass to No. 4, No. 1 breaks toward the basket. As he breaks toward the basket, No. 1 receives a screen from No. 3, which will free him as he breaks for a return pass from No. 4. No. 3 executes a reverse pivot after the screen on No. 1's opponent and follows No. 1 toward the basket. If No. 3's defensive man does not switch to No. 1 as he cuts to the basket, he will be open for the pass. If the switch is made, then No. 3 should be open as a trailer, providing he executes the screen-and-roll correctly. No. 5, meanwhile, has also executed a screen-and-roll, which, if done correctly, will also result in another player being freed for a pass from No. 4. No. 4 has three opportunities to pass to players who might be free to receive the pass and have a good scoring opportunity as a result—Nos. 1, 3 and 5. If none are free, then he must pass to No. 2.

Diagram 2-15. In this diagram, No. 1 makes the pass-in to No. 3, who breaks toward the ball from the free throw line area. No. 4 cuts behind No. 3 and sets a screen for No. 1 as he cuts for the basket, as shown in the diagram. No. 2 moves out toward the center of the court from a position near the basket to help clear the area, and screens for No. 5. No. 5 fakes a drive to his right, and then breaks toward the left side of the basket, off the screen set by No. 2. If he is free, he may receive a pass from No. 1 or 3. No. 3, upon receiving the pass from No. 1, makes a return pass as No. 1 makes the cut to the basket. No. 2, after screening for No. 5, rolls out to the mid-court area for defensive balance. No. 4 will execute a reverse pivot and roll-off toward the base line and corner area after he has screened for No. 1. No. 3 may now pass to No. 1, 5, 4 or 2. Quick opening possibilities can come from this play.

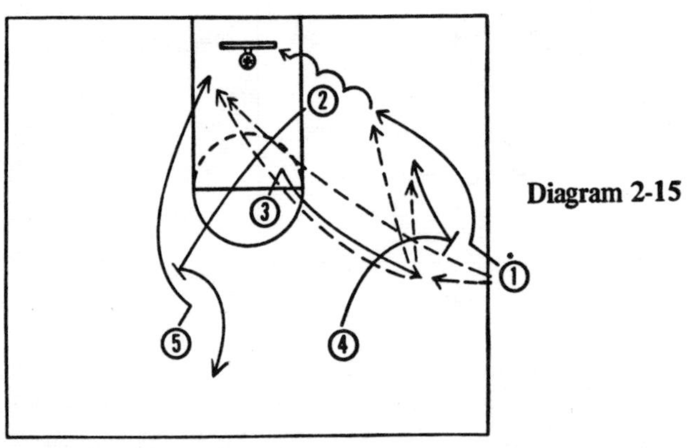

Diagram 2-15

Diagram 2-16. In Diagram 2-16, No. 1 passes to No. 2, who fakes toward the basket to throw his guard off balance, and then breaks toward the ball. No. 3, meanwhile, also fakes toward the basket and then breaks out toward No. 2, where he receives the pass, as shown in the diagram. Correct timing in making this move is important, as No. 3 will not receive a screen and therefore must free himself for the pass at the time No. 2 receives the ball and is ready to make the pass to No. 3. After No. 3 receives the pass from No. 2, he then passes to No. 5, who cuts for the basket after receiving a screen from No. 4, as shown in the diagram. No. 4 must hold his position and time his move so that his screen on No. 5's opponent will take place at a time when No. 5 is ready to make his break toward the basket. It must also be at a time when No. 3 is ready to make the pass. If the pass cannot be made to No. 5, it can possibly be made to No. 4, who makes a reverse pivot after screening for No. 5 and cuts toward the basket. If No. 2 cannot make the pass to No. 3, he can pass back to No. 1, who moves into the mid-court area for defensive balance. If No. 3 cannot pass to either No. 4 or 5, he also can make the pass-back to No. 1 in the back-court area.

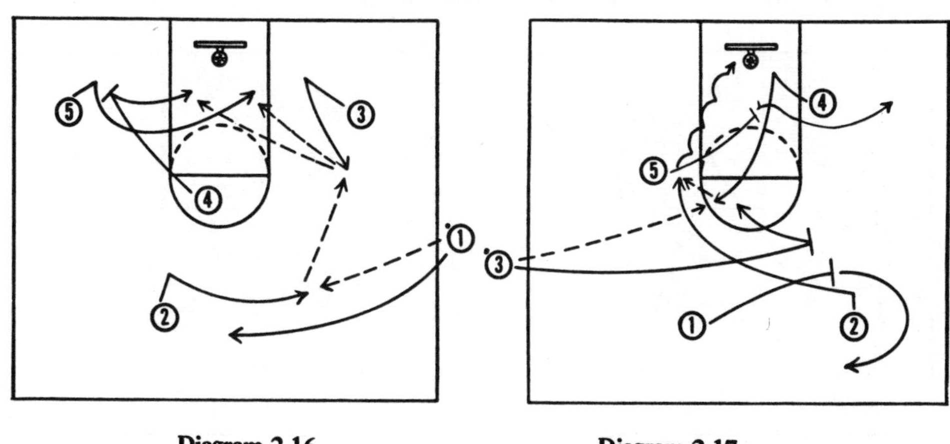

Diagram 2-16

Diagram 2-17

Diagram 2-17. No. 4 breaks diagonally across the free throw lane and toward the top of the circle. No. 5 sets a moving screen for No. 4 at about the center of the lane. This should free No. 4 for a pass from No. 3 at the top of the circle. In the meantime, No. 1 moves toward No. 2 to set a screen, and as soon as No. 3 passes the ball in to No. 4, he moves in with No. 1 to set a double screen for No. 2. No. 2 cuts behind Nos. 1 and 3, and should be open for a pass from No. 4. If No. 3's guard switches to No. 2, No. 3 can roll off on a reverse pivot for an opening over No. 4, and a possible pass from No. 4. No. 1 rolls out to mid-court for defensive balance, and No. 5 pulls over to the side and toward the corner of the court to clear the area.

Diagram 2-18. No. 1 takes the ball out-of-bounds. On the signal to start the play, No. 5 breaks from his position near the basket to an area beyond the free throw circle and near the ball. No. 1 passes him the ball. As No. 5 is breaking toward the ball, No. 3 sets a screen for No. 2 near the top of the circle, and No. 4 screens the defensive man guarding No. 1, as shown in the diagram. After the ball is passed to

No. 5, No. 1 drives hard and sharp for the basket behind the screen which has been set by No. 4, with the expectation of receiving a return pass from No. 5. No. 2 jams his defensive player to the left, and then breaks hard to the right behind the screen set by No. 3. He may be open for a pass from No. 5. If No. 4's defensive man should shift to No. 1, No. 4 should execute a reverse pivot and roll toward the basket for a possible pass from No. 5 as No. 1 clears the area. No. 3 rolls out to the area near the top of the circle for defensive balance.

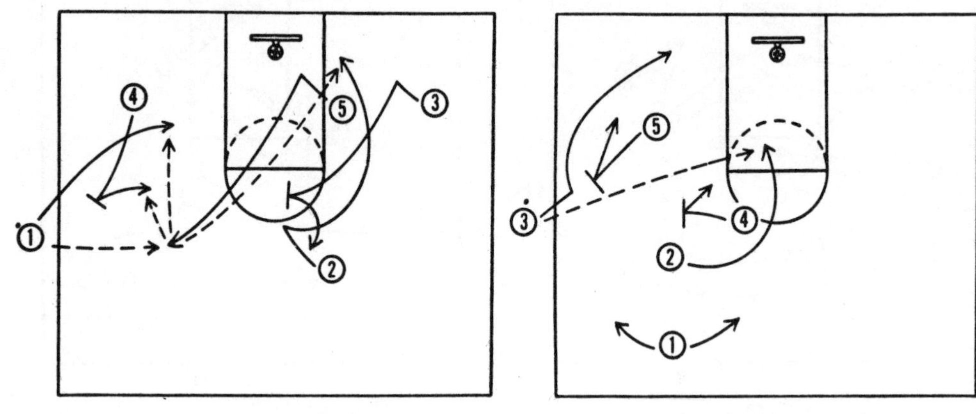

Diagram 2-18 Diagram 2-19

Diagram 2-19. No. 3 takes the ball out-of-bounds. Nos. 1, 2, 4 and 5 line up as shown in the diagram. On the signal to start the play, No. 4 sets a screen on No. 2's defensive man. No. 2 breaks behind the screen and down the free throw lane. He should be open for a pass from No. 3. As the pass-in is made, No. 5 sets a screen on No. 3's defensive man. After passing in to No. 2, No. 3 cuts hard and sharp past the screen set by No. 5, for a possible opening, if No. 2 has not been able to score and needs to make an outlet pass. Nos. 5 and 4 roll off their screens toward the basket to follow up on the play. No. 1 furnishes the opportunity for the outlet pass if it is needed.

Diagram 2-20. If the opposition is using a tight man-to-man defense and the ball is out-of-bounds on the sideline in the front court, this diagram shows a typical quick opener play that can be used with success. No. 1 takes the ball out-of-bounds, and when the signal to begin the play is given, No. 2 jams his man toward the basket and then breaks toward No. 1 and the ball. No. 1 passes the ball to No. 2. No. 3 fakes his man toward the basket and then breaks out toward the ball. He times his moves just in time to receive the ball from No. 2. No. 2 may have to dribble the ball in order to get the timing needed to coincide with No. 3's break toward the ball. When the signal is given, Nos. 4 and 5 break toward the ball and move shoulder-to-shoulder to set a double screen at the top right side of the free throw circle, as shown in the diagram. After passing the ball in-bounds, No. 1 breaks behind No. 2, hard and sharp behind the double screen set by Nos. 4 and 5. The play should be timed so that No. 1 breaks from behind the screen just as No. 3 receives the ball. No. 1 should be open for a pass from No. 3. If the defensive man guarding No. 4 or 5 switches to cover No. 1, then that player should execute a reverse roll to the basket for an opening. Nos. 4 and 5 should both roll for the basket in following up on the play. If No. 2 is not open on the original jam and break toward the ball, No. 1 could make a delayed pass to No. 3. No. 1 can break behind Nos. 4 and 5 for a return pass and drive to the basket. No. 3 can hold the defense in with a dribble delay movement until No. 1 breaks off the double screen for an opening.

Diagram 2-20

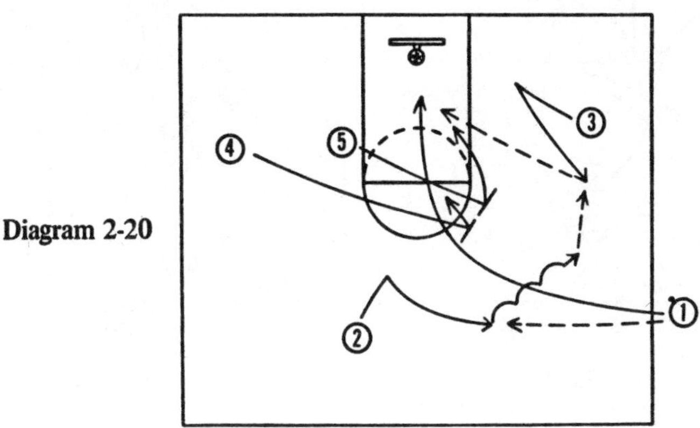

VERTICAL LINE PLAYS

Diagram 2-21. Players 1, 2, 4 and 5 position themselves in a straight line above and directly in front of the free throw circle. When the signal is given to begin the play by No. 3, who has the ball out-of-bounds, No. 4 breaks toward the left corner of the court and then hooks back toward the ball. No. 5 waits for No. 4 to break past him and then cuts behind No. 4 and toward No. 3. No. 5 should time his cut so that he can rub his guard off, using No. 4 as a moving screen. No. 3 passes the ball to No. 5 as No. 5 breaks toward him, and as he sees that No. 5 is open. As soon as No. 3 passes the ball, he cuts quickly and sharply toward the opposite side of the court. When he passes the middle of the court, he angles sharply to his left and toward the basket. No. 5, meanwhile, after receiving the pass, pivots and passes to No. 3, as indicated in the diagram. No. 3 should receive the pass in the vicinity of the free throw line. If No. 3 is unable to pass to No. 5, then he has the option of making the outlet pass to either No. 2, 4 or 1.

Diagram 2-22. In this diagram, the ball is out-of-bounds near mid-court. No. 1 takes the ball out and Nos. 2, 3, 4 and 5 line up in a vertical line facing him, about three to four strides in-bounds. On the signal to begin the play, No. 5 sets a screen on the defensive man guarding No. 4, while No. 2 sets a screen on the defensive man of No.

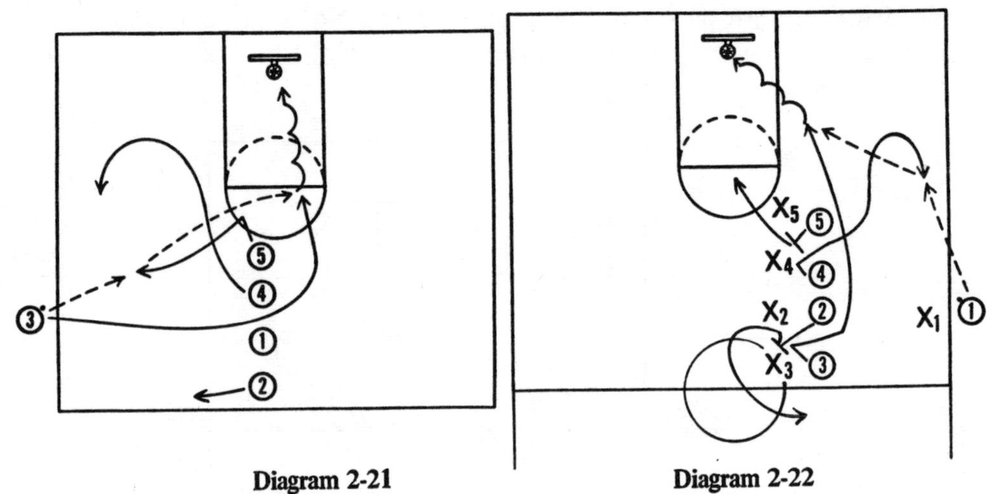

Diagram 2-21

Diagram 2-22

3. No. 4 fakes to drive off the screen of No. 5 toward the center of the court, and then pulls deep down court toward the sideline to receive the pass-in from No. 1. No. 3 fakes also as if to drive toward the center of the floor, and then breaks to the right and down the side in such a manner as to benefit from the screen set by Nos. 2 and 5. He then cuts hard and sharp toward the basket. No. 4 passes him the ball, or he could receive a pass direct from No. 1 if No. 4 is not open for a pass. If the defensive man guarding No. 5 should switch to No. 3, then No. 5 rolls toward the basket for a possible opening. No. 2 rolls out of the screen toward the back court for defensive balance and a possible outlet pass if needed.

HORIZONTAL LINE PLAYS

Diagram 2-23. No. 1 has the ball out-of-bounds as shown in the diagram. Nos. 2, 3, 4 and 5 line up in a horizontal line near the free throw line and circle. No. 5 should be the best position shot. On the signal to start the play, No. 4 sets a screen on No. 5's defensive man, and No. 3 sets a screen on No. 4's defensive man, while No. 2 screens on No. 3's man. No. 5 fakes a drive to the right and toward the basket, and then steps out behind the protecting screen set by Nos. 2, 3 and 4. No. 1 passes him the ball at this position for a good percentage shot. After passing the ball in, No. 1 drives for the basket. As No. 5 shoots, Nos. 3 and 4 roll toward the basket, and No. 2 remains outside for defensive balance.

Diagram 2-24. This play is very much like the one shown in Diagram 2-23, but it provides a little more protection for the position shooter. No. 1 has the ball out-of-bounds. Nos. 2, 3, 4 and 5 line up as shown in the diagram. No. 4 is the best position shooter from the top of the free throw circle area. When the signal is given to begin the play, Nos. 3 and 5 both screen on No. 4's defensive man as shown in the diagram. No. 2 screens on No. 3's defensive man. No. 4 fakes a drive, and then steps back to receive the pass from No. 1. He should have a good shot from this area. After passing the ball in, No. 1 drives for the basket. Nos. 3 and 5 roll toward the basket when No. 4 shoots, or if their defensive men scramble to stop the shot by No. 4, either of them may be eligible for a pass and a possible opening on a roll-off toward the basket. No. 2 rolls off his screen toward the mid-court for defensive balance.

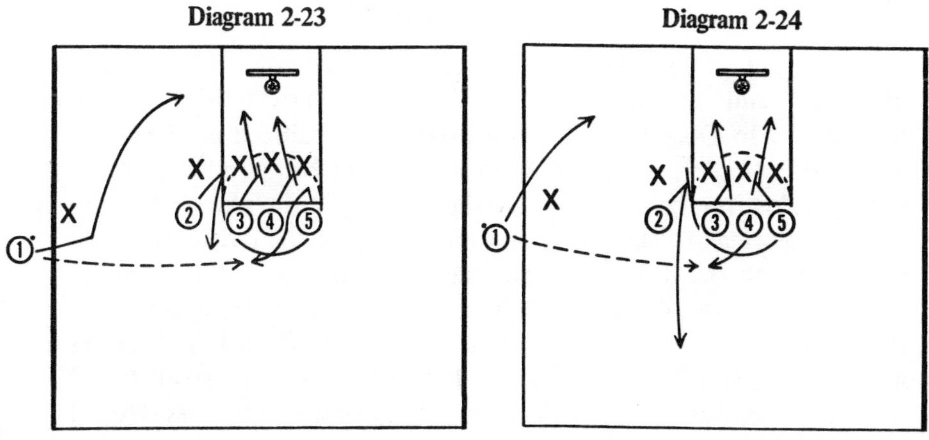

Diagram 2-25. In this diagram, Nos. 1, 2, 4 and 5 line up near the free throw line in a horizontal position. No. 3 has the ball out-of-bounds. On the signal to begin the play, No. 2 screens on No. 1's defensive man, No. 4 screens on No. 2's defensive man and No. 5 screens on the man guarding No. 4. This, in effect, will set up a triple screen. As this is done, No. 1, after faking to the left, breaks behind the three players setting a screen, and then moves sharply toward the basket, where he receives the pass-in from No. 3. He could be wide open for a shot, but in the defensive scramble resulting from a play like this, an opening could come to No. 4 or 5, both of whom should be ready to follow on the play. No. 2 rolls off the screen toward the mid-court for defensive balance and a possible outlet pass if none of the other players are open. No. 3, after passing the ball in-bounds, follows with a hard drive for the basket and a possible return pass and opening.

Diagram 2-25

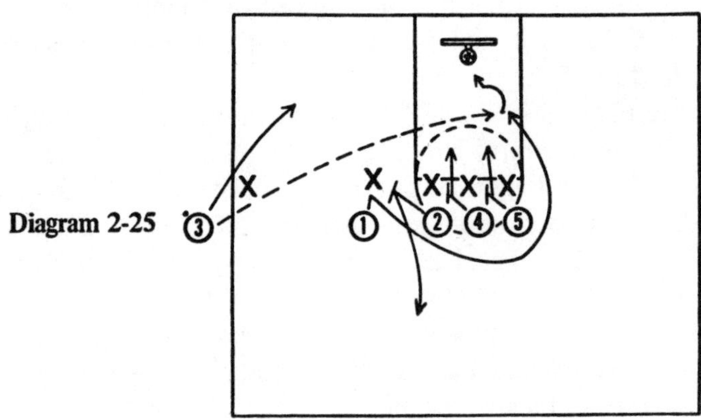

MID-COURT PLAYS

Diagram 2-26. When the ball is taken out-of-bounds at mid-court and the defense is tight, several possibilities present themselves. In Diagram 2-26, No. 3 takes the ball out-of-bounds at mid-court. Nos. 1, 4, 2 and 5 line up facing No. 3, about evenly spaced across the court. When the signal to begin the play is given by No. 3, Nos. 1 and 2 fake a strong move toward their right and then set screens on the defensive men guarding Nos. 4 and 5, as shown in the diagram. Nos. 4 and 5, at the same time, fake strong moves to their left, and then break sharply off the screens which have been set in a move first toward the ball and then toward the basket. No. 3 passes to whichever one is open, and then follows the pass. Nos. 4

and 5 will usually be freed by this move. Nos. 1 and 2 roll off the screen toward the backcourt for outlet passes and defensive balance, in case neither No. 4 nor 5 are open. If there is a switch on defense on the screen move, Nos. 1 and 2 can also pivot and roll toward the ball, and then toward the basket for openings.

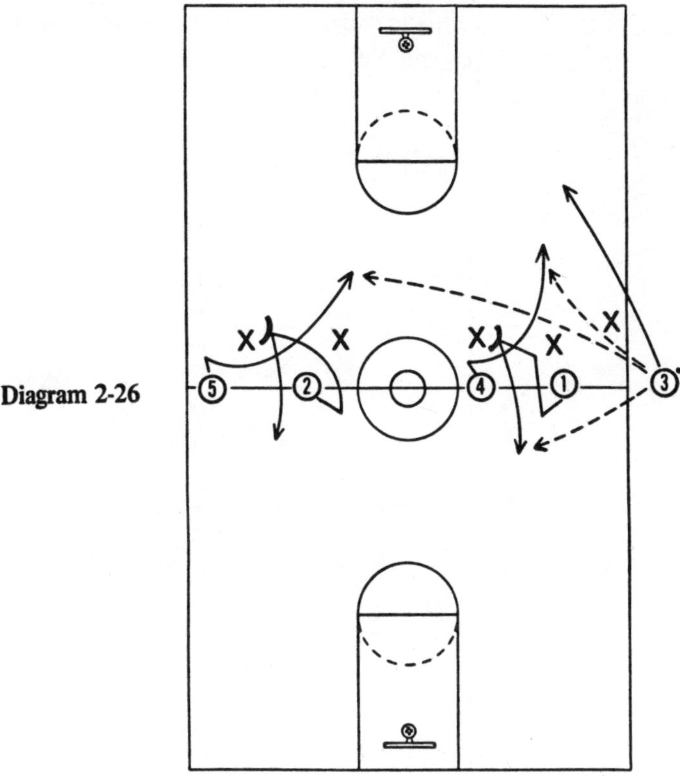

Diagram 2-26

Many scoring opportunities are possible as a result of this play, and in the ensuing scramble which takes place as the play unfolds, it will be difficult to determine which players will be freed for these opportunities. However, continued rehearsal of the play will develop the team's ability in exploiting opportunities that arise from the various situations.

Diagram 2-27. The mid-court version of the horizontal line play can take various options. This diagram gives a very interesting one, and is aimed at freeing one player; in this case, No. 4. The players line up equidistantly apart on the mid-court line facing No. 3, who has the ball out-of-bounds. Nos. 1 and 2 do not do any screening, but, on the signal to begin the play, No. 1 fakes to his right and then breaks to his left into the front court just to get open. At the same time, No. 2 fakes to his left and pulls into the back court for a possible outlet pass. No. 5 fakes right, and then turns to put a screen on No. 4's defensive man. No. 4 holds until No. 5 gets into the screening position, and then he cuts sharply behind the screen and toward the basket. If he is open, No. 3 passes to him. No. 3 could also pass to No. 1, who in turn might pass to No. 4 when he breaks open. After the pass-in, No. 3 breaks hard for the basket. Quick openers are possible from this play.

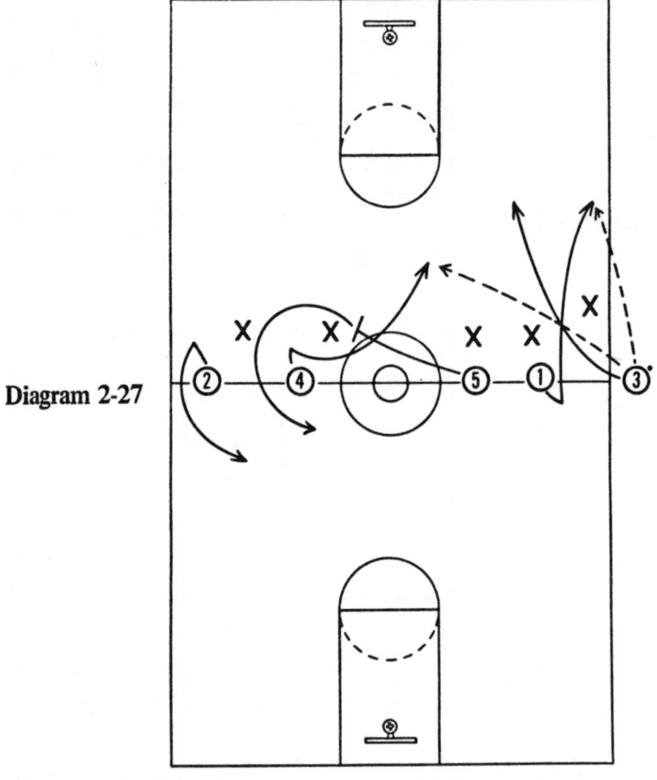

Diagram 2-27

Diagram 2-28. In this diagram, No. 1 takes the ball out-of-bounds. Nos. 2, 3, 4 and 5 line up very close together and on the mid-court line facing No. 1, as shown in the diagram. On the signal to begin the play, Nos. 3, 4 and 5 set a triple screen for No. 2, who is the fastest player on the team. No. 2 breaks hard and sharp past the screen, and then straight down the floor toward the offensive basket. No. 1 passes to him as soon as he is open, and he goes in for the lay-up shot. No. 3 rolls out of the screen to the back court for defensive balance and an outlet pass if needed. Nos. 4 and 5 follow on the shot.

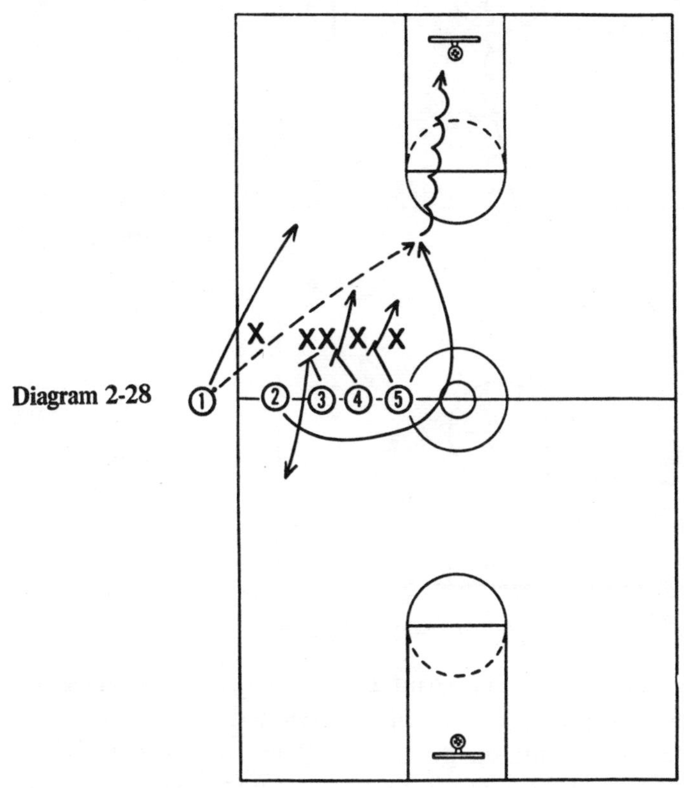

Diagram 2-28

Diagram 2-29. This diagram shows No. 1 taking the ball out-of-bounds at mid-court. The arrow indicates the front court area. Instead of the players taking their regular offensive positions in the front court or at mid-court, Nos. 2, 3, 4 and 5 move to the back court and take their offensive positions as if going for and attempting to score at the defensive basket. If the defense is tight, and if the play is set up like this after a time out, it will often confuse the defense. The defensive players will take positions on the opposite side of the offensive player rather than between him and his basket. If this happens, on the signal to begin the play, all No. 2 has to do is race for his basket, receive the ball from No. 1 and go in for the shot. Nos. 4, 5 and 3 will need to put on a good act, because for all appearances they are setting up a play for the wrong basket. The intent is to confuse the defense and as a result score two easy points.

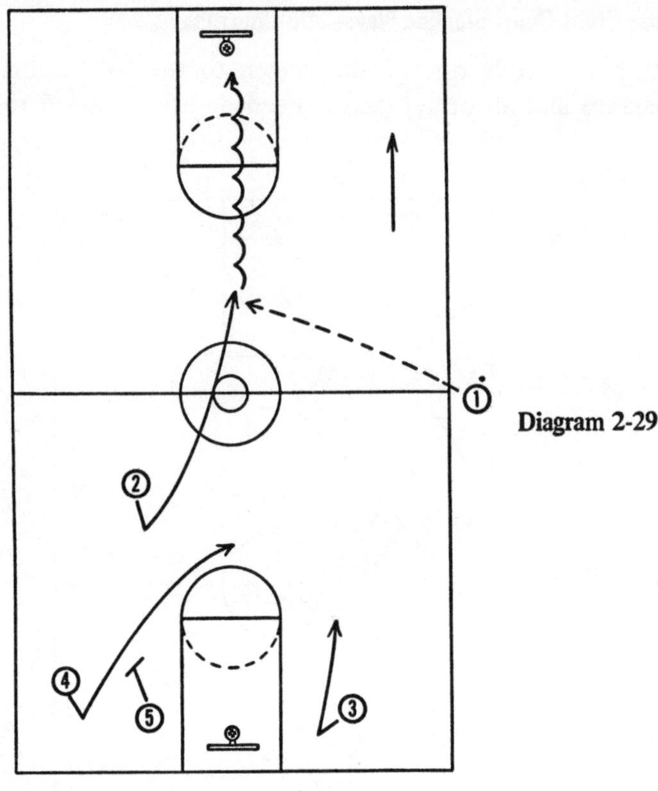

Diagram 2-29

CORNER PLAYS

Diagram 2-30. Every front court offense should have a corner out-of-bounds play. The ball will be awarded there enough times to justify the time spent on practicing it, and it can help the team to obtain "the winning edge." In this diagram, No. 3 has the ball out-of-bounds near the left-hand corner of the court. The same play could be run from a position just around the corner or from the opposite corner. Nos. 4, 5, 1 and 2 line up as shown in the diagram. When the signal to start the play is given, No. 1 sets a screen on No. 2's guard in an exchange maneuver with No. 2. No. 2 moves over to an area on the left side of the floor to receive the outlet pass from No. 3. As this is done, Nos. 5 and 4 move out toward No. 3 and set a double screen shoulder-to-shoulder. No. 3 breaks inside, and over the top of the screen set by Nos. 4 and 5. He could be open, and if so, No. 2 will pass to him for a drive-in and a shot. If No. 3 is not open on this first move, he immediately circles behind Nos. 4 and 5 and comes out behind the screen set by them. No. 2, who has gone into an adjustment dribble, passes the ball to No. 3 as he comes from the underneath side and into position behind the double screen for an unmolested set shot. After the shot, Nos. 4 and 5 follow hard in a roll-off for rebound and follow-up positions on the shot. No. 1 rolls

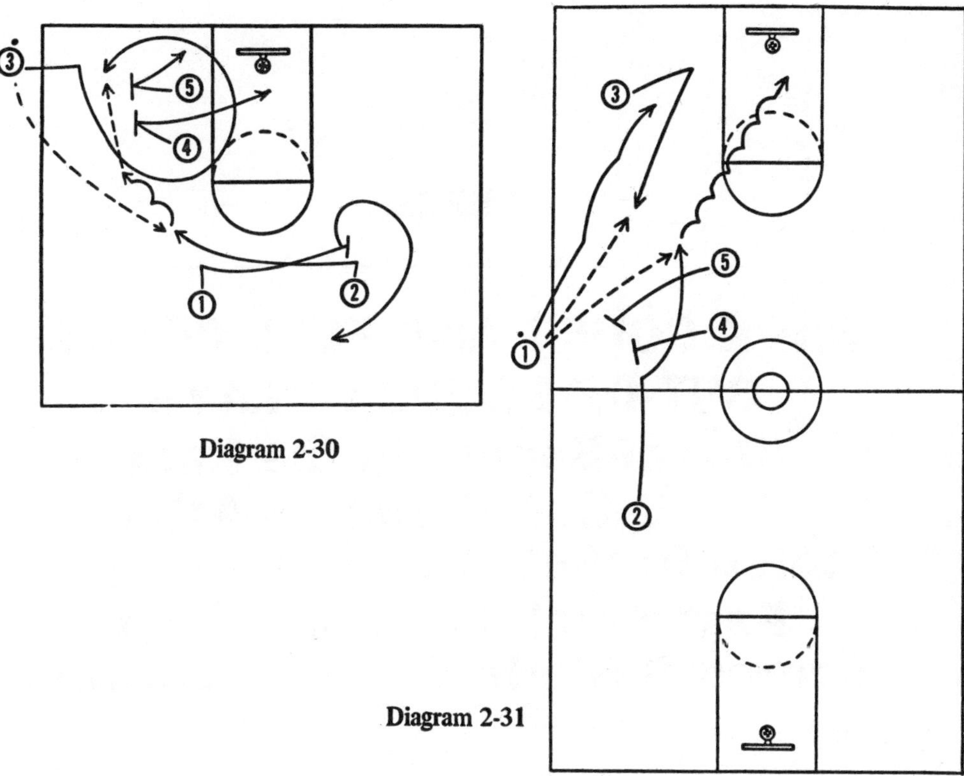

Diagram 2-30

Diagram 2-31

out of the screen set by No. 2 toward the mid-court area to provide for defensive balance.

Diagram 2-31. No. 1 takes the ball out-of-bounds near the mid-court corner. It could be at mid-court, and this play could be termed a mid-court play. The other players line up as shown in the diagram. When the signal is given to begin the play, Nos. 4 and 5 move toward No. 1 as if to get the ball, but, at the last second, they move in and set a double screen for No. 2. Nos. 4 and 5 set the screen shoulder-to-shoulder and about halfway between the center circle and the sideline. No. 2, timing his break, cuts hard and sharp behind the screen, at which point No. 1 passes him the ball. He can now dribble in for a shot. If No. 2 is not open, No. 3, who has delayed his action to coincide with the move of No. 2, after jamming his defensive man toward the basket, breaks out to an area where No. 1 could pass him the ball. If No. 2 is not open, then No. 1 passes to No. 3 and cuts behind him for a possible return pass. Quick openings could come from either option to the play.

THREE

BACK COURT AND FULL COURT OUT-OF-BOUNDS PLAYS (Out-of-Bounds in the Back Court—Out-of-Bounds After Scored Baskets and Free Throws—Fast Break Situations from Scored Baskets and Free Throws)

Establishing a Philosophy on the Use of Out-of-Bounds Plays

In establishing a sound philosophy on the importance of out-of-bounds plays, it is necessary to develop a sound basis for plays which will be successful from any out-of-bounds position on the court. Present day all-court pressing defenses present many problems to the team that is not particularly adept at handling the ball in the back court.

Purpose of Out-of-Bounds Plays in the Back Court

When facing a press with the ball out-of-bounds in the back court, the offensive team's first objective is to get the ball into the front court; its second objective is to score. These objectives can be accomplished through positive thinking, the possession of confidence by every player and a well-planned attack. The offensive players must be ever mindful of the fact that in order for a team to perform efficiently, it must have confidence in its ability to move the ball up court quickly and surely from any position in the back court.

Types of Out-of-Bounds Plays in the Back Court

The out-of-bounds plays discussed in this chapter will be those which will originate from the back-court area, and are designed to help the offensive team who has possession of the ball in this area to move it toward the front court easily and with a minimum chance of interception. These plays can and often do result in scoring opportunities. The primary purpose is to provide the team with a well-conceived pattern of play which will not only accomplish this objective but enable them to move the ball toward the front court in an orderly fashion, helping to provide them with "the winning edge."

The plays will be those which can be executed from the side of the back court and also from the defensive end line. The defensive end line plays will be those which give the ball to the offensive team after a successful shot or free throw, as well as when the opposition touches it last before it goes out-of-bounds. Obtaining possession of the ball out-of-bounds on the side of the back court is usually the result of the opposition touching the ball last before it goes out-of-bounds, the result of a violation by the opponent or putting the ball into play after a time out.

The following plays will be diagrammed and discussed in this chapter: out-of-bounds in the back court; out-of-bounds after scored baskets and free throws; plays for missed free throws; fast break situations and reverse offensive set-ups.

Ingredients for a Successful Out-of-Bounds Play

Up until now, we have discussed out-of-bounds plays from all positions on the court. It is important at this time to emphasize the fact that any good out-of-bounds play should have three things to make it work successfully: (1) at least two pass-in options which will be open in succession; (2) provisions for either switching, non-switching or a zone defense; (3) a safety man who protects against an interception or who can be used for a safety valve pass, should the scoring options not appear or the receivers are all covered.

OUT-OF-BOUNDS IN THE BACK COURT—SIDELINE PLAYS

Every team should develop its offense so that it functions from base line to base line, or, stating it in another way, from the defensive end line to the offensive end line. There will be times during a game when the defense will attack at any or all points between these two base lines and from any position on the court. The offensive team must, therefore, be prepared for this eventuality, and never be without ways and means to combat it. This requires special plays and special preparation.

In the back court, the point at which a team will be awarded the ball out-of-bounds most frequently is on the sideline at the free throw line extended. Awarding the ball out-of-bounds to a team at this spot usually results from the opposing team committing a free throw or a lane violation. Basket interference or goal tending by the offensive team also results in the ball being awarded to the opponent at this particular spot. It is from this point on the sideline in the back court that a team must be prepared to execute out-of-bounds plays. Extreme pressure by the defense may often be applied to these out-of-bounds plays which are used from this spot, depending, of course, upon the game situation and the type of defensive play and defensive philosophy that has been developed and is being used by the opponents. The out-of-bounds plays presented here are all planned with the assumption that pressure is applied by the defense in all out-of-bounds situations. The various plays from the line out-of-bounds formations which are presented here can be used successfully to put the ball into play against the pressure defenses in the back court. These plays can also be used for direct scoring possibilities, as well as a means of bringing the ball down to the front court against the pressure defense so that the regular offensive patterns can be set up and put into use.

Diagram 3-1. In this diagram, the team is awarded the ball out-of-bounds in the back court at the free throw line extended. No. 1, a guard, takes the ball out-of-bounds against a tight pressing defense.

The same line formation as is shown in Chapter 2 can be used in this situation. Nos. 2, 3, 4 and 5 line up in a vertical line facing No. 1, as shown in the diagram. These players should be positioned about three to four strides in-bounds from the sidelines. As the signal is given to begin the play, No. 5 sets a screen on the defensive player guarding No. 4. At the same time, No. 2 sets a screen on the defensive player guarding No. 3. No. 4 fakes a drive toward the center of the court and then cuts deep down court toward the sideline to receive a pass from No. 1. No. 3 fakes a drive toward the center of the court, and then breaks to the right of the screen and down the side of the court in such a manner as to benefit from the screen set by Nos. 2 and 5. No. 3 then cuts hard and sharp toward the basket. No. 4 passes No. 3 the ball, or No. 3 can receive a pass direct from No. 1. No. 1 can also pass to either No. 4 or 3. If neither No. 4 nor 3 are successful in freeing themselves for a pass on this maneuver, No. 2 rolls off the screen he made previously and drives deep toward the back-court end line, in preparation for receiving an outlet pass from No. 1 if it is needed. If the pass is made to No. 2, then No. 1 immediately steps in-bounds, and No. 2 may pass to him, or possibly pass down court to Nos. 3, 4 and 5, who have fanned out on the play and perhaps hooked back for possible outlet pass opportunities. This will help to take the pressure off of the back-court play conditions and also move the ball into the front court scoring areas.

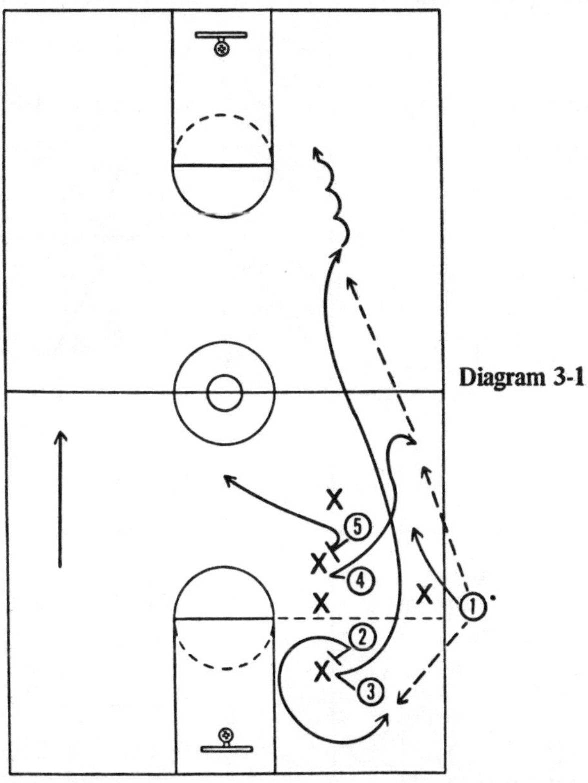

Diagram 3-1

Diagram 3-2. The horizontal line play can be used with success when the ball is out-of-bounds at the sideline in the back court. This play shows No. 3 taking the ball out-of-bounds on the side of the court at the free throw line extended. The defense is playing tight, but a line play such as this leaves them in a dilemma, because they do not know on which side of the player they are guarding to play in order to stop the offensive pass-in. Nos 1, 5, 4 and 2 line up as shown in the diagram. On the signal to begin the play, No. 1 fakes to his right and then breaks toward the front court area to get open. No. 2 fakes to his left toward the front court area, and then goes to his right to provide outlet pass possibilities. No. 5 fakes a move to the right and then sets a screen on No. 4's defensive player. No. 4 cuts sharply off the screen set by No. 5 toward the front court. If No. 4 is open, No. 3 passes the ball to him. No. 1 may also be open for a pass from No. 3. No. 1 could relay the ball to No. 4 if he is open. After executing a screen on No. 4's defensive player, No. 5 reverses his direction and moves back deeper into the back-court area for a possible outlet pass from No. 3 if it is needed. No. 3 has several

Diagram 3-2

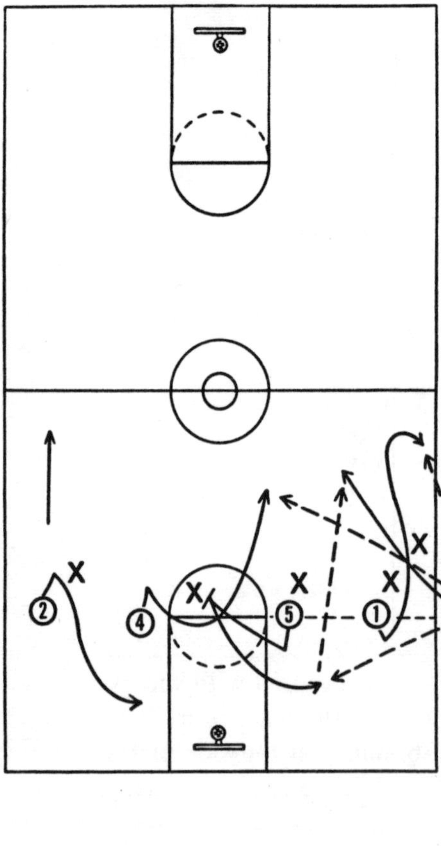

Diagram 3-3

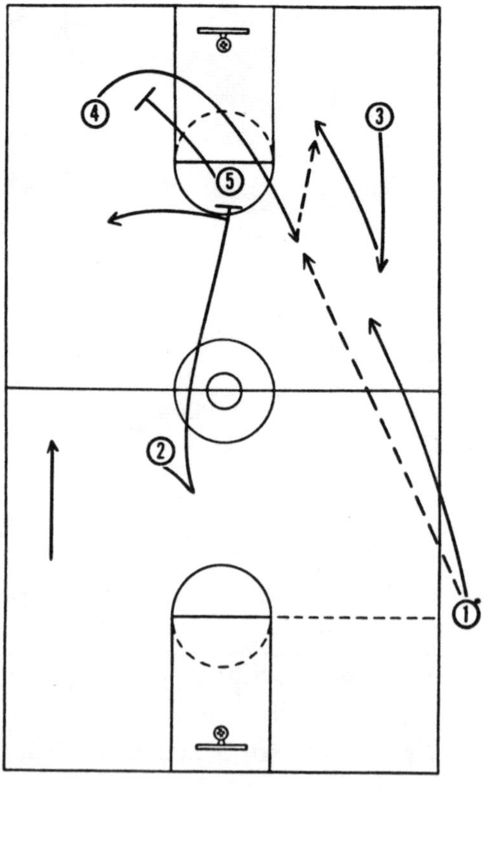

options whereby he may make direct passes to Nos. 1 and 4, either one of whom could be open for the pass and a long, driving dribble to the basket. This play could, however, be used only to provide an opportunity and a means of advancing the ball to the front court area. Nos. 2 and 5 should be open for outlet passes. They should have immediate opportunities to receive passes from No. 3 in the back court. They can then advance the ball using the dribble to the front court area as the pressure is reduced by the defense as a result of the moves made by the offense. No. 3, after passing the ball in-bounds, can drive hard for a return pass if the pass is made by him to either No. 1 or 5. If the pass is made to either No. 5 or 2, No. 3 will need to move in-bounds and use his own good judgment as to where he should go and what he should do to relieve the pressure situation that is being exerted by the defense.

Diagram 3-3. One of the quickest ways to relieve the pressure on the offensive team when it has the ball out-of-bounds along the sideline in the back court is to use the play from the formation shown in this diagram. No. 1 takes the ball out-of-bounds at the free throw line extended in the back court. Nos. 3, 4 and 5 position themselves in their near normal offensive operational areas in the front court. No. 2, the other guard, positions himself near the center circle, to be of help to No. 1 if necessary. On the signal to begin the play, No. 5 goes deep and to the left from his original position to set a screen for No. 4, as shown in the diagram. No. 2 fakes toward No. 1, and then drives toward the basket to set a screen for No. 4 near the free throw line. No. 4 moves in toward the basket, and then behind No. 5, in order to free himself. He then breaks sharply toward the ball and around the screen set by No. 2. He should be free for a pass somewhere in the mid-court area or near the mid-court line, since he had, in effect, received a double screen—first by No. 5 and then by No. 2. If he is free, No. 1 passes him a long pass and follows the pass hard. No. 3, also, on the signal, moves toward No. 1 as if to receive the ball, but, just as No. 4 receives the ball from No. 1, No. 3 reverses his direction and drives toward the basket for an opening on what amounts to a "sucker" or "blind-pig" play. Other scoring possibilities could result from these maneuvers as No. 2 rolls out for an outlet pass and as No. 1 moves in hard to follow his pass. The chief requisite of this play is that No. 1 be able to execute the long pass to No. 4, and that No. 3 is able to time his move so that the time he makes his reverse move to the basket will coincide with the moment No. 4 receives the ball from No. 1.

Diagram 3-4. This play can be used when the ball is out-of-bounds along the sideline in the back court, and the pressure defense is being applied by the opponents. No. 1 takes the ball out-of-bounds at the designated spot, as shown in the diagram. Players No. 2, 3, 4 and 5 form a square or a diamond near the center circle, as shown in the diagram. On the signal to begin the play, Nos. 2 and 4 break toward the ball. Nos. 3 and 5 hold the timing of their break for a

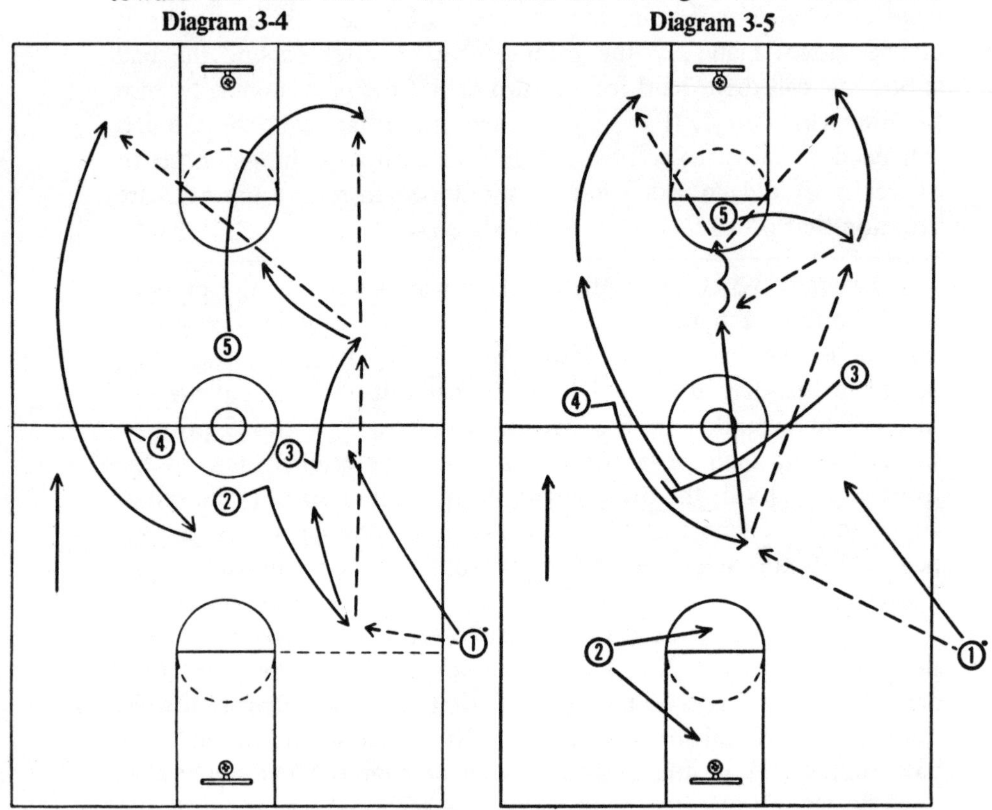

moment to see exactly at what point the ball is going to be passed in-bounds. After the pass-in is made to No. 2, Nos. 3 and 5 then fan out and move to the most advantageous areas to receive deep down court passes from No. 2. This diagram shows No. 1 passing the ball in to No. 2. No. 3 cuts deep down the same side of the court and receives a pass from No. 2. No. 5 has gone deep down court and then moved over to the right side of the court to receive a pass from No. 3. No. 4, after breaking toward the ball and the back court, reverses his direction and breaks fast down the left side of the court for a possible pass from either No. 3 or No. 5, which could result in a scoring opportunity. Nos. 1 and 2 follow the play down court. The object here is for the four players to fan out from the square or diamond formation they have formed around the center circle and move into possible pass receiving areas. This will confuse the defense and make it possible to pass the ball to players in-bounds, and subsequently down court for possible scoring opportunities as a result of the maneuver.

Diagram 3-5. No. 1 has the ball out-of-bounds in the back court and Nos. 2, 3, 4 and 5 take positions as shown in the diagram. On the signal to begin the play, No. 3 breaks toward the middle of the court from his position on the side of the court and over toward No. 4 in such a manner, that No. 4 can cut by him as shown in the diagram. No. 4 can now receive a screen on his defensive man as he moves toward No. 1 and the ball. This should free No. 4 for a pass from No. 1. No. 5, in the meantime, has moved over to the right side and deeper down court in quest of a possible opening. If he is open, No. 4 passes to him and then drives down the middle of the court. No. 3, after screening for No. 4, moves down the left side of the court. This has brought three players into the immediate scoring area for a possible scoring opportunity on a fast break pattern. No. 5 may pass back to No. 4, and from here other scoring possibilities may develop. Nos. 1 and 2 follow the play. If No. 1 is not able to make the original pass-in to No. 4, he can pass to No. 2.

Diagram 3-6. This play can be used to help the offense free itself of the defensive pressure which might be exerted by the opposition when the ball is out-of-bounds in the back court and along the sideline. No. 1 takes the ball out-of-bounds, and Nos. 3 and 2 line up at the free throw line as shown in the diagram. Nos. 4 and 5 line up just at the mid-court line but somewhat farther apart than Nos. 2 and 3. At the signal to begin the play, Nos. 2 and 3 cross, with No. 3 screening on No. 2's defensive man. No. 2 cuts to the base-line side of the screen set by No. 3, preparing to receive an outlet pass from No. 1. This maneuver should free No. 2 for an outlet pass from No. 1. At this same time, Nos. 4 and 5 cross, with No. 5 screening for No. 4. No. 4 breaks to the back-court side of the screen to receive a possible pass from either No. 1 or 2. If No. 2 has received the outlet pass from No. 1, he passes the ball on down court to No. 4. After screening for No. 2, No. 3 rolls out of the screen and cuts down the middle of the court. He should be open for a pass from No. 4 or 2. Nos. 5 and 4 break to the outside lanes, and No. 3 dribbles the ball to the top of the circle in anticipation of any fast break possibilities that might develop as a result of this maneuver. Nos. 1 and 2 follow the play as trailers.

Diagram 3-6

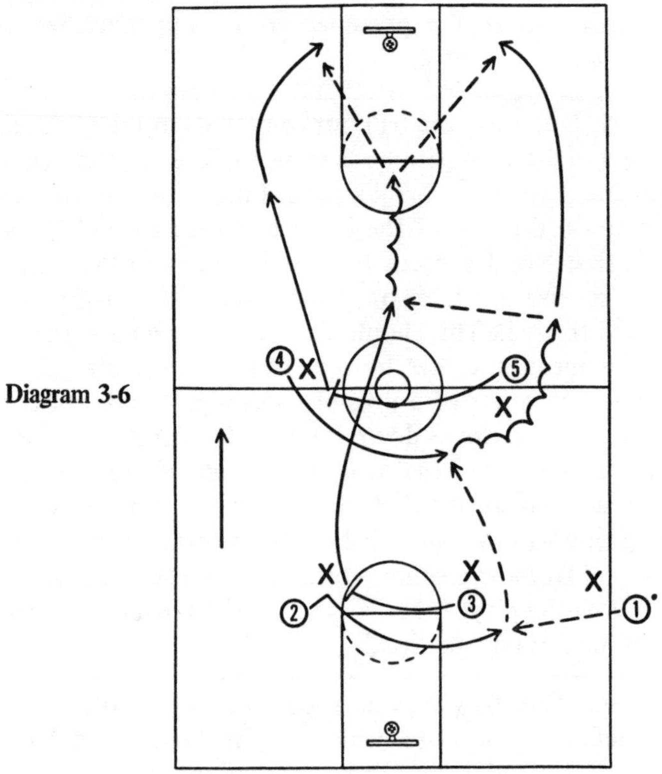

All these plays have been shown from the right side of the floor, and any play shown from one side of the floor can also be executed from the opposite side in using the same player movements.

The timing of this play is important. It should be timed so as to first free No. 2 as a result of the screen set by No. 3. Then, just as No. 2 receives the outlet pass, the timing of the screen set by No. 5 on No. 4's defensive man should be such that No. 4 will be free to receive the pass from No. 2. If No. 2 has not been able to free himself for the pass from No. 1, then No. 1 can make the pass directly to No. 4.

With this quick maneuvering, the pressure point is no longer on the offense, but will be transferred back to the defense because the defense will have to scramble back on defense to protect against the points of attack created by the fast break maneuvers.

OUT-OF-BOUNDS PLAYS ALONG THE BACK-COURT END LINE

The area where a team will be awarded the ball out-of-bounds most frequently will be along the end line in the back court. Every time the opponents score a basket or a free throw, the team is awarded the ball out-of-bounds at this point. The throw-in may be made anywhere along the end line. After a basket or a successful free throw, a player may pass to a teammate anywhere along the end line out-of-bounds. This teammate, in turn, may then make the throw-in. The only restriction which is made in this situation is that the throw-in must be made within the five-second limitation of the rules. The officials are not required to handle the ball in this particular situation, so it is reasonable to assume that the team that has good organization and can advance the ball from this situation into scoring areas as quickly as is feasible, will have a decided advantage and will have provided themselves with a "winning edge."

Violations such as defensive basket interference, goal tending, free throw lane violations, as well as other violations, will result in having the ball awarded to the team along the back-court end line also. Since this area is the most frequent origin of ball possession resulting from these aforementioned circumstances in most games, it should be an area from which the team is thoroughly prepared to execute its maneuvers with speed and precision.

In this chapter, the plays presented which result in getting the ball down court, will be those that could be classified purely as the out-of-bounds type play, which occurs after the ball has been awarded to the team along the end line after a violation, or after a time out has been called immediately following a score by a basket or a free throw. In these situations, the officials do handle the ball. However, it must be remembered that after a score, even though a time out has been called, or other time lapses occur, the team still has the option of throwing the ball in-bounds from anywhere along the end line. Chapter 6 in this book will give a more thorough discussion of offenses against pressing defenses, and, as such, will give a more complete coverage of putting the ball into play after a basket and a free throw in these situations.

The team members must know which player is going to take the ball out-of-bounds in all situations. The player taking the ball out-of-bounds should never attempt to throw the ball in-bounds from directly behind the basket. He should always move to one side of the basket or the other in order to have a clear view. Usually, if the player is right handed, it can be assumed that it might be to his advantage to move to his right side of the basket, but this may not always be true. For the left-handed player, the opposite would be assumed to be an advantage. The player taking the ball out-of-bounds should be the player with the most ability for getting the ball in-bounds under pressure. This requires the quarterback type of player as well as the best passer. He should usually be a guard, but there could be times when it would be advantageous to have a tall player take the ball out-of-bounds in this particular situation.

Diagram 3-7. The play shown in this diagram has been used successfully many times to move the ball down court quickly, utilizing a minimum of passes. This situation could exist after the ball is awarded out-of-bounds from a violation, or after a time out is

Diagram 3-7

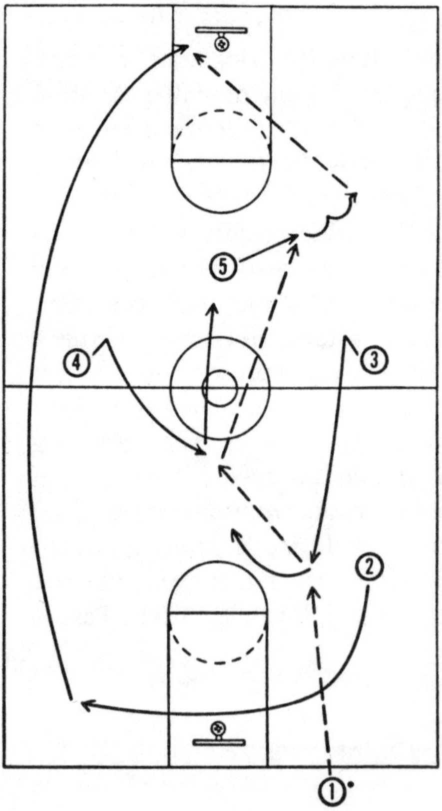

Diagram 3-8

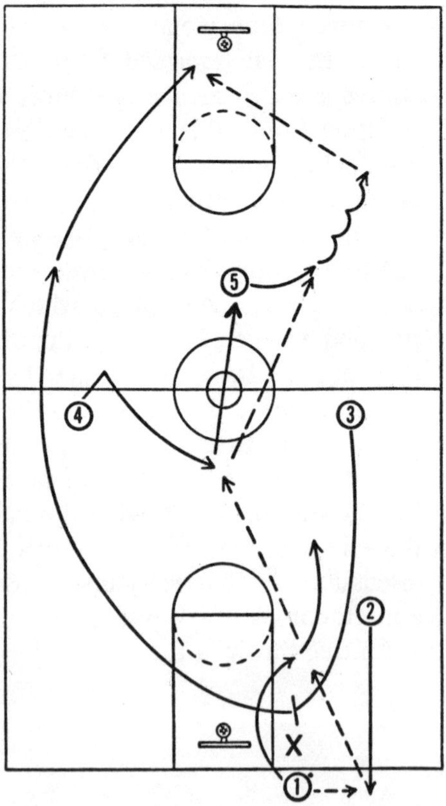

taken after a successful basket or free throw. No. 1 takes the ball out, as shown in the diagram. No. 2 lines up facing and in line with No. 1 at about the top of the free throw circle. Nos. 4 and 3 station themselves at about the mid-court line. No. 5 is positioned deeper and about halfway between the center circle and the free throw circle in the front court. When the play starts, No. 2 breaks toward No. 1 as if to receive the ball, and then clears the area and breaks wide down the left side of the court toward the basket and scoring area. No. 3 shakes his defensive man and breaks hard and fast toward the ball so that he is able to receive the outlet pass from No. 1. No. 4 now breaks toward the ball, and No. 3 passes to him at approximately the spot shown in the diagram. No. 5 breaks to the right side of the court, and the pass could go direct from No. 3 to No. 5, but No. 4 may pass the ball to No. 5 or possibly to No. 2. The timing of the cuts and passes should be made so that No. 2 will arrive in the scoring area in time to receive the pass from No. 4 or 5. This will enable him to move in for an unmolested shot. Against a back-court press, this play can get the ball down the court and into scoring territory very quickly, and if the timing and the player breaks are made properly, the play will usually be successful.

Diagram 3-8. This is a slight variation of the play presented in Diagram 3-7. The ball has been awarded out-of-bounds following a scored basket or free throw. The team still has passing rights along the base line out-of-bounds. The only restriction is the five-second limitation placed on throwing the ball in-bounds. When the play starts, both Nos. 2 and 3 break toward the ball. No. 2 steps out-of-bounds, and No. 1 passes him the ball behind the end line. No. 1 now steps in-bounds and cuts sharply behind No. 3, who provides No. 1 with a moving screen below the free throw line area. This screen should free No. 1 for a pass from No. 2. Nos. 4 and 5 make their cuts as shown in the diagram. No. 1 may pass the ball to either No. 4 or 5. The ball may, however, get to No. 5 by being passed from No. 1 to No. 4, who in turn relays it quickly on to No. 5. After the screening move for No. 1, No. 3 breaks hard and fast down the outside lane on the left side of the court and toward the basket. If his cut is timed correctly, No. 3 should be open for a pass from No. 5 and a scoring opportunity.

Diagram 3-9. Many times, when a team has the ball out-of-bounds along the end line in the back court, and the defensive team is in a pressure defense, they will double team the most likely receiver of the first in-bounds pass or the throw-in pass. The defensive team that does this feels there is more to gain by this double teaming maneuver than by guarding the player taking the ball out-of-bounds. Here, defensive players X1 and X2 double team the most likely receiver, No. 2, thereby leaving No. 1 free and unguarded. Nos. 3, 4 and 5 line up as shown in the diagram. On the signal to begin the play, No. 2 fakes a movement toward No. 1 as if to receive the ball, then moves completely away from No. 1 to the opposite side of the floor. No. 2 must be an excellent actor and make every effort possible to make it appear that he expects to get the ball. He then leads the two defensive players as far away from the ball as possible, and completely out of the area of play. While this is happening, Nos. 3 and 4 must move into the action, and, in doing so, No. 3 shakes his defensive man and comes to meet the outlet pass from No. 1. No. 1 immediately breaks straight down the middle of the court. With the two defensive players having been pulled out of the area by No. 2, No. 1 should be free to make this move unmolested. This maneuver immediately creates a situation whereby the offense will now outnumber the defense down court. No. 3 returns the ball to No. 1, who dribbles quickly down the middle of the court. No. 4 breaks down the left side of the court. No. 5 moves over to the lane on the right side of the court, and, with No. 1 driving to the top of the circle, a 3-on-2 fast break situation is established and a scoring opportunity presented.

Diagram 3-10. If the ball is awarded out-of-bounds after a successful free throw or a basket, even though a time out has been called before the throw-in, the offensive team still has the option of throwing the ball in-bounds from anywhere along the defensive end line. When No. 2 sees that he is pressured by two defensive players, he fakes toward the ball and then leads his defenders to the end line on the opposite side of the basket, at which point he steps out-of-bounds. No. 1 passes the ball to No. 2 along the end line out-of-bounds, and then immediately steps in-bounds to receive a return pass from No. 2. No. 1 will be free to drive the length of the court, or, if the defense shifts to him, he can pass off to a free receiver because the defense will be outnumbered as a result of No. 2 pulling two defensive players away from the play. With No. 1 driving to the top of the circle, a fast break scoring opportunity should be available to the team.

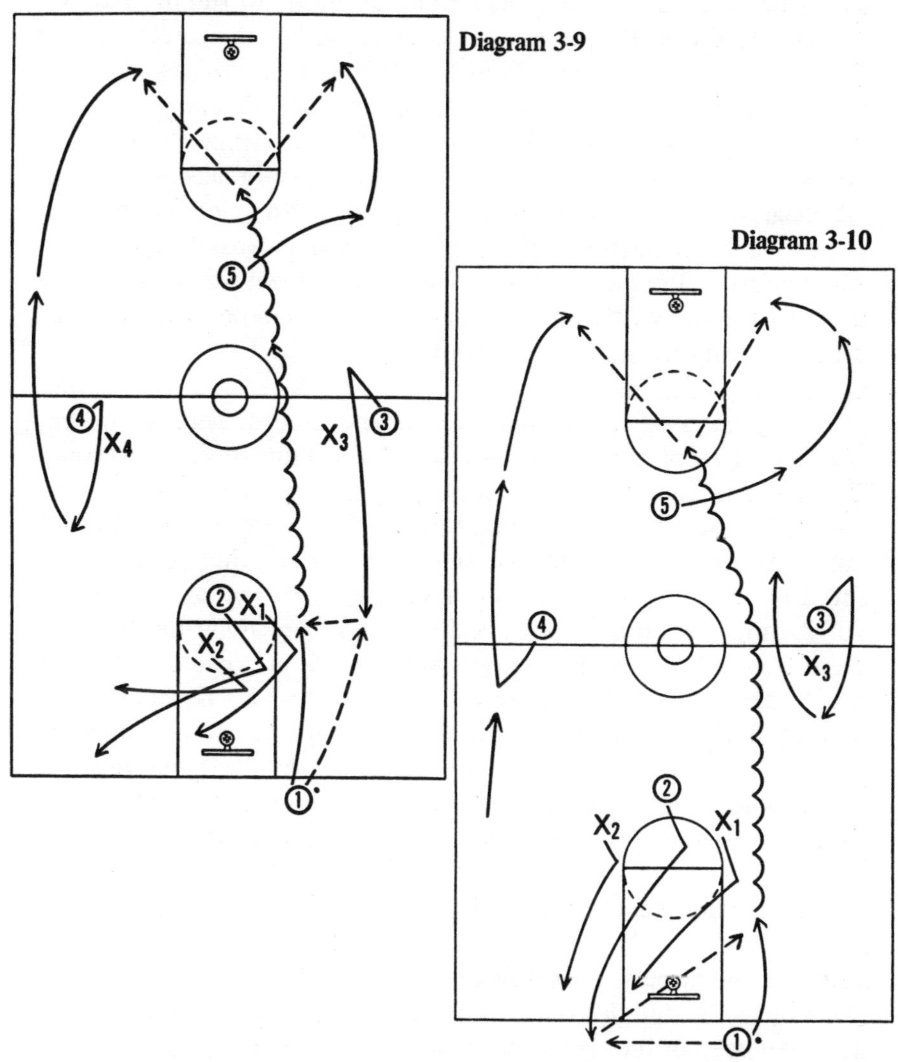

Diagram 3-9

Diagram 3-10

Diagram 3-11. With the defense pressuring the offense when they have the ball out-of-bounds along the back-court end line, the play and maneuver shown in Diagram 3-11 will often free the players for a fast break maneuver and, as a result, a good scoring opportunity. No. 1 has the ball out-of-bounds at the right side of the basket. Nos. 2 and 3 line up at either side of the free throw line, facing No. 1 a lane width apart. Nos. 4 and 5 are positioned at approximately the mid-court line and wider apart. No. 3 executes a screen on No. 2's defensive player and attempts to run his man into the screen. No. 2 then breaks on the ball side of the screen, and he should be open for a pass from No. 1, but if the defense switches, then No. 3 should roll off the screen toward the ball, and he could be open for the outlet pass from No. 1. In the meantime, No. 4 moves across the court to screen for No. 5, who, if he breaks as shown in the diagram, should be open for a pass from No. 2 or 3, whichever player has received the outlet pass from No. 1. Nos. 4 and 2 break down court in the outside lanes. No. 5 drives down the middle of the court to the top of the circle. This maneuver should result in a fast break opportunity and a scoring possibility.

Diagram 3-12. Many patterns can be used in getting the ball down court from out-of-bounds along the end line in the back court. This pattern can be used successfully if executed properly. The players line up as shown in the diagram. No. 2 fakes toward the ball, and then moves wide to the opposite side of the floor. If this out-of-bounds situation follows a successful basket or free throw, No. 2 can step out-of-bounds and receive a pass along the base line from No. 1 who is also out-of-bounds. No. 1 could then step in-bounds and receive a return pass from No. 2, as was done in Diagram 3-10. The optional outlets down court can now be pursued. In this situation, however, the first pass-in shown is being made to No. 3, who first breaks toward the end line and then across to the right side of the court in an attempt to gain a position which will enable him to receive a pass from No. 1. No. 4 has driven down court so that he may receive a long, deep pass which he receives from No. 3. No. 4 passes to No. 5, who breaks deep and toward the basket, as shown in the diagram. Good fast break possibilities are shown here as No. 3 takes the middle lane after passing down court to No. 4, who is stationed deep in the right lane. Nos. 1 and 2 trail the play.

Diagram 3-13. No. 1 takes the ball out-of-bounds. The other players line up as shown in the diagram. No. 5, the center, stations himself very deep to take at least one defensive player very near the

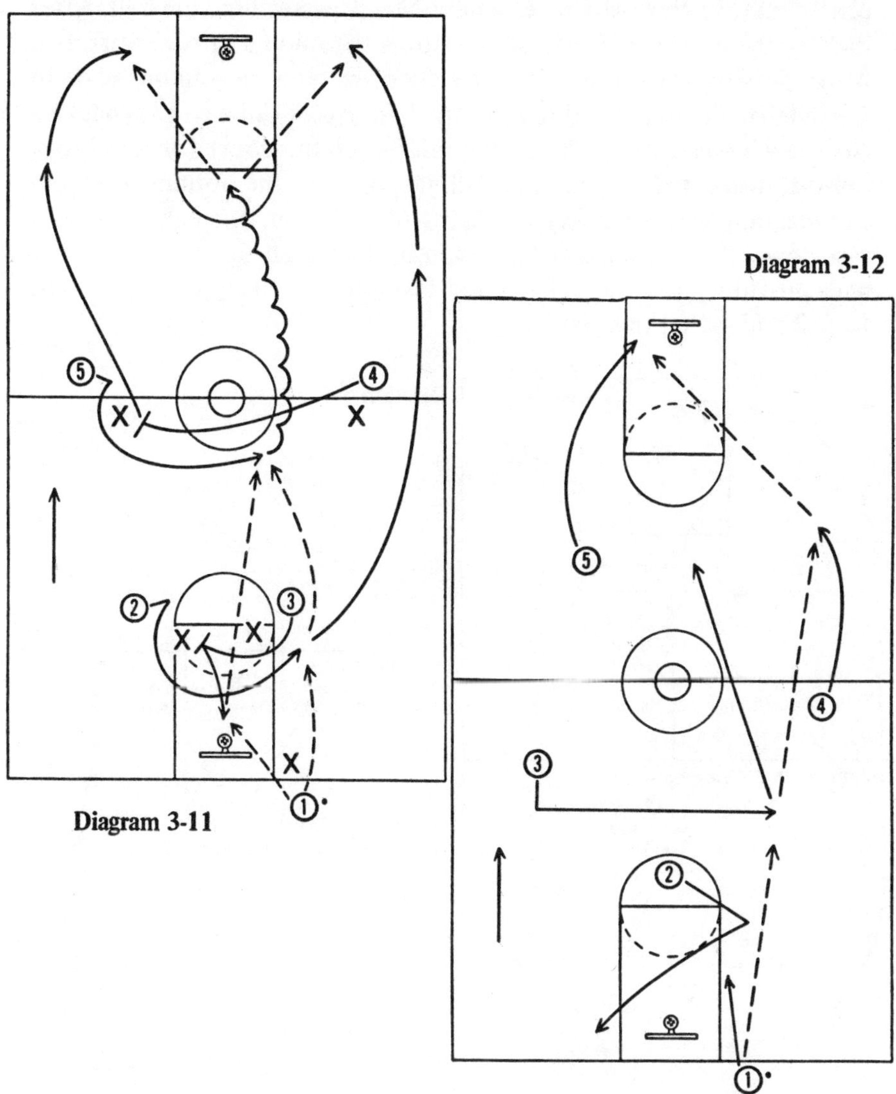

Diagram 3-12

Diagram 3-11

front court basket. No. 2 shakes his defensive man with a fake and breaks toward the ball to receive the outlet pass from No. 1. No. 3, who is stationed on the opposite side of the floor near mid-court, shakes his defensive man and breaks into the center of the court toward the ball somewhere between the center circle and the top of the back-court free throw circle. No. 2 passes him the ball at this point. In the meantime, No. 4 breaks down court past the mid-court center line, in the right lane, where No. 3 passes him the ball. After making the pass, No. 3 drives hard down the middle of the court. No. 4 can possibly pass down court to No. 5, who has moved out wide to the side of the court and toward the ball. No. 4 can also pass back to No. 3, who is cutting down the middle of the court for fast break opportunities. If No. 3 has the ball, he will have the options shown in the diagram. After passing the ball to No. 2, No. 1 breaks hard and fast down the outside left lane thereby filling all three passing lanes and providing the ingredients for fast break scoring opportunities. Nos. 2 and 4 trail the play.

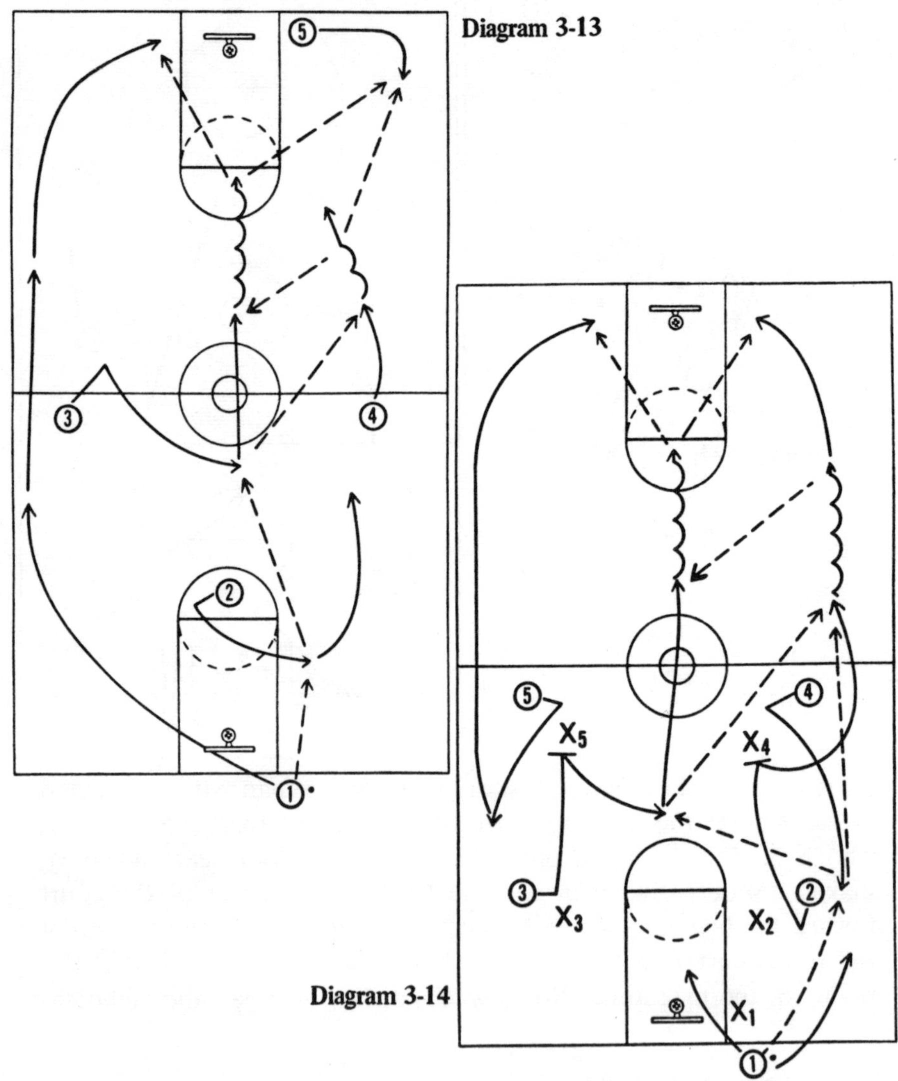

Diagram 3-13

Diagram 3-14

Diagram 3-14. No. 1 has the ball out-of-bounds, and a pressure defense is being exerted by the opposition. Nos. 2, 3, 4 and 5 line up as shown in the diagram. Here the purpose is to free No. 4 or 5 for the outlet pass under pressure by having Nos. 2 and 3 screen for them. When the signal to begin the play is given, Nos. 2 and 3 turn and move down court, screening for Nos. 4 and 5 near the mid-court line. Just before Nos. 2 and 3 execute the screen, Nos. 4 and 5 fake toward the middle of the court and then break to the outside to take advantage of the screen given them. Nos. 4 and 5 could both be open for the outlet pass, but the logical receiver is No. 4, since he is on the same side of the floor as No. 1. In this diagram, the pass is shown going to No. 4. Nos. 2 and 3 can roll out of the screen for possible outlet passes, especially if the defense switches. Here, No. 3 is shown rolling out to the middle of the court and toward the ball for an opening as a result of a switch. No. 2 rolls out of the screen and down court just past the mid-court line. No. 4 can pass to either No. 3 or 2. If the pass is to No. 3, No. 3 may relay the ball down court to No. 2. As soon as No. 5 sees the release pass going to No. 4, he reverses his direction and breaks down court in the outside lane. Here Nos. 2, 3 and 5 lead the fast break. Nos. 1 and 4 follow the play. When No. 4 receives the outlet pass, he follows the play. When No. 4 receives the outlet pass and he cannot pass to No. 3 or 2, he can always pass back to No. 1, who can take passing possibilities to any down court players.

Diagram 3-15. If, as in the play shown in Diagram 3-14, the defense effectively switches on the screen, then the play can be executed as shown here with excellent results. The players position themselves as in the previous diagram. Nos. 4 and 5 fake toward the ball as if to receive the outlet pass, but, just as the defense switches, Nos. 4 and 5 reverse directions and break down court for a longer pass. The defense will be completely fooled by the maneuver at times, and especially if they are aggressive at switching on the screens. Nos. 4 and 5 break down court with the hope or expectation of being open just beyond the mid-court line, where No. 1 throws a long mid-court pass to either of them. No. 3 rolls off the screen for an outlet pass if the long pass cannot be used. Here No. 1 makes the long pass to No. 4, who moves to the middle of the court on a driving dribble. No. 2 moves out of the screen and drives down court in the right lane, keeping wide. Nos. 4, 5 and 2 lead the fast break. If no opening to No. 4 or 5 develops, No. 1 can pass in to No. 3, and possibly receive a return pass, if No. 3 cannot relay the ball down court.

Properly executed, this play will offset the pressure defense exerted by the opposition, and scoring opportunities will develop from it.

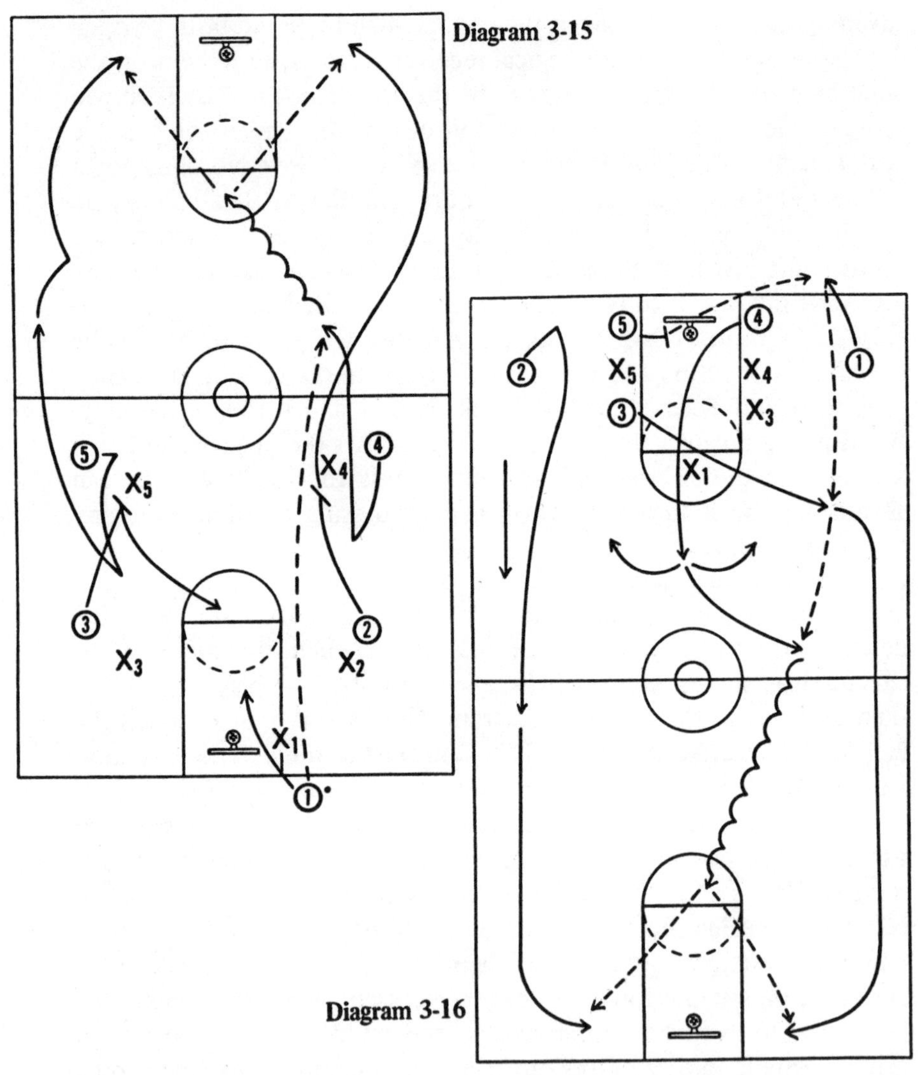

Diagram 3-15

Diagram 3-16

OUT-OF-BOUNDS FROM SCORED FREE THROWS

One of the times a team secures possession or is awarded the ball out-of-bounds at the defensive end line most frequently is after a successful free throw or basket by the opponents. When this situation takes place, the ball may be put into play anywhere along the out-of-bounds end line, and may be passed behind this line by two players, both of whom may be out-of-bounds at the time the pass is made from one player to the other. The only limitation on the use of this type of maneuver is the rule which places a five-second time limit on putting the ball into play from this position once the player takes possession of the ball out-of-bounds. The team that is well organized and prepared to advance the ball quickly down court into scoring territory from this position will not only remove any defensive pressure that may be applied to them, but also will possess the necessary mechanics of play that will give them the "winning edge" in the close games. There are several patterns of play that can be used to advance the ball quickly from this situation which will result in good scoring opportunities.

The following diagrams will illustrate and describe some of these patterns of play that have been used successfully.

The Out Play

In this play the defensive team is putting less concentration on defensive play along the free throw lane, and assumes that the percentages of making the free throws are on the side of the team at the free throw line. Actually, most teams will hit from 60 to 75% of their free throw attempts, so, with this in mind, the defensive team concentrates on preparing its players to get the ball back into play quickly after the free throw is made and bring the ball down court into a scoring situation as soon as possible.

Diagram 3-16. This diagram shows the offensive team at the free throw line, with X1 shooting a free throw. Nos. 4 and 5, the best defensive rebounders, occupy the space next to the basket.

By prearranged signal, one of the players calls the play that is to be used. No. 5, for instance, could call out as the players line up: "I have it out." This means that No. 5 will retrieve the ball as it comes through the basket from the free throw, before it touches the floor if at all possible, and pass it "out" to No. 1, who will step out-of-bounds to receive the ball and put it in play from that position. If No. 4 should call the play, then he would pass the ball "out" to No. 2, etc.

The players will require considerable coaching on the techniques of getting these plays underway quickly. Nos. 4 and 5 must be coached and must practice retrieving the ball from the net before it hits the floor from free throws that are made. Nos. 1 and 2 must acquire the technique of being out-of-bounds at the exact moment they should be, in order to be ready to receive the pass from No. 4 or 5 at a time when they are ready to make the pass. The players who have the ball out-of-bounds must be able to put the ball into play quickly, without a moment's hesitation. They must also be adept at hiding and delaying their intent to perform the act of stepping out-of-bounds as long as possible without endangering the success of the play.

Diagram 3-16 shows that the free throw is made by X1. No. 5, who has called the word "out," retrieves the ball quickly and passes it to No. 1, who, after lining up on the right side of the court, steps out-of-bounds along the end line as the ball is in the net. As soon as it is obvious that the free throw will be made, the other players move into action and perform the duties expected of them.

Number 2 cuts down the outside right lane as deep and as quickly as possible. No. 4 cuts to the right and down the middle of the court to the center circle, where he either stops, reverses his direction and breaks back to help on the outlet pass from No. 1, or cuts into the left lane in anticipation of receiving a pass from No. 1. No. 3 breaks to the side of the court on which No. 1 receives the ball, and moves about as deep as the free throw line extended and midway between the sideline and circle. He must be free to receive a pass if it is at all possible because he is the first player No. 1 looks to for the first outlet pass. If No. 3 is open, No. 1 passes the ball to him. When No. 3 receives the ball, No. 4 breaks into the left lane, as shown in the diagram, to receive a pass from No. 3. No. 4, after receiving the pass, dribbles to the middle of the court and looks for an opportunity to pass down court to No. 2 or 3, both of whom are breaking down the outside lanes on a fast break pattern. If No. 4 dribbles to the center of the court, No. 3 will move into the left lane anticipating the fast break possibility. If No. 4 drives down the left lane, then No. 3 would move into the middle lane. Nos. 1 and 5 will trail the play.

There are other maneuvers which may be used with this pattern. For example, when No. 1 receives the ball from No. 5, he looks first to No. 3 in the area shown in the diagram for the first pass, but, if No. 3 is not open, No. 1 should look next for No. 4, who breaks to the center circle or near this area. No. 4 should always hesitate at this point, and should even hook back so that he may receive a pass from No. 1 if necessary. No. 1 could discover that one of his first opportunities to make a pass could be one to No. 4 at about mid-court or just short of it. From this position, No. 4 could possibly pass to No. 2 or drive into the front court. This maneuver would set up fast break possibilities with Nos. 2 and 3. If No. 1 cannot immediately pass to No. 3 or 4, then he may pass to No. 5, who must always make himself available for an outlet pass in this situation. The pass could then go from No. 5 to players down court, and a possible fast break pattern would result.

Diagram 3-17. This diagram illustrates that the team can concentrate on defensive play along the free throw lane and still use the "out" play. The players line up as shown in the diagram. No. 4

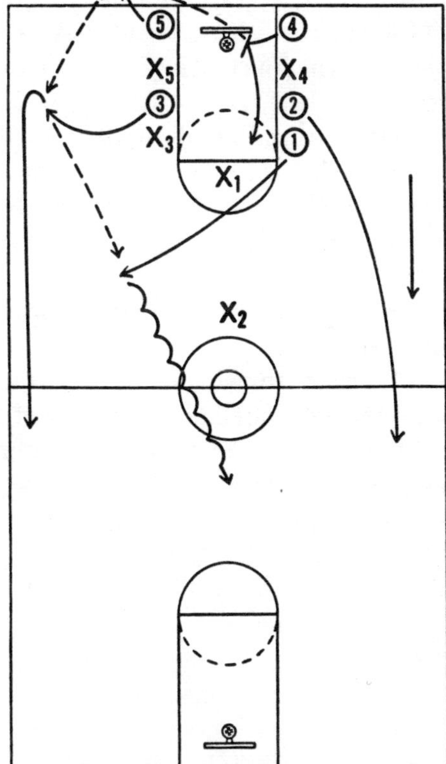

Diagram 3-17

calls out: "I have it out." After X1 makes the free throw, No. 4 retrieves the ball from the net if this is possible. No. 5 steps out-of-bounds as No. 4 retrieves the ball. No. 4 passes No. 5 the ball quickly, and, as this is done, No. 3 breaks to the position shown in the diagram, enabling him to receive the outlet pass from No. 5. No. 1 breaks for the area near the center of the court, so that he will be in a position to receive a pass from No. 3 or perhaps a direct pass from No. 5. No. 2, as soon as it is evident that the free throw will be made, breaks hard and fast down the court in the left outside lane in anticipation of fast break opportunities. No. 1 may pass the ball down the court to No. 2 or dribble the ball down the center of the court. This will set up a three-lane fast break pattern. Nos. 4 and 5 trail the play. If No. 5 cannot pass to No. 3 or No. 1, then he must look for No. 4, who must always be ready to receive an outlet pass if the play cannot be carried out and the ball cannot be passed to No. 3, 1 or 2.

The Keep Play

Diagram 3-18. The only difference between the "keep" play and the "out" play is that the player retrieving the ball from the successful free throw steps out-of-bounds and makes the throw-in himself. In this diagram, No. 5 calls the play by informing his teammates, "I'll keep it." Nos. 1 and 2 are stationed wide, and are ready to move down court. They are not in a defensive position along the free throw lane. As the free throw is made, No. 5 retrieves the ball and steps out-of-bounds with it so that he can make the throw-in. No. 2 breaks fast down court in the outside right lane. No. 1 positions himself for an outlet pass from No. 5, somewhere near the free-throw line extended on the left side of the court, as shown in the diagram. No. 3 moves toward the mid-court line on the side of the throw-in, and No. 4 cuts immediately for the center circle, where he will either hook back or go on down court, as the situation dictates. No. 5 passes to No. 1, who in turn passes to No. 3 at mid-court near the left sideline, or deeper if necessary or feasible. Nos. 3, 4 and 2 proceed down court in a fast break move that should bring scoring opportunities.

Diagram 3-19. This play illustrates a "keep" version that places all the defensive players along the free throw lane when a free throw is being attempted by the opposition. No. 5 calls out, "I'll keep it." When the free throw is made, No. 5 retrieves the ball and steps out-of-bounds on the right side of the basket. No. 3 moves out wide toward the side of the court to be in a position to receive the throw-in from No. 5. No. 1, after taking the precaution to step in the lane area and block X1 in case the free throw is missed, then breaks up the right side of the court to the mid-court sideline area. No. 2 breaks toward the far end of the court using the left outside lane. No. 4 breaks to the center circle, hesitates and then reverses his direction and breaks back to receive either an outlet pass from No. 5 or a pass from No. 3, if this move is needed and No. 3 is unable to pass to No. 1. No. 5 passes to No. 3, who in turn passes to No. 1 (he could pass directly to No. 4), who passes to No. 4. Nos. 4, 2 and 1 move down the court in a fast break pattern that should provide scoring opportunities. Nos. 3 and 5 trail the play.

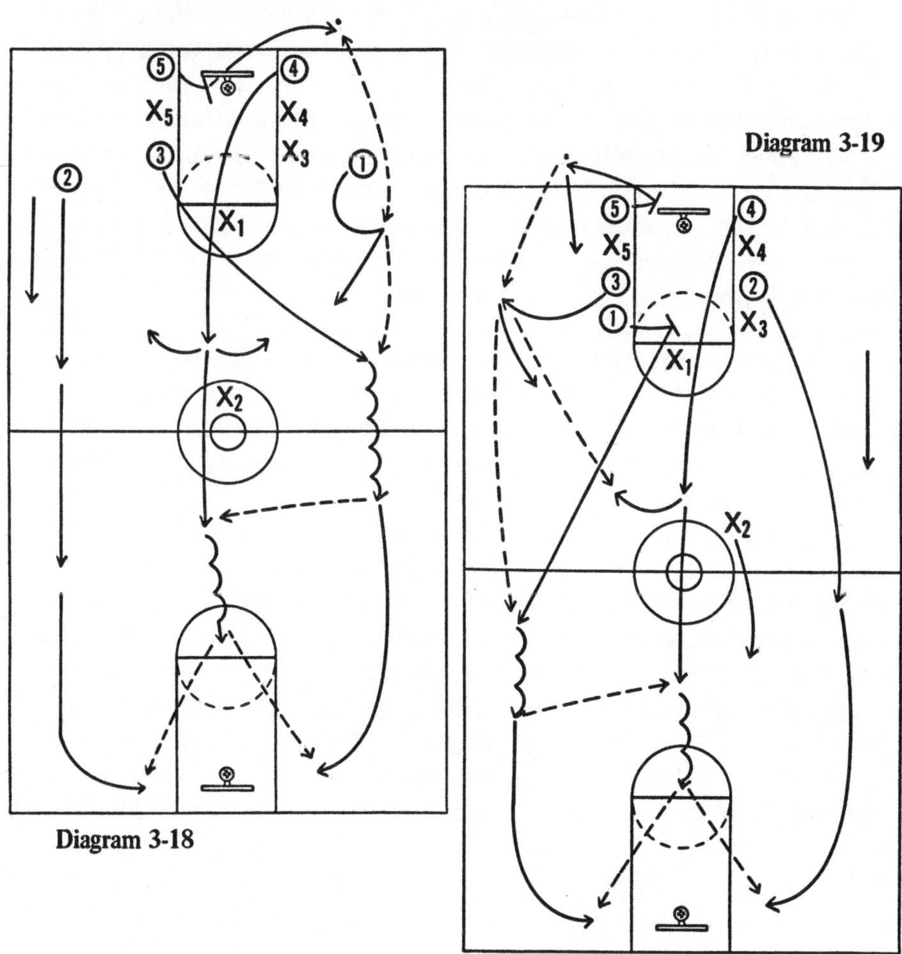

Diagram 3-18

Diagram 3-19

Diagram 3-20. This play shows how the team may elect to move into a more wide-open free-lance type of game from a successful free throw by the opposition. They then put only the two players required by the rule in the free throw lane space next to the basket and end line. The other players can take up positions down court, thereby forcing the free throwing team to compensate for this maneuver and position some of their players off the line also. From this wide-open formation, the team can execute either the "keep" or the "out" version type of play. In this play, Nos. 4 and 5 take the defensive lane positions on the inside. No. 3 takes a position at the top of the free throw circle just behind the free thrower, X1. Nos. 1 and 2 take up positions deep down in the front court, as shown in the diagram. No. 5 calls the "keep" play version, and as the free throw is made, he retrieves the ball and steps out-of-bounds in preparation for the throw-in. No. 3 breaks to the right side of the court to receive the pass-in from No. 5. No. 4 breaks to the center of the court, and either moves deeper down the court for a pass or hooks back toward the passer, No. 3, whichever meets the situation most adequately. Nos. 1 and 2 cross underneath the offensive basket, a maneuver which will confuse the defense and provide the offense with a better opportunity to receive a pass from No. 4. No. 5 passes to No. 3, No. 3 passes to No. 4 and No. 4 passes to No. 2. Nos. 4, 1 and 2 move down court on a fast break pattern that should provide scoring opportunities. Nos. 3 and 5 trail the play.

Diagram 3-21. This diagram shows another play which can be used with considerable success from the wide-open formation. Nos. 4 and 5 may decide to use the "keep" or the "out" version of the play. If they decide on the "keep," then the player retrieving the ball steps out-of-bounds and throws the ball in-bounds. If the "out" version is used, then one player retrieves the ball and the other player steps out-of-bounds and executes the throw-in pass after receiving the ball from the retriever. No. 3 can break to either of the areas shown in the diagram to receive the pass-in. No. 4 or 5 can break to the center of the court and execute the options shown in the diagram, depending upon the situation. No. 1 or 2 can take a position deep down court, as shown in the diagram. They may, however, take a position at mid-court, or in the areas to the side of the free throw lanes, if they wish to do so. They can break from these positions into

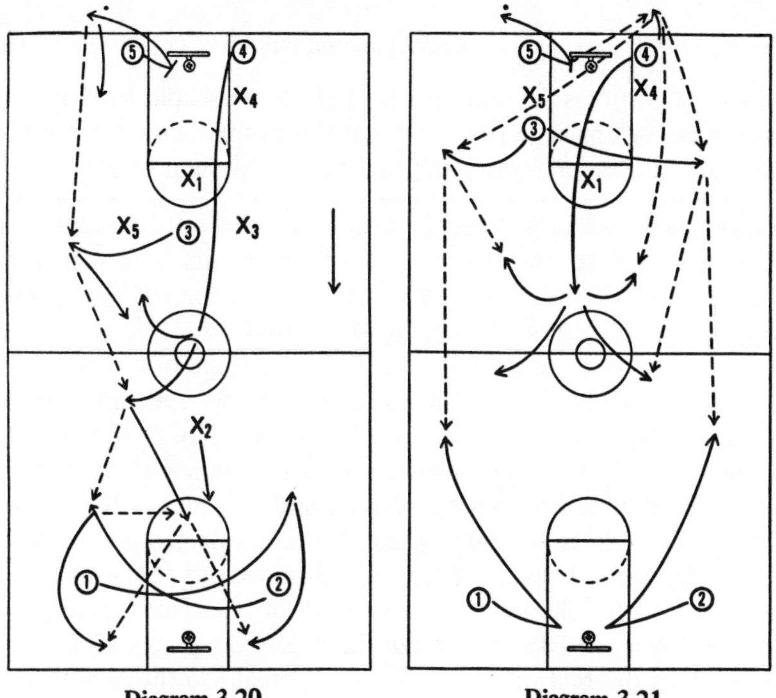

Diagram 3-20

Diagram 3-21

patterns, crosses, screens and maneuvers, which will result in a fast break situation and possible scoring opportunities from the free throw made by the opponents.

Diagram 3-22. This diagram shows another version of the "keep" play after a successful free throw by the opposition. No. 5 retrieves the ball and quickly steps out-of-bounds on the side of the basket farthest from his original position on the free throw lane. No. 2 immediately moves out of his position on the free throw lane and to the side of the court, as soon as he is sure that the free throw is successful. No. 3 steps in front of the free thrower, X1, and holds his screening position until he observes that the free throw is successful. No. 3 then moves to the side of the court, as shown in the diagram. No. 5 passes the ball in-bounds to No. 2, who in turn passes to No. 3. No. 1, meanwhile, has cut quickly down the right side of the court as soon as the free throw was made so that he may be in a position to receive the pass made by No. 3. No. 3 dribbles down the left side of the court until such time as No. 3 is in a position where he can execute a pass. No. 1 cuts under the basket and toward No. 3 so that he can receive the pass. No. 3 cuts to the middle of the court after making the pass. Meanwhile, No. 4 cuts quickly down court after the free throw is successful and into the right lane vacated by No. 1. No. 1 may now pass back to No. 3, who at this point occupies the middle lane position. Several scoring opportunities become possible.

Diagram 3-23. A "keep" version of the out-of-bounds play following a scored free throw by the opponents is shown in this diagram, with the defensive pressure being released by a double screen used to free a player for the outlet pass. No. 4 calls the "keep" play, and, after retrieving the ball, steps out-of-bounds to make the throw-in. Nos. 2 and 5 step into the free throw lane to form a momentary shoulder-to-shoulder screen. No. 3, after stepping in front of X1, the free thrower, to block him out, now breaks around the double screen set by Nos. 2 and 5 to receive the throw-in from No. 4, as shown in the diagram. No. 1 has started down court as soon as the action began, and now No. 2 moves out to the free throw line extended on the right side of the floor, and No. 5 breaks hard and fast down the left side of the floor. No. 3 passes to No. 2, and No. 2 relays the ball on to No. 1. No. 2 breaks to the middle of the floor. The three lanes are now occupied, and the fast break pattern is in operation with Nos. 1, 2 and 5.

Diagram 3-22

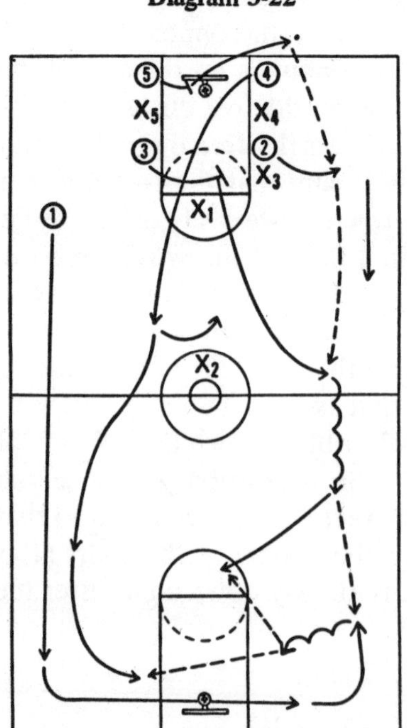

Diagram 3-23

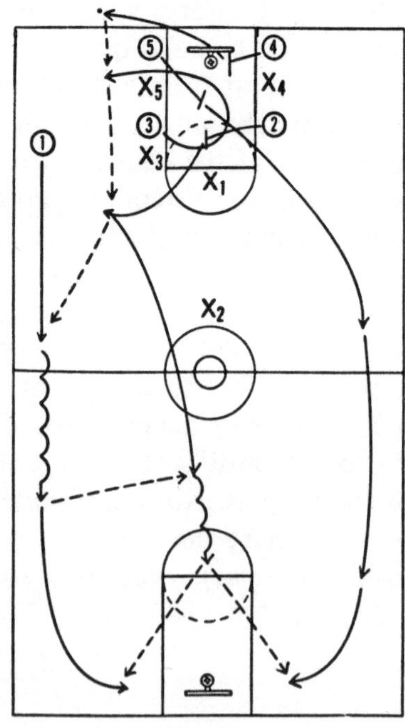

FOUR

JUMP BALL SITUATION PLAYS (Defensive and Offensive Alignment in Jump Ball Situations; Jump Balls in the Front Court; Jump Balls at Mid-Court; Jump Balls in the Back Court; Special Tip Plays for Beginning Quarters, Halves and Overtimes)

While it is generally true that jump ball situations in the game of basketball do not occur nearly as frequently as they did in the past, it is to the advantage of any team to be prepared for the times that these situations do arise and be ready to take advantage of them. As a result of this preparation and the successful use of special plays, the team may gain for themselves "the winning edge" and the coveted margin of victory.

Number of Jump Balls During a Game

Although the number of jump balls that occur during a game has been reduced considerably from what it used to be, the number is not significant enough so that this phase of the game should be neglected. At one time, statistics supported the evidence that there would be an average of 20 jump ball situations in a high school basketball game. Today, state tournament statistics can reasonably support the evidence that there will be from 10 to 12 jump ball situations per game. The number will vary from game to game, but no coach can afford to neglect the phase of the game that would give his team an opportunity to gain possession of the ball this number of times and could result in a direct scoring opportunity.

Outcomes of the Held Ball

Set plays can add to the players' confidence. Preparation in all phases of the game gives the players the feeling of being ready; they are anxious to meet the situation and overcome the obstacles confronting them. The confidence and the knowledge it gives them can create a decided advantage over the opponents. Often the cheap basket originating from a held ball situation can be the margin of victory. The fast break basket from the held ball situation can often temporarily break the morale of the opposing team. If it comes at the right time, it can completely demoralize the opposing team for a short period of time, during which a tremendous advantage may be gained. This advantage can be very difficult to overcome.

Determining Factors in the Use of the Jump Ball

The determining factor in the use of the jump ball situation play will be whether the jumper is able to control the tip. Naturally, controlling the tip will give the team an extremely valuable advantage and will enhance the success of the held ball play immeasurably. However, success in this instance does not necessarily mean that a score can be obtained as a direct result of the play. Ball possession as a result of the play can be interpreted to mean that the play was successful. Any results obtained beyond just ball possession can and are "frosting on the cake." The cheap basket is always desirable, but it is not always attainable unless provision is made to see that it becomes so. The jump ball play will provide this opportunity, and its results will more than justify the time spent in practicing and preparing for it, not only in the points it might produce but also in the psychological effects it has on the players using it.

Jump Ball Plays in the Back Court

The jump ball situation plays in the back court will, of necessity, be those which will be defensive in nature. The primary concern of the back-court defensive team is to prevent a successful tip-off play being executed by the front-court offensive team which will result in a quick basket. In order to offset the advantage that the offensive team has when the jump ball play is executed in the front court, the defensive team should attempt to tip the ball forward or away from the basket if at all possible. The type of play used in this area will depend a great deal upon the score and the time left to play in the game. Usually the scoring play used from this area will be a fast break type of play.

Jump Ball Plays at Mid-Court

Almost every team will attempt to use mid-court tip-off plays, although all of them will not be scoring plays. The ball-possession type play is also popular from this area. However, the scoring type of play can be used to advantage if the center can control the tip and the play is properly executed. There is always danger, however, that the opposition will also be attempting to score from the tip-off, so this will need to be taken into consideration when a scoring play from this area is attempted. With this thought in mind, it should be remembered that on every held ball situation where the scoring play is being attempted, provision should be made to protect against the other team obtaining ball possession, and, as a result, affecting a scoring play on their own. To offset this development, a player should always be assigned to stay back and protect the defensive basket.

Jump Ball Plays in the Overtime Game

Many coaches do not adequately prepare for the overtime game. They spend many hours on offensive and defensive play but neglect to plan the necessary strategy for the overtime. Preparation for this period begins with complete understanding of the rule which governs overtime play. There should be no confusion as to what plays should be used. These plays should be reviewed during the practice period.

Jump Ball Plays in the Front Court

The jump ball situation plays in the front court should be designed primarily as scoring plays, because although the element of risk of interception may be the same as the back or center court, it cannot immediately result in a scoring opportunity for the opposition. This is primarily true because the distance from the opposing basket gives the opposition an opportunity to recover defensively and move to their defensive positions, in time to prevent the scoring opportunity which might result from the interception of the ball from the tip-off. Therefore, it is possible to design and use plays which will stress scoring with almost a complete disregard for the fact that the opposition might gain possession of the ball on the tip-off. The front court team can utilize their entire effort in executing the scoring play, and yet have time to recover defensively if the play does not materialize or the opposition gains possession of the ball on the tip-off.

DEFENSIVE AND OFFENSIVE ALIGNMENT IN JUMP BALL SITUATIONS

The proper placement and alignment of the players on jump ball situations will determine the success of the play. The appropriate formation to use will be determined by the situation. The use of a certain play from a specific formation will be determined by a particular need for such a play. There are various situations which will influence the selection and use of a particular formation.

Factors to Be Considered in the Use of the Jump Ball

Some of the factors which should be taken into consideration, and ones which will influence and determine the selection and use of a specific formation, can be listed as follows:

1. The ability to control the tip.
2. The desire to score from the play.
3. The desire to want ball possession only.
4. The desire to score quickly from the play.
5. The possibility of securing the ball after the tap.
6. The rebounding ability of the players.
7. The amount of time left to play in the game.
8. The score at the time the play is to be used.

Held Ball Formations

These formations can be divided into five categories; namely: the circle formation, the box formation, the cross formation, the diamond formation and miscellaneous formations. All plays should be begun from one of these formations so that every play used will look the same until after the tip is made, at which time each player performs the task which is called for in that particular play. There are advantages in the use of plays from each formation as well as from the use of the formation itself. Certain formations are more adaptable to specific situations as well as to the personnel available. Therefore, selection of a particular formation to be used, as well as its use of a specific play, may determine the success of a play.

Each jump ball must be analyzed in terms of the possibility of controlling the tip. Height and jumping ability are the major factors in determining the type of play that is to be used. All jump ball situations must fall into one of three categories:

a. Potential control rests with team A.
b. Potential control rests with team B.
c. Control is indefinite and either team may gain the tip-off.

Standard Jump Ball Situations

Since jump balls may be called from any one of the three circles, and since the three situations are possible at each of the three circles, then there are nine standard jump ball situations.

It is essential that all members of the team have a common understanding of the jump ball situation each time the ball is put in play in this manner, and a member of the team should be designated to analyze the jump ball situation and to call the signal designating the formation and play to be used. For example, if the jump ball is in the defensive end of the court, with a tall opponent jumping against a much shorter member of the defensive team, the designated player should select and give the signal for the use of a formation and play which will be of a defensive rather than offensive nature. Even though many jump ball situations are evident, it is sound practice to have one designated player to identify all jump balls, so there will be no confusion in the selection of a play. If he is totally unsure of the jump, he should call a defensive formation.

Basic Principle of Jump Ball Situations

The basic principle of all jump ball formations, as is true in all out-of-bounds situations, is first of all to get possession of the ball. If a scoring play can be the result of a successful jump ball situation, so much the better. The following formations with plays for each of them are presented with this in mind:

THE DIAMOND FORMATION

Most teams prefer to tip the ball forward or to the right or left, because it is much easier to do so. There are occasions, however, when a team may wish to protect a lead or slow down the tempo of the game. Typical situations would be in a tie game with a few seconds to play, or an overtime game. When this is true, the team may wish to tip the ball back to the guard. The alignment of players in the diamond formation presents an opportunity to tip the ball backward, as well as forward and to either side. If the ball is tipped backward, it practically assures ball possession with very little risk of interception because there are three defensive players in the back-court area to protect against such an occurrence. Proper placement of the players in the diamond formation will contribute to its success. The three back men should be the best rebounders, with the player stationed in the middle of the three back players being the best all-around ball handler.

Even though the ball is sometimes tipped backward, there are enough defensive players stationed in the back-court area to assure adequate defense against interception.

While the diamond formation provides the opportunity to tip the ball backwards, it is also just as effective when the ball is tipped forward and to the side.

The alignment of players in the diamond formation can be changed to fit the ever changing situation.

Diagram 4-1. This diagram shows the ball being tipped to No. 1, who goes high in the air to get the ball. No. 3 drives by and receives a pass from No. 1. No. 1 makes the pass while still in the air, but the ball must be passed and not batted. He should catch the ball or at least semi-catch it before passing it to No. 3. Possession of the ball is most important. After receiving the ball, No. 3 drives as far as possible down court using the dribble, and then passes to No. 2, who remains stationary until he is sure No. 3 has the ball. After No. 2 is sure of ball possession by No. 3, he then cuts hard into the offensive end of the floor where he receives a pass from No. 3. After receiving the ball, No. 2 may have several options to pass to No. 1 or 3, who cut down the left side of the floor, or No. 4, who will be going in the opposite direction on his drive toward the basket. The play can also be used on the opposite side of the floor, with No. 1 passing to No. 2 and No. 2 driving down court and passing to No. 3. This play will also work well in the back court when the team is sure of the tap and ball possession. The play gives ample opportunities for quick offensive thrusts down the floor ahead of the guards.

Diagram 4-2. In this diagram, No. 3 tips the ball to No. 4, who goes high in the air to receive it. No. 1 fakes toward the center to get the ball, then reverses his direction and cuts toward the basket. If he does not receive the pass, he then cuts to the side of the court. Usually No. 4 can pass to No. 1 as he is cutting toward the basket, but if this is not possible, he can make the pass as No. 1 makes the cut to the sideline. No. 2 drives rapidly down the floor toward the offensive basket after being sure No. 4 has possession of the ball. No. 3, the jumper, goes the opposite way from the tip, and then drives down the floor toward the offensive basket. No. 4 may also drive in toward the basket for a return pass from No. 1, who will have several option pass possibilities. The same play may also be used on the other side of the floor, with No. 2 receiving the tip and No. 1 cutting to the opposite side of the floor. No. 3 would then drive in the direction opposite to that in which the ball is tipped. Many times, it

Diagram 4-1

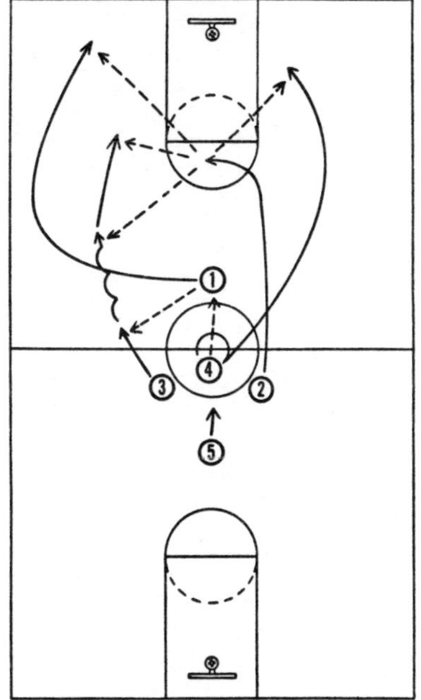

Diagram 4-2

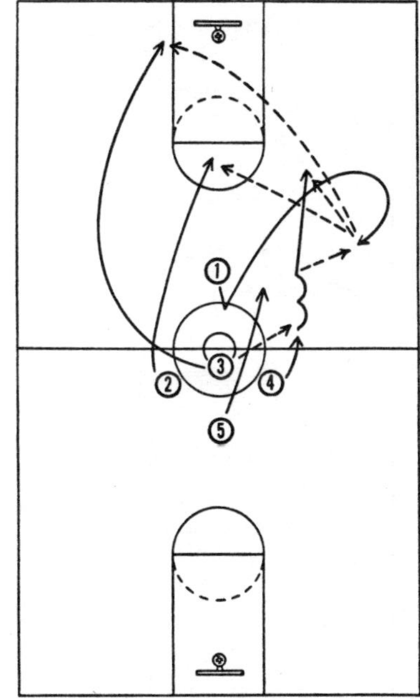

is possible to use this particular play if the players are able to secure the ball from the opponent's tip. It is possible, upon interception of the ball, for players to go right into the offensive thrusts from the position at which the ball is recovered, regardless of what signal is called.

Diagram 4-3. This diagram shows a variation of the two previous plays, and can be used successfully should the opponents be expecting the ball to be tipped forward as in Diagram 4-1, or to the side as in Diagram 4-2. Should the opponents be pressing hard to beat the players to the tip in these areas, the play shown in this diagram can be used successfully, because, by doing this, they will leave the area to the rear of the jumper open. In this play, No. 3 fakes as if going in to get the tip on the side, thereby protecting that area. Instead of getting the ball, he drives on down the court toward the offensive basket. No. 1 fakes, as if going in for the tip, and then cuts down the floor and to the side, as shown in the diagram. The ball is tipped by No. 5 backward to No. 4, who is stationed directly to the rear of the jumper. No. 4 dribbles to his left and passes to No. 1, who has faked toward the center, and then cuts down the floor and to the side, as shown in the diagram, to be in a position to

Diagram 4-3

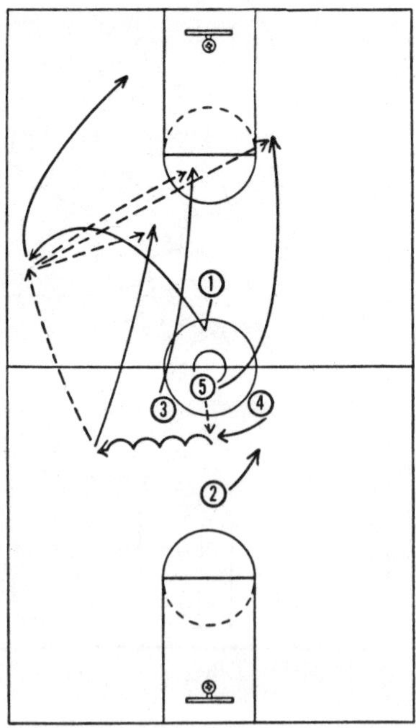

Diagram 4-4

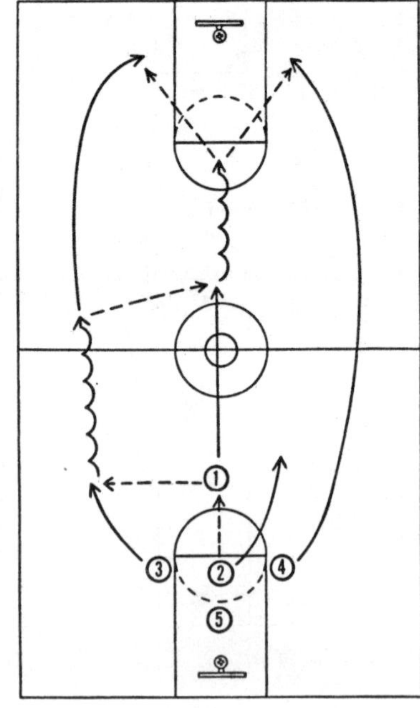

receive the ball from No. 4. No. 4 cuts hard down the center of the floor toward the offensive basket in anticipation of a return pass from No. 1. No. 5 drives down the side of the floor opposite to that on which the ball is passed. No. 1 will have many options and possibilities from this area. This play may also be reversed to the other side of the floor. These variations will keep the opponents guessing.

Diagram 4-4. This diagram shows a jump ball situation from the back court, which, if properly executed, will result in a fast break pattern and enable the team to move the ball down the court and into scoring position very quickly. The ball can be moved to either side of the floor on the initial pass-off from No. 1 after he has received the tip from No. 2. In this diagram, No. 3 moves out to the side of the court as soon as he is sure that No. 1 has possession of the ball after the tip from No. 2. This is an important move because neither No. 3 nor 4 can afford to leave their defensive positions too soon, as the position of the ball in the back-court area will allow an easy basket if the area is left unguarded and the opposition gains possession of the ball from the tip. After receiving the pass from No. 1, No. 3 moves down the side of the court in a fast dribble. No. 1, after making the pass, moves down the center of the court toward the offensive basket. No. 4 moves down the opposite side of the floor from No. 3. No. 3 passes the ball to No. 1 as soon as he is able to do so and as soon as No. 1 is free to receive the pass. The movement of Nos. 3, 1 and 4 provides for a three-lane fast break pattern which allows No. 1, who has the ball at the free throw lane area, to either shoot from the free throw line, drive in for a lay-up or pass off to No. 3 or 4.

Diagram 4-5. This diagram illustrates a possibility that may be worked when the team has absolute control of the tip in the back court and the opponent's guards are in close to the jump ball area. No. 1 breaks in toward the ball and receives the tip from No. 2. As soon as No. 3 is sure that No. 1 has possession of the ball, he breaks out to the side of the court and down the sideline. No. 1 passes the ball to No. 3 as soon as he is able to do so. No. 3 dribbles down the side of the court until he is able to pass the ball to No. 4, who moved straight down the court for a short distance and then broke into the center of the court. After No. 4 receives the pass from No. 3, he dribbles to the free throw line, at which point he stops, unless he is

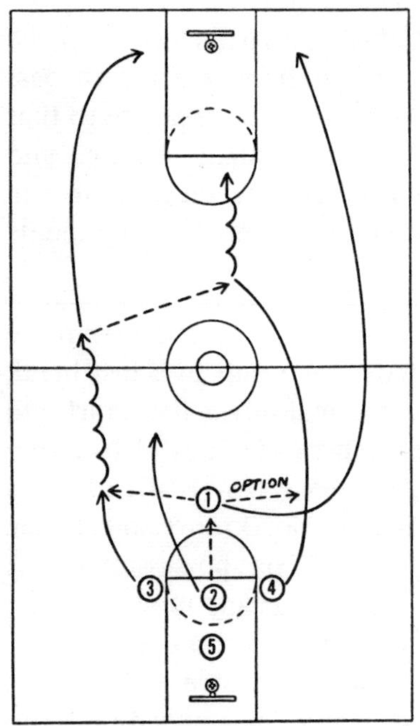

Diagram 4-5

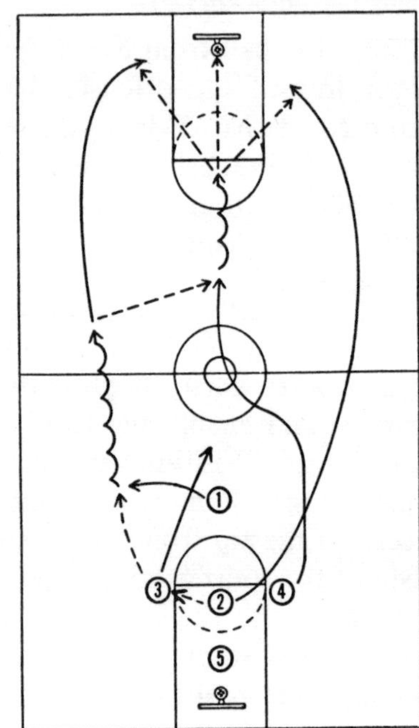

Diagram 4-6

able to drive all the way in for the lay-up. If No. 4 is unable to drive in or shoot from this position, he can pass off to No. 3 or 1, both of whom are driving down the sides of the court. No. 1 moves to the side of the court after making the pass to No. 3.

Diagram 4-6. This diagram shows another version of the same type of play from the jump ball situation in the back court depicted in the previous diagram. No. 2 tips the ball to No. 3, who in turn passes to No. 1, who cuts to the side of the court from his previous position, which he took at the inception of the jump ball. No. 1 dribbles hard down the side of the court. No. 4 moves straight down the court toward the offensive basket until he is able to cut to the center of the court and thereby be in a position to receive a pass from No. 1. After having tipped the ball to No. 3, and making sure that No. 3 has possession of the ball, No. 2 moves out to the right side of the court and continues his drive toward the offensive basket. No. 4 dribbles to the free throw line area and if possible drives all the way in for a lay-up shot, stops for a jump shot at the free throw line area or passes off to No. 1 or 4, who are in excellent positions for an "out" court shot or a drive-in.

Diagram 4-7. This diagram shows a jump ball situation in the front court free throw circle. A maneuver by No. 2 uses the referee and the jumpers as a screen and will often free the player for a shot in close, when the ball is tipped to No. 1 and he in turn passes to No. 2. No. 2 cuts behind No. 3 as soon as the tip is made. No. 3 remains stationary after the tap so that No. 2 may use him as a screen. No. 2 can brush his guard off using No. 3 if he cuts close to No. 3. No. 2 should be open for a good percentage shot if No. 1 is able to get the ball to him at a time when he is free to receive the pass and obtain the shot. No. 5 remains in his original position, so that he can protect against an interception by the opposition or if his teammate "jumping center" is not able to control the tip and get the ball to No. 1. No. 4 moves in the opposite direction to No. 2, so that he is not in the scoring area and is able to receive a pass from No. 1 should No. 1 not be able to pass to No. 2. No. 1 should be the tallest player, unless he is the jumper.

Diagram 4-8. This diagram shows a jump ball situation at the free throw circle in the front court area. After the ball has been tipped a few times successfully to No. 1 from this position, the

Diagram 4-7

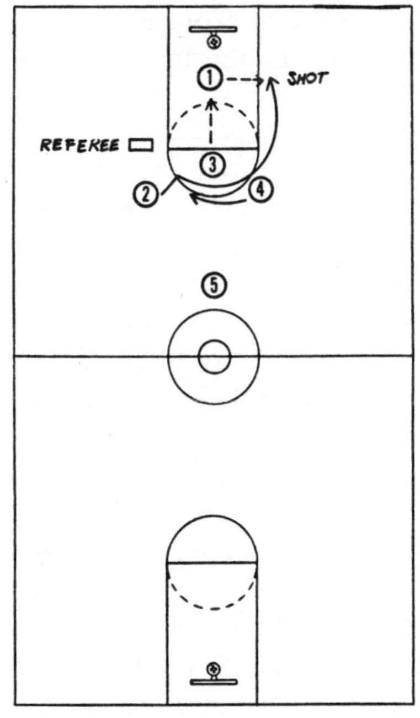

Diagram 4-8

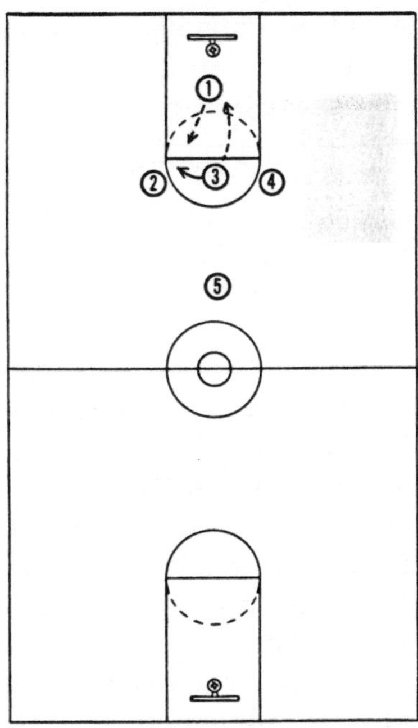

opponent jumping with No. 3 will often, in an effort to tie up No. 1, get into the habit of turning his back on No. 3, leaving him open. No. 1 may tap the ball quickly back to No. 3, who has an excellent shot from the free throw line. The success of the play, therefore, depends upon the action of the defensive player jumping against No. 3. If this player does not turn his back on No. 3, then No. 1 is faced with the possibility of making the pass to either Nos. 2, 4 or 5. He can and should, of course, shoot the ball himself if he is free to do so, and feels that a good percentage shot can be executed at the particular time he is able to take it. The pass to No. 3 can be high so that No. 3 may shoot while still in the air after having received the pass from No. 1.

Diagram 4-9. This play is similar to the previous two plays, inasmuch as the ball is tipped forward to No. 1. If No. 1 cannot shoot, he may pass off to No. 2 or 4. No. 3 remains in his original jumping position after the tap, and No. 2 cuts behind him after the tap has been made. No. 4 cuts off of No. 2, and the pass can be made to whichever player is open. The cuts by Nos. 2 and 4 must be made quickly, otherwise No. 1 will be tied up by the opposition or remain in the lane too long a period of time. No. 5 remains in the back area to protect against interception, or, in some cases, not being successful in obtaining possession of the ball from the tap. The success of the play is in direct proportion to the team's ability to gain possession of the ball.

Diagram 4-10. The diamond formation can be changed to become more of an offensive threat by bringing the back man up on the circle, as shown in this diagram. Here, No. 1, instead of remaining in a deep defensive position, moves up to take a position on the circle in back of the jumper. In this situation, the team not only has men positioned for a quick offensive thrust, but also in fine defensive positions. If the defensive team should position their men around the circle, as shown in the diagram, then both teams would have what might be termed an "open area" in which to receive the tap. In this situation, the "open area" is stipulated as being between Nos. 4 and 1 for the offensive team. No. 5 could tip the ball between these two players, and they could, by blocking out X4 and X1, be assured of obtaining possession of the ball from the tip. Teams should always be alert for these "open area" situations, especially when possession of the ball is all important. Likewise, in this same situation, the defensive team has an "open area" in which to receive the tip. This

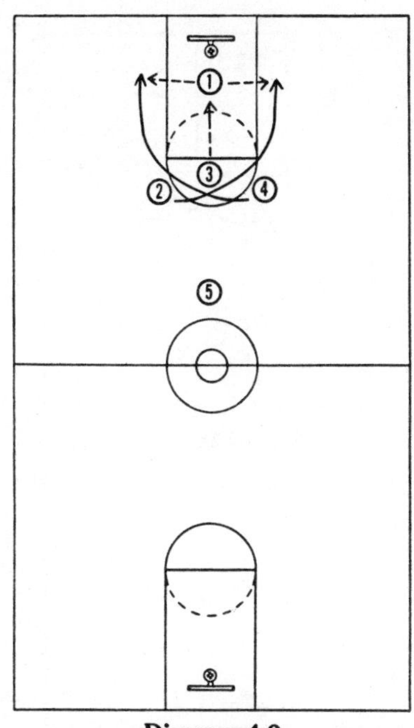

Diagram 4-9

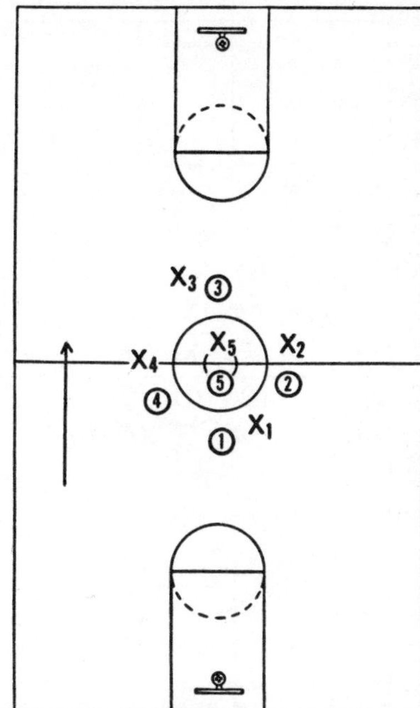

Diagram 4-10

area would be between X3 and X4. If X5 can control the tip and tip the ball between these two players, one or the other would virtually be certain of obtaining possession of the ball. The following diagram gives a further explanation of this situation.

Diagram 4-11. This closed diamond formation shows No. 1 taking a position on the circle behind the jumper. The defensive team has spaced its players so that there are no "open areas" for either team. This means that there is a defensive player stationed between all offensive players, and neither team has an "open area" to which they can tip the ball. However, a closer look at the formation reveals two things: (1) If the offensive team should be able to control the tap, so that No. 3 can receive the ball, then Nos. 4 and 2 can drive quickly down the court. This maneuver could immediately provide the offensive advantage of a 3-on-2 situation. This situation could even be possible with the tip going to the side to either No. 4 or 2. (2) However, if the defensive team should be able to control the tip, and X5 should tip the ball to either X4 or X1, or far down the floor over the heads of all the players, the defensive team would almost immediately have a 2-on-1 scoring situation, with No. 1 having to defend against X4 and X1. All these situations should be watched for and guarded against, depending upon the game conditions at the time.

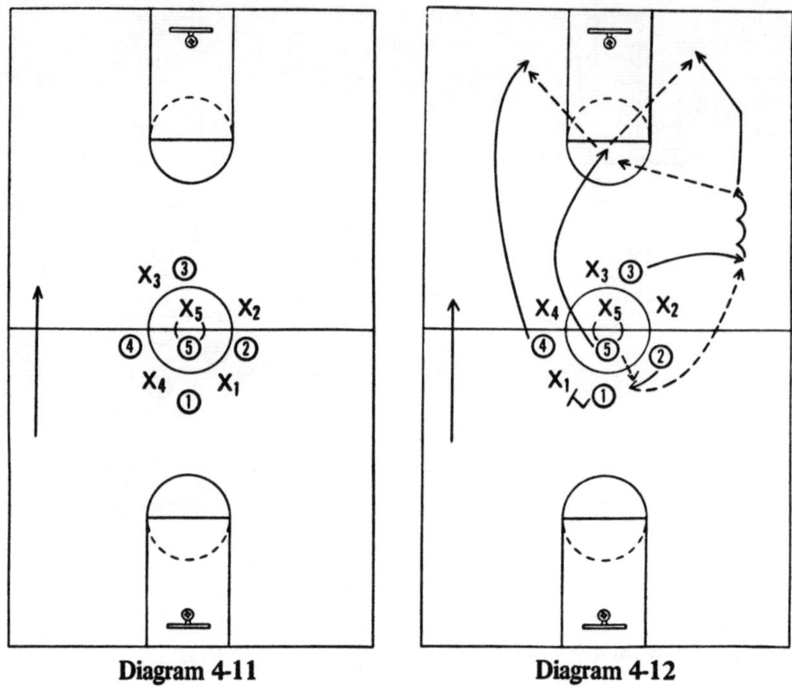

Diagram 4-11

Diagram 4-12

Diagram 4-12. This diagram shows both teams lined up in a close diamond formation, positioned in a manner that will allow both of them to have "open area" tip possibilities. The offensive team is able to turn an "open area," sure-control tip into a quick offensive thrust, as shown in this diagram. No. 5 tips the ball to the open area, and with No. 1 blocking out X1, No. 2 goes for the ball. No. 3 moves deep down the right side of the court, and No. 2 quickly passes him the ball. No. 4 moves down the left side of the court. No. 5 drives down the middle of the court to receive the pass from No. 3. A fast break pattern now exists between Nos. 3, 4 and 5, as shown in the diagram. Nos. 1 and 2 trail the play.

Diagram 4-13. Here again, the offensive team takes the close diamond formation, with No. 1 positioned in tight on the circle. The defensive team places their players so that both teams have an "open area" to which they can tip the ball. However, here the defensive team has chosen to play Nos. 2 and 4 tight, using X4 and X2 to guard them. This leaves an open space on the jump circle to the right side of No. 3. X3 is playing No. 3 tight, but with a sure tip control by No. 5, he could tip the ball forward and to the right of No. 3. No. 3 should block X3 out momentarily, just as he would on a rebound situation, and then go for the ball. Nos. 2 and 4 drive hard down the court to help No. 3. As a result of this maneuver, quick scoring opportunities could develop. Nos. 5 and 1 follow the play.

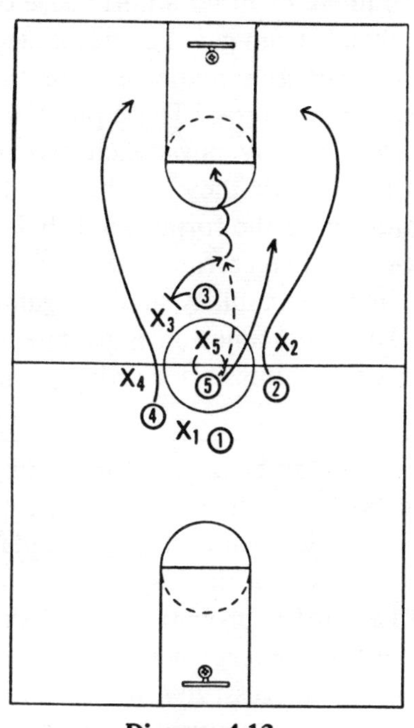

Diagram 4-13

Diagram 4-14

THE CROSS FORMATION

The cross formation will provide many scoring opportunities and is varied enough so that numerous plays can be used from it. It is especially adaptable to the quick scoring type of play, providing the team is sure of getting the tip. This is true because the placement of the players makes it possible for three players to be in a position to break quickly down the floor and be in good scoring position. This formation lends itself very well to a wide variety of plays, especially if the team is sure of getting the tip. It is also a formation which will provide for a 3-on-2 situation. It does give adequate back-court protection because there is one player always present in the back-court position. The two players stationed on the two sides of the jumpers are always in a position to move in either an offensive or defensive direction, dependent upon which team gets ball possession after the tip. The cross formation is given this name because the players are stationed in positions resembling a cross. These positions can vary depending upon the situation. The players on each side of the circle can be lined up on the center line, or they can be on the offensive or defensive side of the center line if the formation is being used at the center circle. The back-court player can also vary his position, depending somewhat on his maneuverability and the game conditions which exist at the time. His main function is to defend the back-court area, and he should position himself accordingly and as the situation dictates.

Diagram 4-14. This shows a play that can be used for beginning the game, a quarter, the second half or an overtime game. It is one of several sequence plays that can be used from this particular formation. It also stresses the tipping of the ball directly in front of the center position. Tipping the ball forward is probably one of the most difficult tasks for the center to perform, except perhaps tipping to his outside. If this can be accomplished successfully, it places the defense in a vulnerable position and immediately gives an advantage to the offense. This is true because it places the ball in the front court in an area where the offense can place three men in a position which will immediately challenge the defense, as can be seen in the diagram. All three can be in a scoring position very quickly. No. 1 tips the ball forward to No. 5. As the official tosses the ball up for the center jump players, Nos. 2 and 3 fake toward the defensive basket. They immediately cut back toward the offensive basket, as shown in the diagram. No. 5 turns and makes a pass to No. 2. Immediately after making the pass to No. 2, No. 5 moves down the center of the court toward the offensive basket as quickly as possible, so that he will be in a position to receive the return pass from No. 2. After No. 2 makes the pass to No. 5, he continues his cut to the basket. In the meantime, No. 3 is also cutting toward the offensive basket on a parallel path to No. 2, as soon as he sees that No. 5 has possession of the ball. After No. 5 receives the ball from

No. 2, he may pass to either No. 2 or 3, as shown in the diagram. If the area is clear, No. 5 may dribble on into the basket area. If he passes to No. 3, No. 5 may continue his drive toward the basket for the rebound. No. 3 will dribble for the basket in the hope that he may be free for the lay-up.

Diagram 4-15. It should be remembered that the placement of the players will be dependent upon whether they are able to obtain these positions prior to the tip. Even though this may not be possible, the play can be executed with success. The important player in this diagram is No. 5. It is to his advantage to be situated directly in front of No. 1, as it will enhance No. 1's efforts to tip the ball to him a great deal. It is much easier to tip the ball directly forward than it is to tip it either to the left or right. It is, therefore, necessary for No. 5 to assume this position immediately, before the jump ball situation takes place. The play can, however, be used effectively if No. 5 is forced to take a position to the left or right of the desired one. The control of the tip will be the determining factor in No. 5's success in obtaining the ball. After No. 5 receives the ball from the tip by No. 1, he turns immediately and dribbles toward the offensive basket as quickly as he can. His success in this maneuver will be determined by the amount of opposition he encounters from the defense. If an opposing player lays back on defense, then No. 5's task will become more difficult and he will be forced to alter his offensive tactics. It will force him to change his dribble from a direct drive to the basket to a more indirect path.

Diagram 4-16. This shows the ball being tipped to No. 3, who sets up approximately 6 feet from the circle. No. 3 breaks toward the circle, and, then, as he approaches the circle, he veers to his right. He times his move so that he can receive the tip at the position shown in the diagram. Timing is important because the tip must be made so that No. 3 can receive the ball approximately 4 feet from the circle. This is a quick scoring play, and one that can be used successfully when the jumper is sure of controlling the tap. No. 4 moves in toward the ball and the circle as the ball is tipped. He then reverses his drive and moves down court as soon as he sees that No. 3 has gained control of the ball. No. 2 holds his position until he is sure No. 3 has the ball and then he also moves toward the offensive basket. After No. 3 receives the ball, he dribbles quickly down court if he is able to do so. If he cannot dribble all the way, he can pass to either No. 4 or 2. If executed correctly and No. 3 is able to gain possession of the ball from the tip, it will usually result in a move which will set up a 2-on-1 situation in the event that No. 3 is not completely free.

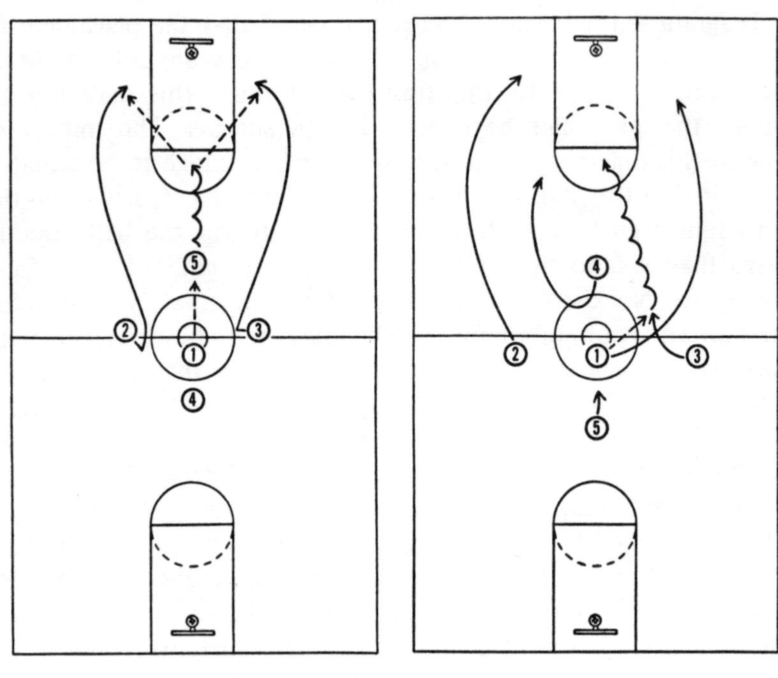

Diagram 4-15 Diagram 4-16

Diagram 4-17. This shows a long pass play which can be used from the same formation as in the previous diagram. The players are stationed in the same positions. Just before the official tosses the ball up for the tip, No. 4 cuts as fast as he can toward the offensive basket. No. 1 tips the ball forward to No. 2, who stations himself directly in front of No. 1 and as close to the center circle as possible, using a wide stance to insure himself plenty of room. After receiving the ball, No. 2 passes to No. 4, who is well on his way down court. The pass made by No. 2 can be a "back over the head" type pass, or, if this is impossible, then No. 2 may turn and make a one-handed pass. The intention of this play is to break No. 4 free and clear for a quick drive to the basket. No. 2 follows his pass so that he may be in a position to assist No. 4 if a defensive player lays back. No. 2 can also be in a position for a rebound should the basket be missed. No. 3 moves down court as soon as he sees that No. 2 has received the tip. No. 5 remains in the back court for defensive purposes.

Diagram 4-18. The cross formation, if used in the back court on a jump ball situation, is a strong defensive formation because it positions four players close to the defensive basket. However, it does present strong possibilities for fast break opportunities if the tip can be controlled and either No. 3, 4 or 2 gains possession of the ball from the tip-off. However, its main attribute must be considered to be one of defense rather than offense. This play shows No. 1 tipping the ball to No. 4, who in turn passes to No. 5, as shown in the diagram. No. 5 must be careful not to leave his defensive position until he is certain that No. 4 has possession of the ball; otherwise, it will weaken the defense considerably. No. 2 moves to the side of the court to receive the pass from No. 5 when he is sure No. 5 has possession of the ball. No. 2 may cut directly out toward the

Diagram 4-17

Diagram 4-18

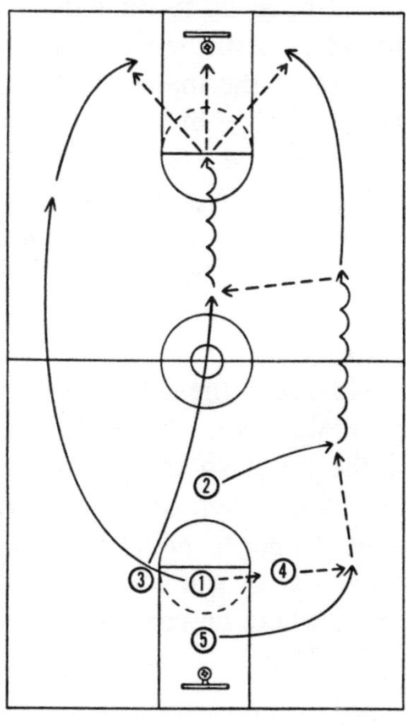

sideline, or he may advance toward or away from the defensive basket as the occasion demands. No. 3 cuts toward the middle of the court, with the expectation of receiving the pass into the center of the court by No. 2. However, No. 3 does not leave the defensive area until he is sure No. 5 has received the pass from No. 4 and actually has possession of the ball. No. 1, by the time No. 5 gains possession of the ball, has recovered his balance from the jump ball and is able to cut toward the left sideline. The three lanes are now filled and the fast break is in operation. No. 3 now has the ball in the center of the court near the center circle. He dribbles hard down the center of the court until he reaches the free throw circle area, where he stops, unless he is able to drive all the way in for the lay-up. He can also pass off to No. 1 or 2, who are breaking down opposite sides of the court toward the basket.

Diagram 4-19. Oftentimes, the ball will be tipped backward from the cross formation when the jump ball tip-off takes place in the back court. As was previously mentioned, this is a dangerous procedure because of the close proximity of No. 5 to the opponent's basket. A mistake in ball handling, an interception or the inability of the jumper to control the tip could result in an easy basket for the opposition. It is important, therefore, that careful consideration should be given to the indiscriminate use of this play. Possibly its use should be restricted to times when No. 5 gains possession of the ball, because of the inability of the jumper to control the tip and the fact that the ball should have been tipped to either No. 3 or 4. The play could then be executed in the same manner as when the tip should have gone to No. 3 or 4. The important thing to consider in the use of any play from any formation is to be sure, first of all, that ball possession is obtained and then proceed from this point. The play can be used, however, with equal effectiveness if the jumper can control the tip. If the tip goes to No. 5, he passes to No. 3, who moves out to the side of the court away from the congested area near the basket. No. 3 passes to No. 2, who has also moved out to the side of the court so that he may be in a better position to receive the pass. No. 2 then dribbles down the side of the court until such time as he is able to pass to No. 4, who has moved from his position up the center of the court. No. 4 dribbles to the top of the free throw circle, where he can either drive all the way in for the lay-up or stop

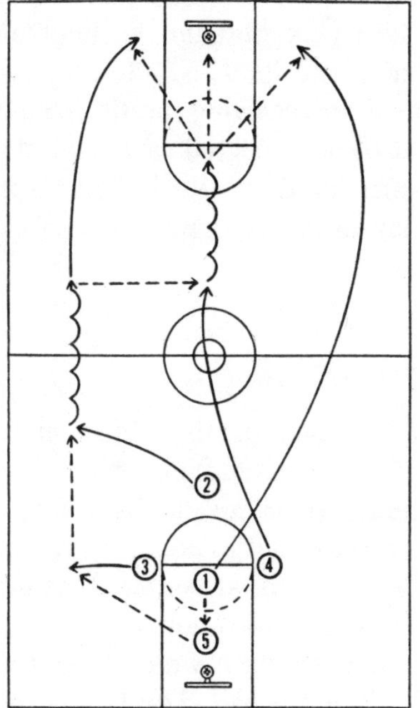

Diagram 4-19

Diagram 4-20
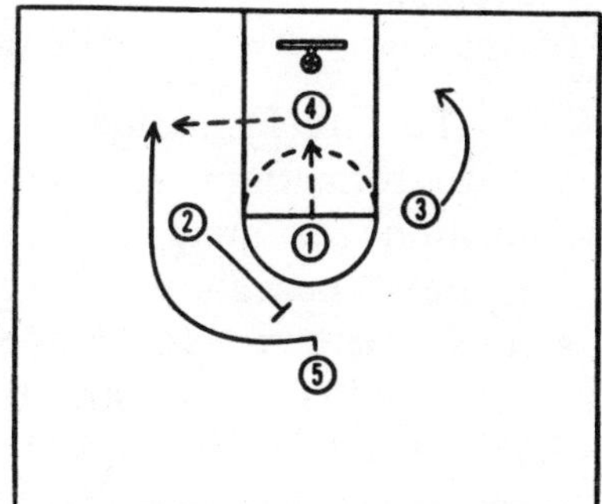

and shoot from this position. He can also pass off to No. 2 or 1, who are breaking toward the basket using the outside lanes, as shown in the diagram.

Diagram 4-20. This play shows a front court jump ball play from the cross formation. Its success depends upon proper timing between Nos. 5, 4 and 2. Just as the ball is tipped by No. 1 on the jump, No. 2 moves, as shown in the diagram, to execute a screen for No. 5. No. 5 also breaks straight in toward the basket at the same time. The cuts should be timed so that Nos. 2 and 5 meet at a point shown in the diagram. This is very important, and the success of the play will depend upon this timing because it will enable No. 5 to change his direction and break to his left. By so doing, his guard will be screened off by No. 2. No. 5 now breaks to his left and receives a pass from No. 4. No. 5 may either execute a jump shot at the point where he receives the pass from No. 4, or he may drive in for the lay-up. If No. 2's guard switches to pick him up, he may make a return pass to No. 4. If the timing is excellent, No. 4 may make the pass to No. 5 while still in the air after receiving the tip from No. 1. This exact timing, of course, is not to be expected each time the play is used. No. 2 will move out toward the defensive basket to protect against interception, or, if the play does not materialize, No. 3 can move in for the rebound.

THE BOX FORMATION

The box formation is probably one of the oldest and most popular formations, and it is used more extensively than any other formation for jump ball situations. It is given the name "box formation" because the players are stationed in positions resembling a square or box before the ball is tossed up at center. It is popular because of its overall strength. The team does not have to sacrifice defensively in order to gain offensive strength which would enable them to use a scoring play from the jump ball. The box formation can be used from all three circles, depending upon the situation and circumstances underlying its use. It also provides opportunities offensively and yet furnishes adequate protection defensively. Because of the player arrangement, offensive plays can be used successfully, yet this same placement of the players results in good defensive positioning. These standard box formations provide many offensive options which can result in a score as a direct result of the play; they insure that possession of the ball is obtained, and yet they provide the defensive strength that is needed to protect against an opponent's scoring possibilities. The arrangement of players in the box formation is important. The back guards should be the best defensive players, with the front men being the best rebounders. The ball can be tipped in almost any direction and still have a receiver in a reasonably good position to retrieve the tip. Its worth lies principally in its strength in both defense and offense.

Diagram 4-21. This play can result in a quick basket if properly executed. The play will work to advantage if the opposition is expecting to get the tip and as a result are playing their guards, X3 and X4, up tight as shown in the diagram. If this is true, it will be an easy matter for No. 5 to slip behind the guards in a quick action move and receive a long pass from No. 3. This play cannot be expected to work each time as shown, because much of its success will be determined by the play of the two defensive guards. However, even though one of the guards lays back instead of playing up tight, or moves back after the tip, it is entirely possible for No. 5 to maneuver after he has received the ball, in such a way as to drive past the guard, outmaneuver him or pass off to a teammate. After No. 3 passes to No. 5, he cuts toward the basket in an effort to help No. 5 in any way possible. No. 1 also moves toward the offensive basket after he sees No. 3 has controlled the tip and is ready to make the pass to No. 5. No. 2 moves back to a guard position to provide defensive balance, in case No. 1 does not control the tip or the pass is intercepted. After the screen, No. 4 can either move down court, remain stationary or move back to a guard position.

Diagram 4-22. The success of this type of play will be dependent upon the ability of the center to not only be able to outjump his opponent so that he can tip the ball to No. 3, but he

Diagram 4-21

Diagram 4-22

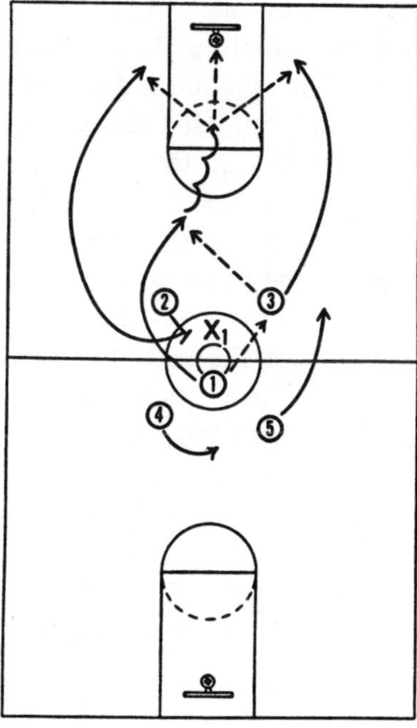

also must be fast enough to move down the court quickly after the tip. No. 1 tips the ball to No. 3. No. 2 screens for No. 1, who cuts around him, taking advantage of the screen, and drives down the center of the court. No. 3, after receiving the tip from No. 1, turns and passes to No. 1. It may be necessary for No. 3 to hesitate before the pass is made to No. 1, in order that No. 1 may have enough time to make his cut and be in the right position to receive the pass from No. 3 when No. 3 is ready to make it. This may necessitate some skillful maneuvering on the part of No. 3 to enable him to control the ball for the desired length of time, that time being the amount necessary to make the pass to No. 1 when he is ready to receive it. No. 2 screens for No. 1, enabling No. 1 to free himself. After the screen is executed by No. 2, he does a reverse pivot and rolls off down the left side of the court. No. 3 also drives down the right side of the court after making the pass to No. 1. No. 1 dribbles in for the lay-up if he is able to do so. If not, he can make the pass-off to No. 2 or 3 as they move down court. No. 4 moves to the back court to protect on defense. No. 5 waits until he can determine what his actions should be as a result of the way the play is progressing.

Diagram 4-23. This play is one in which the opposition gains possession of the ball on the tip and a defensive adjustment must be made immediately. Every team using special tip-off plays must be prepared to assume a defensive position quickly if the tip is lost to the opposition. This play gives the defensive team a 50-50 chance for ball possession on the tip. However, if X5 clearly outjumps No. 5 and is able to tip the ball to X3, then Nos. 3 and 4 must be ready to move into their designated defensive positions, as shown in the diagram. They can do this by cutting through the circle and straight down the court after they are aware that the opposition has secured possession of the ball. This move must be executed quickly, so that they are able to pick up their assigned opponents and then move quickly to help Nos. 1, 2 and 5 in any defensive situation that may develop as a result of the tip to X3.

Diagram 4-24. In this diagram, No. 5 tips the ball to the right side near the center line. No. 3 moves out to receive the ball at this point. No. 1 cuts off X4 after faking him, and goes just outside No. 3

to receive a hand-off from No. 3. As the ball is tipped, No. 4 screens on X5, the opposition jumper. After the tip, No. 5 breaks past the screen set by No. 4 and goes deep down court. No. 3 could pass directly to No. 5 as No. 5 breaks down the court, or the pass to No. 5 could come from No. 1 after No. 3 has passed off to him. Quick scoring possibilities could come from this play. No. 3 trails the play.

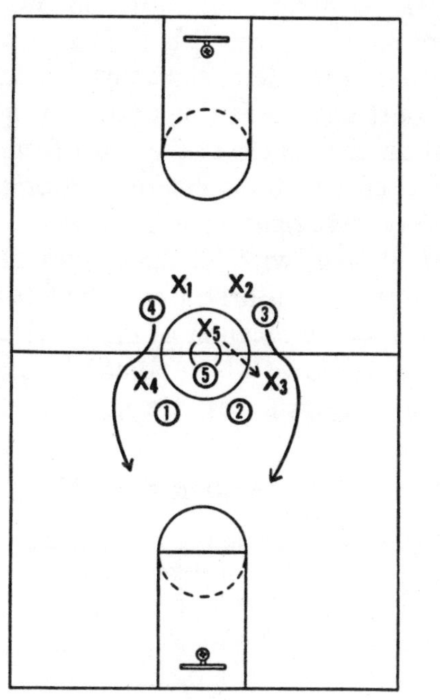

Diagram 4-23

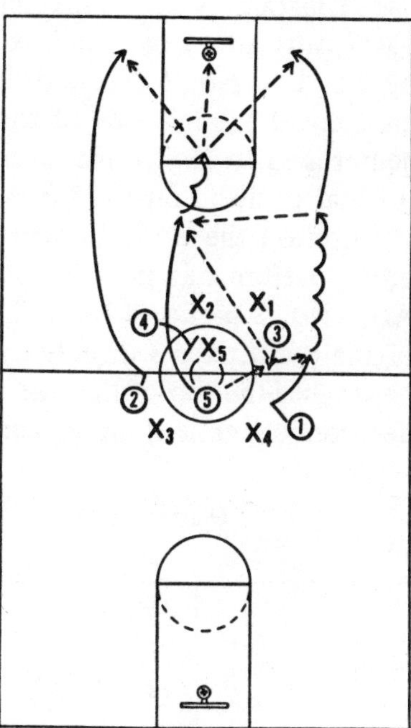

Diagram 4-24

Diagram 4-25. This diagram shows a jump ball situation in the back court, where the jumper, No. 5, has almost certain control of the tip, enabling the team to use a fast break pattern. The X team is defensive minded and in defensive formation. No. 5 tips the ball to No. 2. No. 1 breaks to an area where he will be open, which is shown in the diagram as the middle lane. No. 1 receives a pass from No. 2 at this position. No. 2 then breaks down the outside right lane, while No. 5 drives down the outside lane on the left side. Nos. 3 and 4 follow the play and may enter into it. An example could be that if No. 1 was not open, No. 2 could possibly pass to No. 4 as he moves down the court. No. 4 could possibly pass to No. 1 down court, or drive down the middle himself on the fast break resulting from the play. The object of the play is to provide a fast break opportunity from the jump ball at the free throw line in the back court.

Diagram 4-26. This shows a jump ball situation in the back-court area from the box formation. The ball is tipped forward by No. 1 to No. 2. No. 2 dribbles to the side of the court. He drives hard down the left side of the court until he is able to pass in to the center area to No. 3. No. 3 cuts up the center of the court from his original position on the tip. No. 5 cuts to the right from his original position on the tip and down the outside right lane. A three-lane fast break pattern has now been established, with all three lanes filled. After No. 2 passes to No. 3, he continues his drive down the left side of the court. No. 3 dribbles hard down the center of the court until he reaches the top of the free throw circle, at which point he makes a decision dependent upon certain circumstances. He now has four

Diagram 4-25

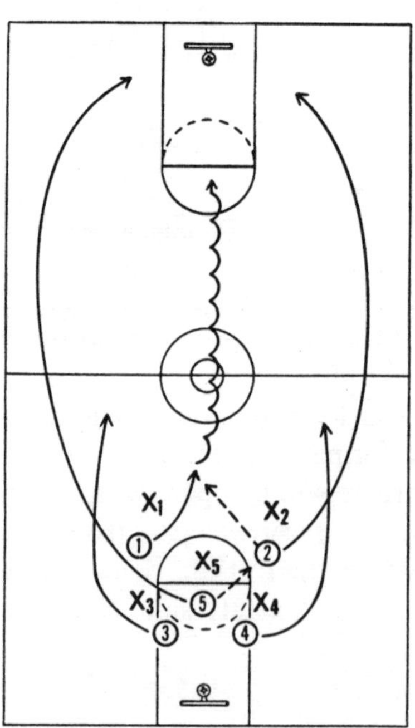

Diagram 4-26

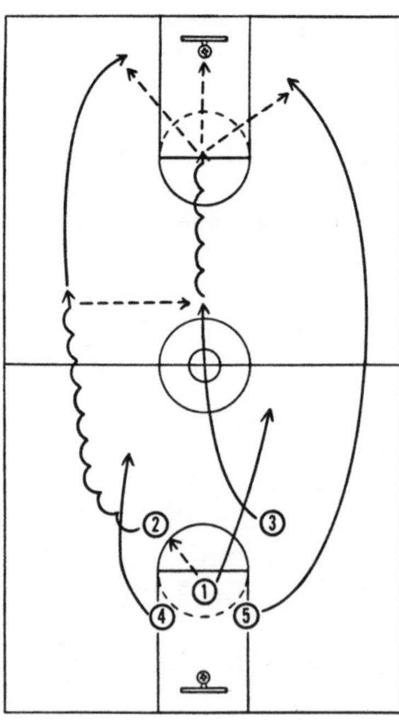

options: he can shoot from this position, drive in for the lay-up, if this is feasible, or he can pass off to No. 2 or 5, both of whom are breaking toward the basket.

Diagram 4-27. This play is a fast break pattern from a jump ball situation in the back court, from the box formation. The ball is tipped back to No. 4, or No. 1 may lose the tip and it is intercepted by No. 4. As soon as No. 2 is sure that No. 4 has obtained possession of the ball, he moves out to the side of the court where there is less congestion and he will be in a good position to receive the pass from No. 4. After receiving the pass, No. 2 dribbles hard down the side of the court. He is able to dribble quickly down court because he will not be molested and harassed nearly as much in this area. As he approaches the center area, he passes in to No. 3, who has cut quickly up the center of the court to be in a position to receive the pass from No. 2 at the center circle area. This area will also be less congested so that the pass can be made without too much danger of interception. No. 3 dribbles hard down the center of the court to the top of the free throw circle, where he can shoot, drive in or pass off to No. 2 or 5, as shown in the diagram. No. 5 drives down the right side of the court. All three players should stay wide and not bunch up in the center of the court.

Diagram 4-27

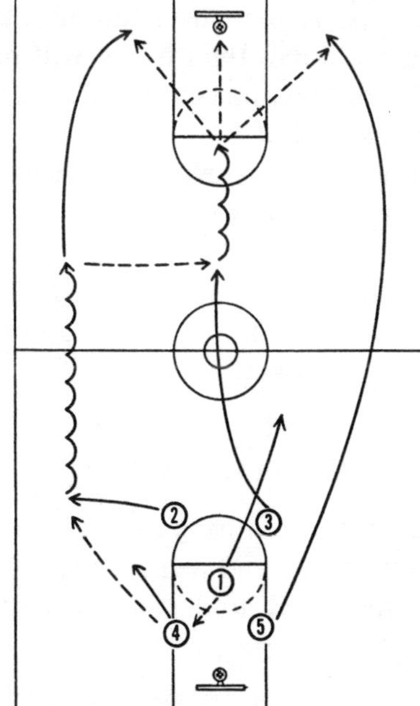

Diagram 4-28. Usually, an attempt is made to tip the ball forward on a jump ball situation in the front court. This depends, of course, on several factors which have been discussed previously. This play shows the ball being tipped forward to No. 3. No. 5 cuts behind No. 1. (He begins his move as soon as the ball is tipped by one of the jumpers.) No. 5 must be careful not to move into the restricted area before the ball is actually tapped by No. 1. As soon as No. 5 moves across the top of the circle, No. 4 makes his cut directly behind him. If the cut is timed and executed correctly, No. 4 should be open for a jump shot in the area indicated in the diagram.

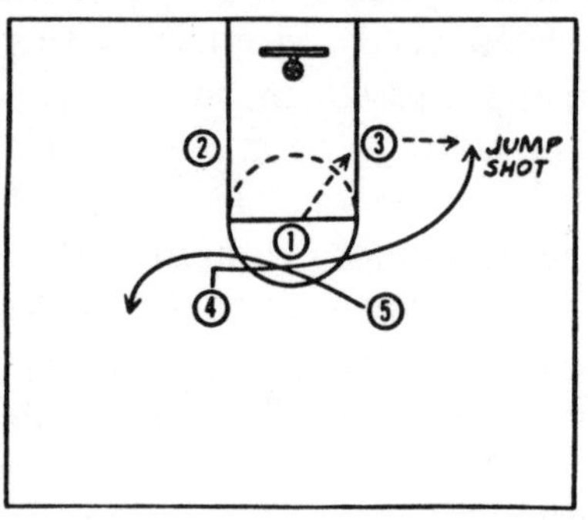

Diagram 4-28

The same type of maneuver can be executed by tipping the ball to No. 2. If this is done, then No. 4 will make the cut to his right, and No. 5 will move behind No. 4 and be open for the pass from No. 4 and the subsequent shot.

If the ball is tipped to No. 3, then No. 5 will need to move to the back court after he has made his initial cut. He must do this so that he will be in a position to provide defensive strength in case the play does not materialize as planned and the opposition gains possession of the ball, either from the tap or from mishandling of the ball, resulting in a turnover.

MISCELLANEOUS FORMATIONS

There are occasions during a game when circumstances are such, or situations will call for and justify, a specific play which is different from those categorized under the several formations previously discussed.

Certain teams may include players that adapt themselves more readily to a particular type of play. This play makes use of a specific skill which this player may possess. A particular situation which may exist during a specific time of the game may also require a play which will fit the situation better than any one which may be used from the previously mentioned formations. The plays described in this chapter can be used as the situation dictates and are classified under miscellaneous formations.

Diagram 4-29. This diagram shows a tip-off play that may be used for a quick basket and yet will not be a dangerous play should possession of the ball not be obtained. No. 3 tips the ball directly ahead to No. 4, who in turns flips the ball to No. 5, who cuts for the basket after he has cut around a screen set up by No. 1. No. 1 drops back to guard the defensive basket after he has screened for No. 5. No. 2 moves in the direction of the ball. If the tip is successful and No. 4 obtains the ball, No. 2 will move toward the offensive basket. No. 3 keeps his position until he is sure that the tip has been successful, then he moves down court as a trailer. In case No. 5 is not able to drive all the way in for the basket, he may pass off to No. 2, who has moved into position on the side of the court and is driving

Diagram 4-29

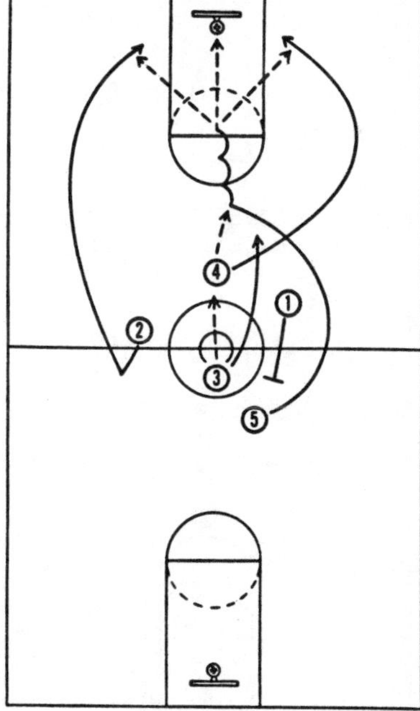

toward the basket. In order to execute the play successfully, it is necessary that No. 1 makes his move to screen off No. 5's guard just as soon as the ball has been tipped on the jump. No. 5 should be moving at the moment the ball is being tipped to No. 4. No. 4 can turn and make a one-hand baseball pass or an "over the head" two-hand pass, whichever is the most desirable and necessary for the particular situation. No. 5 will need to use his own judgment as to whether he can drive all the way to the basket after he has received the pass from No. 4 or pass off to No. 2. It is fairly improbable that the opposition will not keep a defensive player back to guard against this kind of play. However, a 1-on-1 situation almost always favors the offensive player, and this should be the sought-after situation. The play cannot be expected to result in No. 5's obtaining a clear path to the basket. A 1-on-1 or a 2-on-1 situation is quite satisfactory.

Diagram 4-30. This play utilizes the ability of the jumper to move down the floor quickly after the tip. If the jumper is fast, the play can be very successful because a great deal depends upon the reaction and speed of this particular player. He is the key to the success of the play. No. 1 tips the ball to No. 2, who, as the ball is

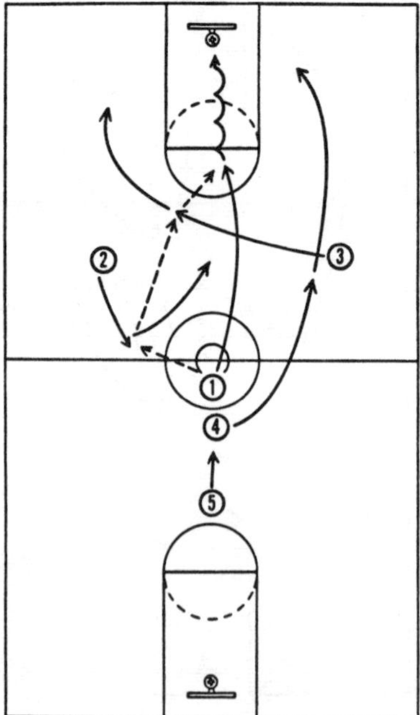

Diagram 4-30

being tossed up by the official, breaks toward the back court and to a position about 6 feet from the side of the center circle. He should receive the ball at this position. No. 3 cuts diagonally across the court to a position shown in the diagram as soon as the ball is tossed up by the official for the jump. No. 1 moves down court as soon as he makes the tap and is sure that No. 2 has possession of the ball. He attempts to time his cut so that he goes behind No. 3 as No. 3 cuts across the floor. In this way, No. 1 can use No. 3 as a moving screen and can brush his guard off if the cut is timed properly and executed correctly. No. 2 is now ready to pass to No. 3, who has positioned himself as shown in the diagram. No. 3 should also time his cut and his movement across the court so that he will arrive at the desired position at a time when No. 2 is ready to make the pass to him. If he arrives too soon he may not be free to receive the pass, and, if he arrives too late, No. 2 may not be able to make the pass. After receiving the pass, No. 3 passes to No. 1, who has cut quickly down court and is in a position for a drive to the basket. Nos. 4 and 5 remain in their original positions until the play materializes, and then they move down court. If the ball is intercepted, both move back on defense.

Diagram 4-31. This shows a delayed jump ball play which has several options. No. 1 tips the ball to No. 3, who breaks toward the back court and about 6 feet to the side of the center circle. No. 3 pivots and passes to No. 4 in the area shown in the diagram. Before he receives the pass, No. 4 breaks toward the back court and the center circle to make it appear that he will receive the tip at this point. He then stops and breaks sharply toward the center of the court midway between the center circle and the free throw circle, at which point he receives a pass from No. 3. After the tip, No. 1 moves out to the right side of the court and breaks toward the basket, with the intention of receiving a pass from No. 4. No. 2 breaks toward the left side of the floor and to the outside of No. 3. No. 2 should wait until No. 3 has received the ball from the tip, so that he does not flood the area where the tip is to be made to No. 3. No. 3 can then fake the pass to No. 2 as he breaks past him. No. 4 now has three options: he may drive in if he is free to do so, or he may pass to No. 2 or 1 as they break down the sides of the court. No. 5 remains back on defense.

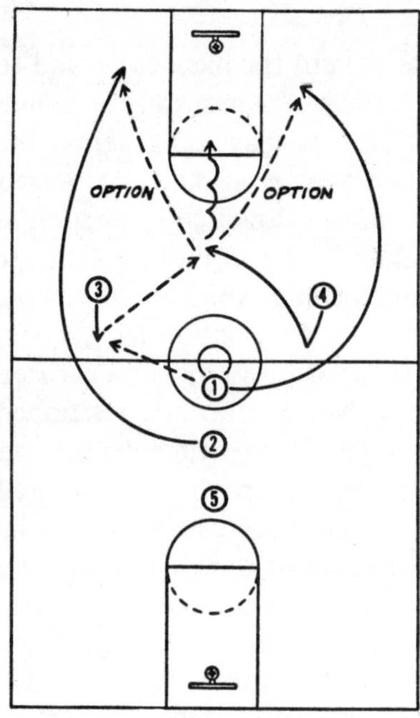

Diagram 4-31

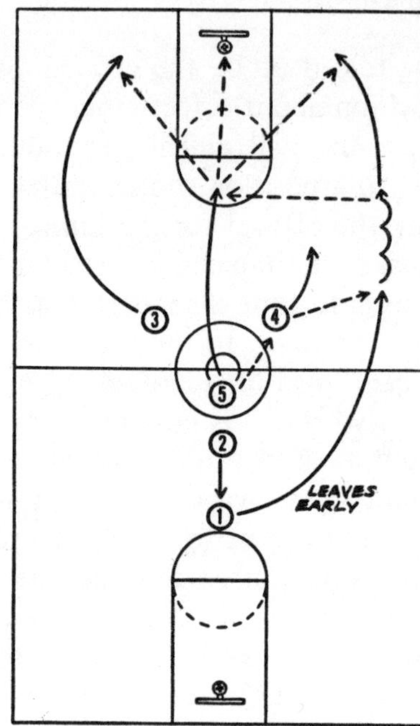

Diagram 4-32

Diagram 4-32. There are many formations that can be utilized from a jump ball situation. The following miscellaneous grouping is sometimes called the "Y" formation. It can be used successfully at either the front, back or mid-court circle. Certainly, if it is used in the back court, adjustments for closer defensive coverage would have to be made. Nos. 3, 4 and 2 take positions around the circle as shown in the diagram. No. 1 takes a deep defensive position behind No. 2. As the official is getting ready to toss the ball, No. 1 breaks down the right side of the court toward the offensive basket. No. 1 times his move so that he is in the position shown in the diagram at a time when No. 4 receives the ball from the tip made to him by No. 5. No. 4 flips the ball quickly to No. 1 as he moves past him. No. 5 quickly drives down the center of the court after the tip, so that he will be in a position to receive a pass from No. 1 at the top of the free throw circle. No. 1 can pass to No. 5 or possibly drive all the way to the basket. With the pass going to No. 5, fast break possibilities are in the making, with No. 3 breaking wide down the left side of the court and No. 4 possibly following the play. No. 2 covers the area behind the jumper for defensive balance.

Diagram 4-33. This play shows a slight variation from the previous jump ball situation described in the miscellaneous "Y" formation. No. 1, the back guard, covers the defensive area behind the jumper, and No. 2 moves down court early to be in position to receive the pass from No. 3. Because of the present rule concerning the movement of jumpers around the circle, once the official is ready to toss the ball up at center, No. 2 must move out of the 3-foot area straight back. After he has cleared the area, he then moves down court in the left outside lane. If it has been established that No. 5 will control the tip, he then tips the ball to No. 3, who in turn passes to No. 2 as he moves past him to the outside. No. 4 quickly moves to the middle of the court after seeing the tip being received by No. 3. No. 5 quickly breaks down court, moving wide to the right side. No. 2 can drive or pass to the middle of the court to No. 4. The three passing lanes are now filled. The ball is in the possession of No. 4, who may exercise the many options that are available to him as shown in the diagram.

Diagram 4-34. The safety tip to the back can quickly develop into a fast break opportunity when executed as shown in this diagram. No. 5 tips the ball back for safety to No. 2, who quickly

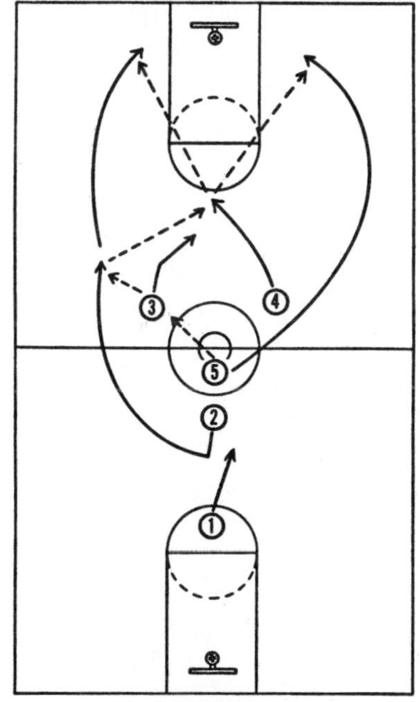

Diagram 4-33

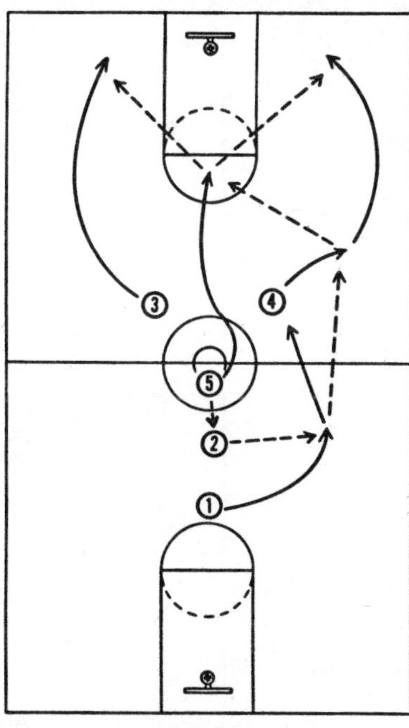

Diagram 4-34

passes it out to No. 1 on the side of the court. No. 1 leaves his defensive position early to reach the point shown in the diagram at the moment No. 2 is receiving the ball. As the tip is made backward, No. 4 moves wide and down court on the right side. No. 1 quickly passes the ball down court to him. No. 3 has also left his position just as the tip was made. He cuts down court on the left side. No. 5 quickly drives straight down the middle to be eligible for a pass from No. 4. Fast break scoring opportunities are now possible for Nos. 3, 4 and 5. No. 1 trails the play, and No. 2 takes care of the defensive situation in the back-court area.

Diagram 4-35. Here the "open area" tip formation can be used by having two of the offensive players take "tight positions" next to or adjacent to each other on the circle. There is a loophole in the rule code here which states that if an opponent should ask for a position between the players, the official must make the offensive players let him have the position. However, he must make this request before the official is ready to make the toss. Many times, the opponent will not make the request. As shown here, No. 5 tips the ball to the tight "open area" between Nos. 3 and 4. No. 4 takes the tip. No. 3 cuts down court. No. 2 left the circle early and is already down court. No. 5 drives down court after the tip, and the fast break is underway.

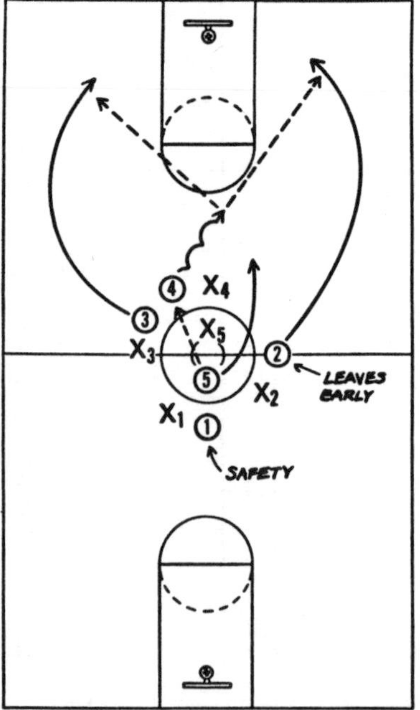

Diagram 4-35

Diagram 4-36. This play is the same as the previous diagram, except that Nos. 1 and 2 take the tight positions to receive the "open area" tip behind the jumper. Nos. 3 and 4 move down court quickly as the tip is made from No. 5 back to No. 2. No. 2 dribbles to the side and passes to No. 4, who has moved out to the right side of the court. No. 3 moves to the middle lane, and No. 5 moves to the left side of the court. No. 4 passes to No. 3, who can either dribble in for a shot or pass to either Nos. 5 or 4, who are breaking for the basket.

Diagram 4-37. This play has a triple option possibility. No. 5, in the front court free throw circle, is sure of controlling the tip. He tips it high and forward to No. 3. No. 3 goes high in the air to get the ball, and then either tips it to the side to No. 4 or to No. 2, as shown in the diagram. He may either tip the ball or semi-catch it and pass it to either of them while still in the air. His third option, and perhaps one of his best, is a pass to No. 5. Many times when the ball is tipped forward in this manner, the jumper opposing No. 5 turns to watch or follow the ball or help double team No. 3. This leaves No. 5 open, and No. 3 can tip or semi-catch and pass the ball right back to No. 5, who will in most instances have an unmolested shot (a high

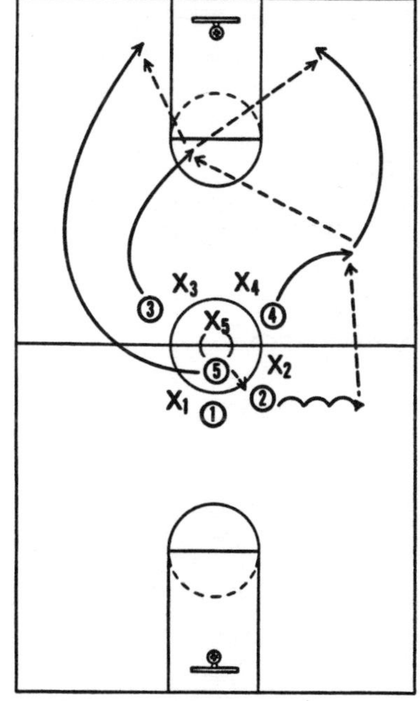

Diagram 4-36

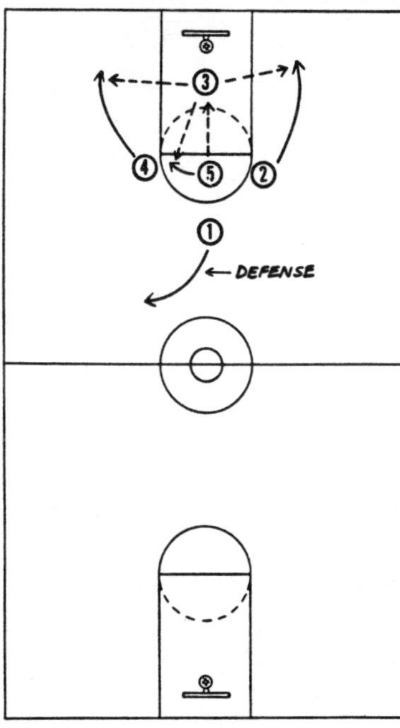

Diagram 4-37

percentage one) from the free throw line. No. 3 may, of course, pass to No. 4, 2 or 5. If none of these maneuvers materialize, No. 3 can always pass the ball back to the defensive area where No. 1 is stationed, for the purpose of assuring defensive balance and to protect against loss of the ball.

Diagram 4-38. If the team wishes to gain ball possession in the front court free throw lane, they can use the play shown here in Diagram 4-38. For safety reasons, No. 5 tips the ball to No. 4 on the back and left side of the circle. No. 4 moves out to get the ball and takes it on a sweeping dribble to the right side of the court. No. 3, after faking to get the tip, moves toward the right corner, where No. 4 passes him the ball. No. 2 cuts in behind the jumper to the left side of the basket. No. 5 breaks quickly down the lane and pulls up just to the right of the basket where he may receive a pass from No. 3, which in turn might result in a quick two points. There is also an opportunity to execute a pivot-post play by having No. 3 follow his pass to No. 5, with No. 4 breaking in behind the pivot-post play, as shown in the diagram. This maneuver turns a safety tip into a quick scoring thrust. No. 1 must remain in a defensive position at all times for defensive purposes.

Diagram 4-38

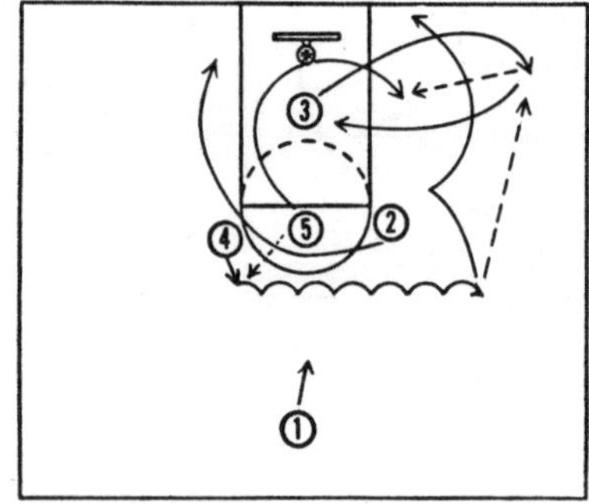

FIVE

DELAYED OFFENSIVE PLAYS

The word "stall" has often been used in basketball to describe an offense that is used by a team that holds the ball or stresses ball possession. Through this medium, it is the desire of the team using such tactics to protect a lead. The authors of this book have never believed in using the word "stall" in coaching this phase of the game. Rather, they have preferred to use the term "delayed offense." It should never be the sole purpose or intent of any basketball offense to "stall" or ever actually quit trying to score.

Strategic Time for Use of Delayed Offense

There can be strategic times or periods during a game when the style, tempo and execution of the offense can and should, perhaps, be changed or altered. The situations where this may be true will vary, but usually they occur during the late phases of the game. They will usually occur late in the fourth quarter of a high school game, or late in the second half of a college game. One team will obtain a lead and then wish to "assure themselves the victory" by using ball control tactics. They believe they can make victory "more certain" by controlling the ball, and thereby dictating what the "defense" must do by forcing them to change their defensive tactics. The answer is "ball control" and making sure that ball possession is exchanged only for points. Thus they make it very difficult to figure actual game statistics in a present day game. Most statistics will substantiate the belief that possession of the ball is worth one point. However, if a team scores a basket for two points and then surrenders possession of the ball, they actually have statistically only gained one point. In some situations, it is possible that possession of the ball is worth more than one point–and it is on this basis, and for this reason, that a team uses the "delayed offense." There can be specific times during a basketball game when possession of the ball is so important that only by obtaining a sure two points can a team afford to surrender possession of the ball to the opposition.

The offensive team should never place itself in a situation whereby the purpose of a maneuver is anything other than an attempt to score. The coach should never allow his players to feel that the purpose of the "delayed offense" is anything other than a means of obtaining two points. The "delayed offense" can, however, be used when needed to change the tempo of the game in such a manner as to bring about a different response and the use of different tactics by the defense. This response and change of tactics by the defense, which is being forced upon them, will, it is hoped, make it easier for the offense to score. By controlling the ball in this type of situation, the defense often becomes careless, and, in its desperation to get the ball, oftentimes allows an offensive player to "get loose" for the easy lay-up.

Oftentimes, when the score is close late in the contest, these points are valuable and can many times put the game out of reach of the opposition.

A change in the basketball rules' code for the season of 1971-72 has brought into focus the question that perhaps the expanded held ball coverage in Rule 4, Section 14 might make it more difficult to run a delayed offense. The rule change has added a five-second count on a dribbler who is closely guarded in the fore-court. As before, the rule combines the count on a player in possession of the ball for holding and/or dribbling the ball in the mid-court area, if he is closely guarded. A continuous five-second count allows a "held ball." However, the player gets a new count when he moves the "ball from mid-court to fore-court," and in the fore-court he is also given a separate count for the dribble and for holding the ball. Also the count is off any time the defense loosens the play to less than a "closely guarded" position. Formerly the rule allowed a count in the "fore-court" for holding the ball while closely guarded only, but there was no such count for a closely guarded dribbler, unless he was in a corner, or surrounded by teammates. With this change, there is also a change in Rule 10-A-2(c) and in "Comments on the Rules," which state that if the score is tied, or if behind in the score, the defense must be "continuous and aggressive" in their attempting to secure the ball, This is a change from the former wording, which stated that the defense must "be reasonably active in an attempt to secure the ball."

The above rule change, in effect, places more responsibility on the defense for forcing action and play when the score is tied, or when behind in the score. The change will not effect or hinder a "delayed offense," but will require response in defensive action, and will help eliminate a one-man dribble show. In effect, it will in reality require more organization and planning by the offense, and could possibly even make a "delayed offense" a more effective and efficient weapon. The defense must act–the offense must act—is what the rule change says in effect.

It is the intent of this chapter to present a variety of "delayed offenses" that can be used in game situations. Some could be used for very special situations. Others would fittingly be more useful for ball control situations using certain types of personnel. Each will be explained in its entirety and in detail. All of the delayed offenses are not presented here, but rather, the "delayed type offenses" that are good and that can be used in most situations are shown. These will be illustrated and described.

It is the opinion of many coaches that no offense should ever be employed without intent to score. The offensive attitude should always be that of operating with intent to score. The momentum may be changed, the tempo cut down, but only for the purpose of dictating a change in the defense that will enable the offense to score more readily in the given situation. When the moment arrives, it is the "trump card"–and the offense should play it. If the defense is not strong enough to counter the change dictated, then they should have to pay the price.

FUNDAMENTAL GUIDELINES FOR THE DELAYED OFFENSE

Any time a team goes into this offense, there has to be certain fundamentals and guidelines which govern the team and its conduct in this maneuver. When the team uses this play, it must be a "never miss" play. The team must be schooled and drilled to perfection in the execution of this play. This means that the team must practice a part of every day on this offense. Part of every practice should be used to perfect the timing and execution of the offense. There will have to be some different fundamental executions and practices so as to be able to apply the offense against both the man-to-man, zone presses and two-timing defenses that will be used against the "delayed offense." The following guidelines usually can be applicable in using the offense:

1. Keep the players well-spread so as to get a full coverage from the defense, and to spread them thin.
2. Against man-to-man defenses, work clearing plays; with 1-on-1, the offensive player should be able to beat his opponent, or at least retain possession of the ball.
3. Keep the ball moving as much as possible–it puts the pressure on the defense. Make passes sharp and crisp.
4. Save the dribble until needed. Dribbling needlessly will lead to trouble. Saving the dribble and using it at the proper time to beat the defensive player will give the delayed offense a much needed balance.
5. Never let the opponents two-time the offense. Stay away from any situation where two-timing the ball handler can be done easily and quickly by the defense.
6. When the defense makes a declaration, player movement and action by the offense should be sharp and hard.
7. The situation usually dictates that only a high percentage shot should be taken. At times, the shot may be limited to a sure conversion of two points. The players *must* be aware of what the percentage shot is that is to be taken in this situation.
8. Keep the middle open, and be alert for drives into this area at all times.
9. It is an absolute must that the receiver move sharply to meet all passes.

10. When the ball is received, the player should square off and face the defensive man.

11. Stay away from danger areas–such as a position adjacent to a boundary line or the corners. Avoid the 3-second lane area.

12. Avoid long passes and cross court passes. These are passes the defense tries to work the offense into making.

DELAYED OFFENSIVE PLAYS: THE 1-ON-1 SERIES

The various delayed offenses are similar to other types of offenses inasmuch as their effectiveness must be judged by their success. Therefore, they must be styled and patterned to meet and combat different situations. The particular situation is determined to a large extent by the defenses the opponents use, how they attempt to break up a delay, and, of course, by the talents of the offensive players using the delayed offense.

The first delayed offense which will be explained in this chapter is a simple spread pattern. This offensive pattern is based on the assumption that the team using it has five players who are capable of handling and passing the ball well enough to warrant its use. It is an offense which should be used when the team is ahead and the time is appropriate for its members to want a change in the defensive play of the opponents. If this is the case, then its purpose would be to force the opposition into a tight man-to-man defense. This, in turn, would result in a 1-on-1 situation. As a result of this defensive change by the opponents, it is hoped that one of the offensive players with the ball will isolate a weaker defensive opponent and beat him for a two-point scoring play. The intent and purpose of the offense is not to hold the ball and let the time on the clock run out. Rather, it is the intent of the offense to force the players out of a tight, compact defensive situation into a spread formation, and, by so doing, be able to slip past them for scoring opportunities. In most situations where this offense is to be used, it is assumed that the offensive team is leading in the score at the time, and that the time factor is such that they choose to dictate the type of defense the opposing team is to use. This is done by drawing the defense out into a spread formation and forcing them to attack the ball or lose the game.

The present basketball rules favor the offensive team in this type of situation. These rules divide the front court into two areas–the area farthest from the basket is called the "mid-court," and the area of the court near and including the basket is called the "fore-court."

If the offensive team is ahead or the score is tied, and they hold the ball in the "mid-court" area, the defensive team must bring at least two defensive players to the mid-court if the offensive team has two or more players in the area. Furthermore, at least one of the defensive players must attempt to gain control of the ball. The defensive team must initiate this action within 10 seconds or receive a warning from the officials. After being warned, the action must be initiated within 5 seconds or it is a technical foul. Under these rules, the defense must come out and attempt to meet the spread put on by the offense. They must bring about action in an effort to secure the ball and break up further scoring attempts by the offense. The present rules result in a tremendous advantage to the team using the delayed offense. They also provide a great deal of variety to both offensive and defensive maneuvering, that can and does occur in this type of situation.

Diagram 5-1. In order to use the "1-on-1" delayed offense, which will force the opponents into a "1-on-1" situation, the offensive players should position themselves as shown in this diagram. The players spread out and keep the middle open as much as possible. The offensive player moves into the basket area only if he has eluded his guard and is free. No. 1 brings the ball to the position shown in the diagram. At this point the players invite the defense to attack, hoping to obtain an isolated 1-on-1 player situation that will result in a score. The offensive players should stay spread out and as far apart as possible at all times. No. 1 has possession of the ball and is stationed in the center of the mid-court area, near the division line. He must not, however, get too close to the division line, and should have enough room in which to maneuver without flirting with the possibility of stepping on the line. Nos. 2 and 3 are stationed wide, as shown in the diagram, but deeper toward the basket and in an area near the mid-court area markers. They should be one or two strides from the sidelines, in order to allow themselves some freedom of movement without being in danger of being pushed too far to the sidelines, making it difficult to maneuver. Nos. 4 and 5 are stationed in the deep corners and about two strides out from the end line and sideline. These positions will allow them freedom of movement without being in danger of stepping on a boundary line.

Diagram 5-2. This diagram shows a continuation of the pattern and the continuity of play which will be instrumental in forcing the defense into a 1-on-1 situation. The following diagrams will show how the pattern develops. It will also show the player movements which are essential to its success. It should be remembered that the key to the offense is movement. No. 1 has the ball and is challenged by the defense. He passes the ball to No. 3, who shakes loose from his defensive man and breaks to receive the pass. After passing to No. 3, No. 1 fakes to his left and then moves on the ball side of his defensive man quickly down the middle of the court toward the basket. If he can free himself from his defenders and is open, then No. 3 should pass him the ball. If No. 1 is not free to receive the pass, he then tails out to the right-hand corner of the court toward the position formerly occupied by No. 5. No. 3, who has the ball,

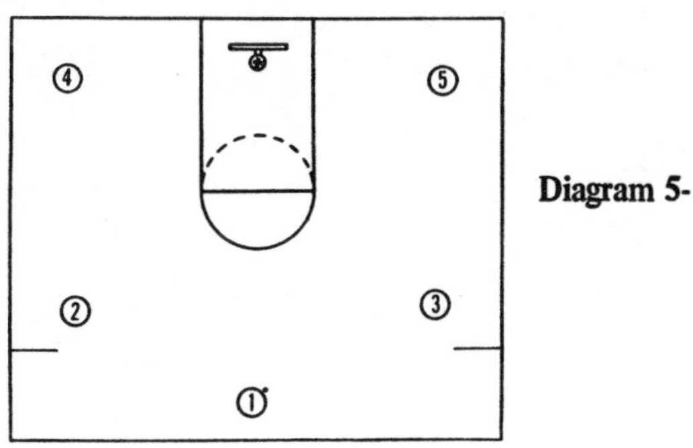

Diagram 5-1

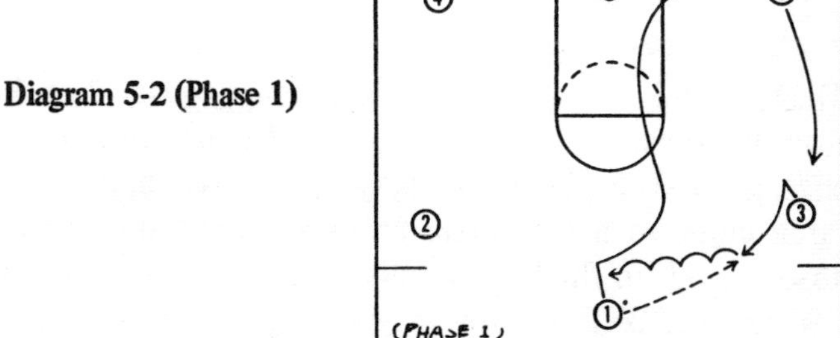

Diagram 5-2 (Phase 1)

now dribbles toward the center of the floor and positions himself in the area formerly occupied by No. 1. No. 5 moves up to the position just vacated by No. 3.

Diagram 5-3. After the maneuvers shown in the previous diagram have been completed, the players are positioned as shown in Diagram 5-3. If No. 3 should pass to No. 2, then No. 3 would drive down the center of the court as No. 1 did in the previous diagram. Nos. 2, 4 and 3 would then make the same change of positions as Nos. 1, 3 and 5 did previously. This movement could be continued and could result in good scoring opportunities. This circulation pattern should be continued, with the ultimate result being a scoring situation which can develop by a player getting loose for a shot underneath the basket.

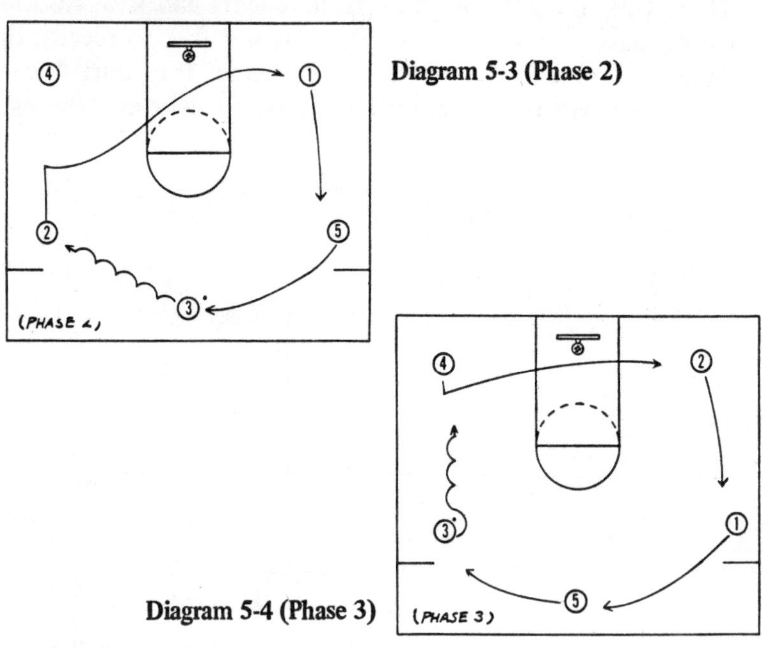

Diagram 5-3 (Phase 2)

Diagram 5-4 (Phase 3)

In Diagram 5-3, No. 3, instead of passing to No. 2 or 5, takes a driving dribble toward No. 2. One of the fundamental concepts of this offense is for the players to stay spread out and to not break into an area close to a teammate so as to draw another defensive player close enough to the ball handler to two-time him or double up on him. When No. 3 drives toward No. 2, No. 2 vacates the area, breaking at first toward the base line, and then laterally across the court toward the basket and the opposite corner now occupied by No. 1. The purpose of No. 2's cut is to get open for a pass and possible score. If he is open, No. 3 should pass to him. However, if no scoring opportunity develops, the players rotate positions as shown in the diagram. No. 3 is now in the position formerly occupied by No. 2, and No. 2 moves to the corner previously occupied by No. 1. No. 1 moves out to the position formerly occupied by No. 5, and No. 5 moves over to the center of the floor into the position previously occupied by No. 3 at the beginning of the play. The players maintain the spread formation by just filling the positions as they are vacated and rotating as shown in the diagram. Other variations and possibilities will develop as the pattern unfolds and the continuity of the play continues.

Diagram 5-4. After the "Phase 2" movement shown in Diagram 5-3 is completed, the players are now stationed in positions shown in Diagram 5-4. No. 3 has the ball as shown in the diagram. While this is not a dribbling offense, nevertheless the dribble can be used to isolate a player in a "1-on-1" situation. As a result, the offensive player can many times beat his defensive opponent and score. If No. 3 should continue to dribble toward No. 4, then No. 4 vacates his position and moves toward the basket. If No. 4 is open, No. 3 should pass to him. If No. 4 is not open, he fills the corner position now occupied by No. 2. The players rotate or fill positions as shown in the diagram, with No. 2 moving out to No. 1's position, No. 1 moving to No. 5's position and No. 5 filling in the position formerly occupied by No. 3. No. 3 has now dribbled toward the left corner of the court. If he can drive the middle and beat his man, he should do so. He should, however, be careful not to let himself get trapped in the corner by his defensive man.

Diagram 5-5. After the player movement in Diagram 5-4, Phase 3 is completed, the players are stationed in the positions shown in Diagram 5-5. Several possibilities might be open to No. 3 as a result of the maneuvers made by the weak-side players, Nos. 2, 4 or 1. These players are all in excellent positions for quick breaks to the basket and a pass from No. 3. They should be constantly alert and ready at all times to execute these maneuvers, which will be brought forth as a result of the opponents' efforts to obtain the ball. This type of situation will provide the opportunity for the offense to beat the defense and score. If these options do not materialize, then No. 3 passes the ball to No. 5. These two players may now begin a shuttle series. This is done by having No. 3 move along the base line toward the basket. He then reverses back to receive the ball on a return pass from No. 5, as shown in the diagram. After No. 5 makes the pass, he breaks to the free throw lane area and down the lane toward the basket. If he is open, No. 3 passes the ball to him. If he is not open, No. 3 dribbles out to the position vacated by No. 5. No. 5 hooks back to the position vacated by No. 3. This shuttle maneuver can be repeated, or the regular pattern can be continued and other options used. In the shuttle, Nos. 3 and 5 just exchange positions as shown in the diagram. The decision to use this maneuver is made by these two players, and only if the situation dictates its use.

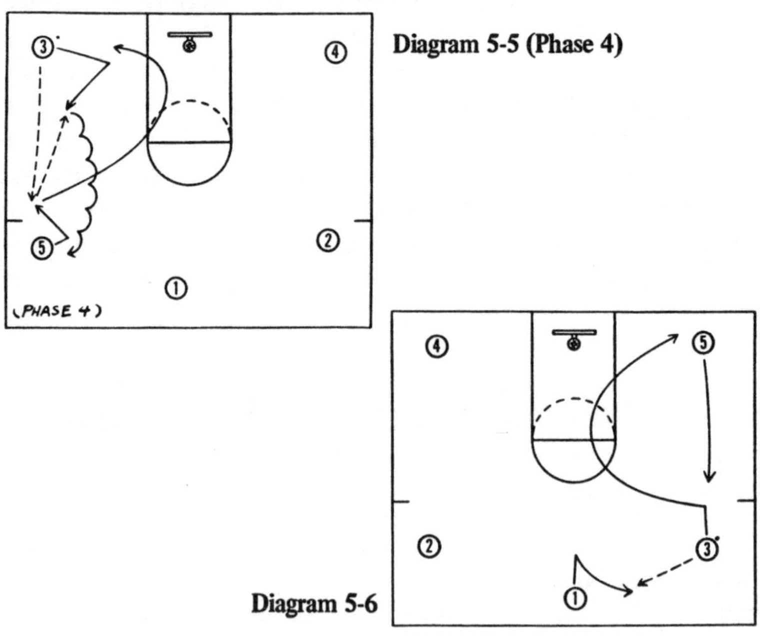

Diagram 5-5 (Phase 4)

Diagram 5-6

Diagram 5-6. If the ball is in the possession of a player in the wing position, such as No. 3, as shown in Diagram 5-6, and the pass is made to No. 1 from this position, then No. 3 after making the pass, should cut to the free throw line and down the free throw lane to the basket. If he is free to receive the pass, No. 1 should pass the ball to him for a clear drive to the basket. If No. 3 is not open, No. 3 and No. 5 exchange positions, as shown in the diagram, with No. 3 hooking into the right corner and No. 5 moving out to the position vacated by No. 3. A fundamental principle of this offense is that when a player passes to another position, he drives down the middle and toward the basket. The position left vacant by the drive will be filled as shown in the diagrams. Another principle is that should a player with the ball dribble toward another position, the player in that position vacates it with a drive to the middle and toward the basket. This makes for a good 1-on-1 isolation procedure and can bring scoring opportunities with lots of movement of both the players and the ball.

Diagram 5-7. In this situation, No. 3 passes from the wing position to No. 1 and makes his cut. Not being open, No. 3 and No. 5 start their exchange movement to fill the positions vacated by No. 3. No. 1 has been challenged by his defensive man and starts a dribble movement toward the position vacated by No. 3. When No. 5, who is moving up the side of the court, sees that No. 1 is dribbling toward the position vacated by No. 3, he immediately makes a reverse cut across the court and toward the basket, as shown in the diagram. If No. 5 is open, No. 1 can pass him the ball. No. 2 now fills the position vacated by No. 1. If No. 5 does not receive the pass, he continues his drive out of the free throw lane area toward the left corner of the court. No. 4 now moves out to the position formerly occupied by No. 2, and No. 5 takes the position No. 4 vacated. If the players will pass, cut and fill the positions vacated by their teammates, a good continuity of movement consisting of passing, cutting and dribbling can be maintained. These maneuvers will bring out the defense and provide scoring possibilities and opportunities.

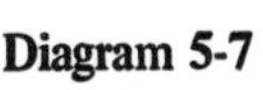
Diagram 5-7

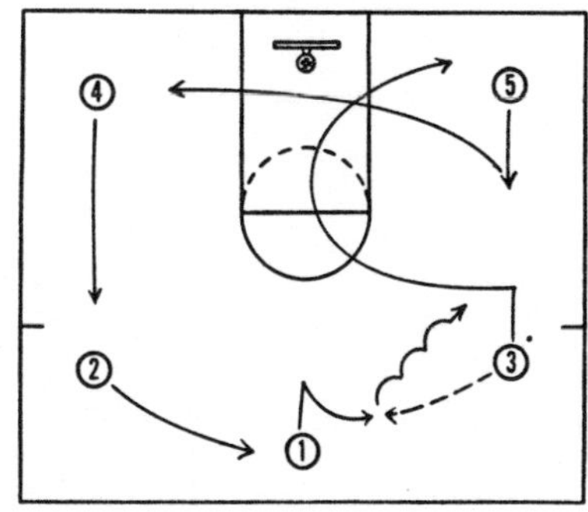

Diagram 5-8. The players in the No. 4 and 5 positions should always be alert to "flashing" the pivot-post position. In other words, they should break quickly into this high post position in anticipation of receiving a pass from No. 1. No. 1 starts the play in Diagram 5-8 by dribbling towards No. 3, who in turn cuts toward the free throw circle area, as shown in the diagram. This movement starts the interchange of positions between Nos. 3 and 5. No. 4 is positioned in the weak-side low position. Just as No. 3 starts his hooking movement into the opposite corner after driving the lane, No. 4 fakes a move toward the basket and then flashes into a high post position in the outer half of the free throw circle. No. 1 passes No. 4 the ball if he is in a position to receive it. Several option scoring plays can result from this maneuver, but the one to *always* look for is the "sucker play" or "back door play," which has No. 2 breaking down to the back side and eluding his defensive man for a clear drive to the basket and a pass from No. 4 for the easy lay-up. If this option does not materialize, other options can come as a result of No. 5 reversing his direction for a cut to the basket, or No. 1 could drive straight in for openings. The players can always fill the positions vacated by cuts, and, if necessary, No. 4 can dribble the ball out to the No. 1 position and start over from there. "Flashing the pivot" at every opportunity should be a fundamental principle of the offense also.

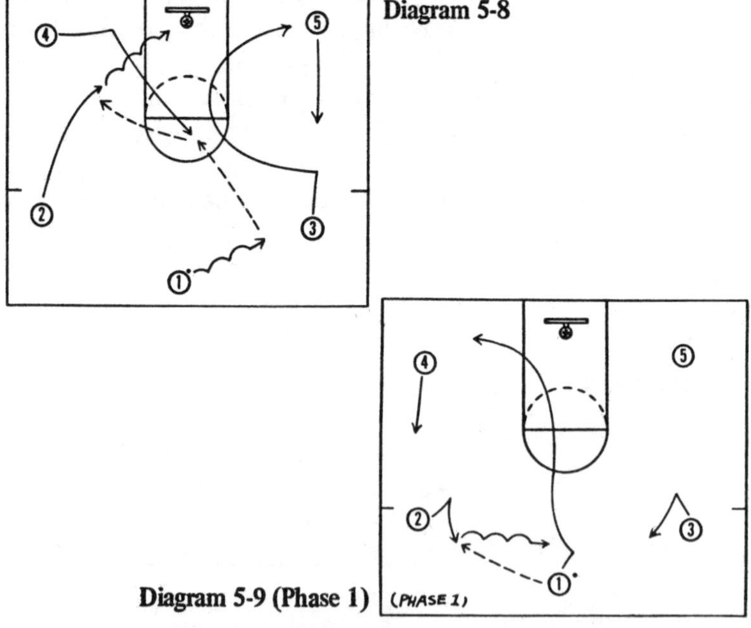

Diagram 5-8

Diagram 5-9 (Phase 1)

THE FIGURE OF EIGHT

The old "figure of eight" play has been and still can be used effectively as a delayed offense. It is very similar to the "1-on-1" series, with some variations and perhaps more emphasis on staying with a set pattern of movement.

Diagram 5-9. The players line up to start the offense exactly as they do in the "1-on-1" series. To start the movement, No. 1 passes to No. 2 and cuts down the middle of the free throw lane, then over to the left corner of the court. No. 2 starts a dribble toward No. 1's position, and No. 4 moves up to fill the position vacated by No. 2.

Diagram 5-10. The players have now arrived at the positions shown in Diagram 5-10. No. 2 passes to No. 3 and cuts down the middle of the free throw lane, then out to the right corner of the court or to the same side of the court to which the pass was made. No. 3 makes an adjustment dribble to get into position for his next pass, while No. 5 moves to the position vacated by No. 3 and No. 2 moves into the position formerly occupied by No. 5.

Diagram 5-11. No. 3 now passes to No. 4 and drives to the left corner of the court to the position vacated by No. 1. No. 1 moves into the No. 4 position as No. 4 dribbles the ball toward the middle

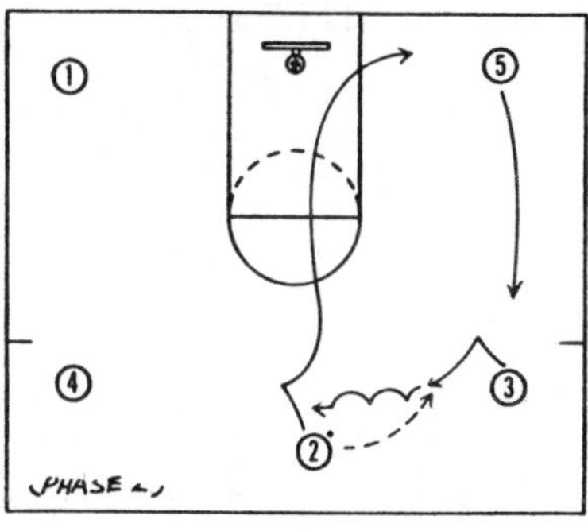

Diagram 5-10 (Phase 2)

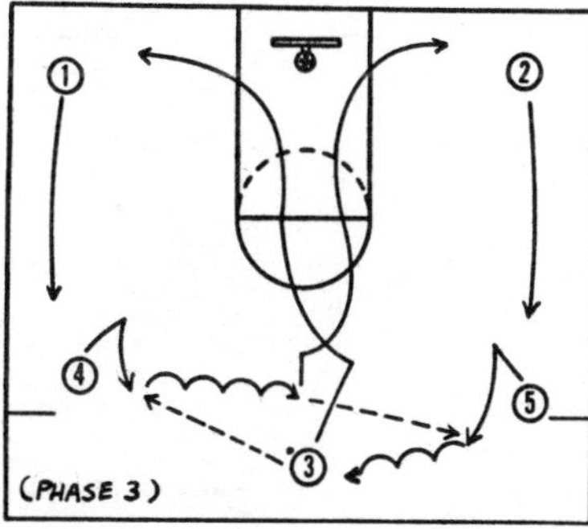

Diagram 5-11 (Phase 3)

of the court, and then on toward No. 5 as the figure of eight circulation movement continues. After six passes or interchanges of positions, the players will arrive back in their beginning positions, except that they will be stationed on opposite sides of the floor. No. 1, however, will be in the center outside position again. Actually the "figure of eight" is really very similar to the "1-on-1" series. The "1-on-1" series does have some cuts or maneuvers resembling the figure of eight moves, but it also has other options and moves that are individualistic and some that depart from the "figure of eight" circulation pattern. It must be remembered that the objective of the "figure of eight" is to score and not just to circulate in the "figure of eight" pattern. The players always make their moves with the intention of scoring and not just to maintain ball control. The use of the dribble should be kept at a minimum, and, as shown in Diagram 5-11, if No. 4 can make the pass to No. 5 without using the adjustment dribble, he should do so. The determining factor in the use of the dribble is the distance the ball must travel. If No. 4 can pass the ball without fear of interception, he should do so immediately, and then make a cut down the middle and to the right corner of the court. This would speed up the movement. However, if the adjustment needs to be made, the dribble should be used wherever needed.

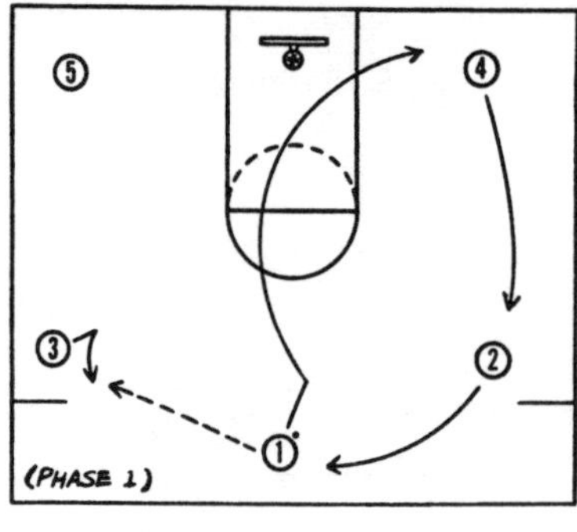

Diagram 5-12 (Phase 1)

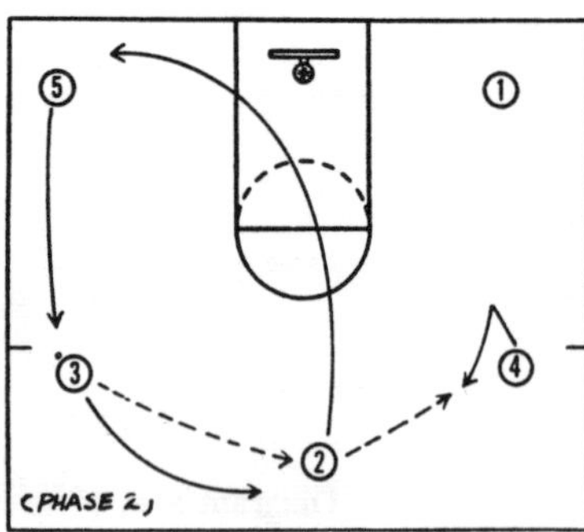

Diagram 5-13 (Phase 2)

Diagram 5-12. The "figure of eight" can also be executed using a reverse circulation pattern. Diagram 5-12 shows No. 1 passing to No. 3 in the wing position and then cutting down the middle of the court toward the basket. If he does not receive a return pass from No. 3, he moves to the opposite or right corner of the court. The positions are now filled by the rotation of Nos. 2 and 4. No. 2 fills the center position left vacant by No. 1, and No. 4 moves up to the wing position vacated by No. 2. No. 1 moves into the opposite or right corner position which was vacated by No. 4. This is a "reverse move" by No. 1 to the opposite corner of the court in relation to the direction in which the pass was made. It differs from the moves shown in Diagrams, 5-9, 5-10 and 5-11, in that the center player in those diagrams moved to the corner of the court in the direction of his pass after making the center drive. His position was then filled by the wing player, who used the dribble to move into the area.

Diagram 5-13. This diagram shows a continuation of the reverse circulation pattern using the "figure of eight" offense. No. 3, the wing player, has the ball but is unable to make the pass to a player in a scoring position, so he passes the ball back to the middle position, which is occupied by No. 2. No. 2 passes to No. 4, the right wing player, and then moves down the center of the court through the free throw lane and on to the opposite corner of the court. If he is free and a pass is made to him, his actions are governed accordingly. No. 3 fills the center position after making the pass to No. 2, and No. 5 moves out to the wing position formerly occupied by No. 3.

Diagram 5-14. In continuing the circulation pattern and to show the options possible, No. 4 in Phase 3 passes the ball back to the center position to No. 3. No. 3 passes to No. 5, who is stationed in the left wing position, and then drives to the middle, continuing through the free throw lane and into the right-hand or opposite corner of the court. The change of positions is made again, but, as No. 4 starts his movement toward the center position, he reverses his direction and cuts down the middle of the court toward the basket. No. 5 has the option of passing the ball to him as he cuts to the basket, or quickly relaying the ball on to No. 2, who is stationed in the left wide post position, as shown in the diagram. No. 2 may now

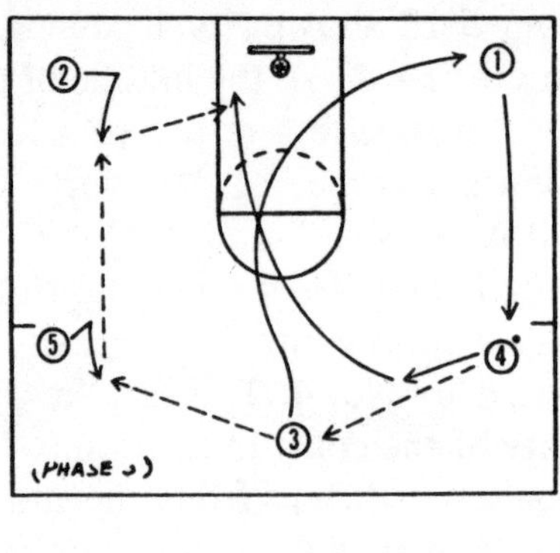

Diagram 5-14 (Phase 3)

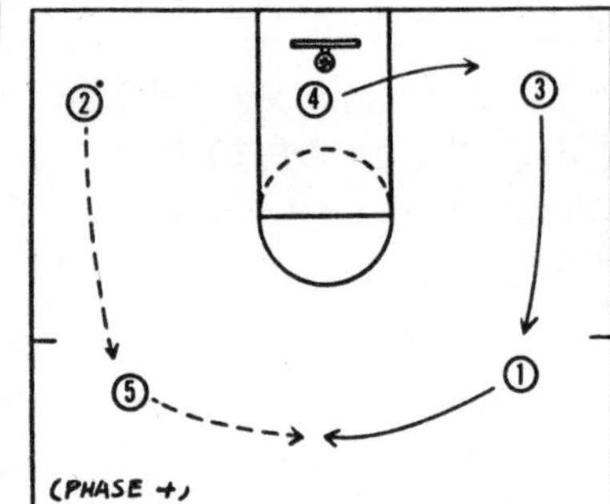

Diagram 5-15 (Phase 4)

pass the ball to No. 4, who is moving quickly down the middle of the court toward the basket. Phase 4 will show the follow-up rotation pattern and continuity sequence.

Diagram 5-15. If No. 5 or 2 finds that No. 4 is not free to receive the pass as he cuts down the middle of the court, as shown in the previous diagram, the pattern of continuity is continued as shown in Diagram 5-15. No. 4, after he has reached the basket area and has not received the pass, continues to the opposite corner of the court or the wide post position. No. 3 moves out to the right wing position which No. 1 is about to vacate. No. 1 will move over to the center position. No. 2 quickly passes the ball out to No. 5, and No. 5 passes to No. 1 in the center position. The "figure of eight" continuity pattern may now be continued in the "near corner" or the "far corner."

There are many other options which will result from the use of this pattern. Ball possession may be easily maintained, but, at the same time, scoring opportunities are always present. If the defense lapses, it can result in an easy lay-up for the offensive team.

Diagram 5-16. If the players who are stationed in the wing positions have difficulty getting open for passes from the player who is stationed in the center position, it is possible to free themselves by creating a movement of the players or an exchange of the players who are stationed in the wide post positions, as shown in Diagram 5-16. If the player in the center position dribbles toward one of the wing positions, the player stationed in this position has the opportunity to vacate, rotate or fill positions, as shown in Diagrams 5-3 and 5-4 of the "1-on-1" series. Also an interchange of positions, as shown in Diagram 5-16, will nearly always free one of the players. Nos. 2 and 3 move down toward the corner wide post positions. Nos. 2 and 3 maneuver in such a manner so as to provide a moving screen for Nos. 4 and 5 as they move up the sidelines in an effort to free themselves for a pass from No. 1. If No. 1 can pass to either of them, he does so, and the regular pattern is continued, with passing and scoring opportunities being a constant possibility.

Diagram 5-17. Any "delayed offense" which leaves the free throw lane area leading to the basket open, makes it possible for the middle player, as shown in the diagram, to elude his guard and drive straight to the basket for a lay-up. This possibility should never be overlooked, and it brings out one theory in present day basketball that many coaches believe in; that is—a good offensive player can

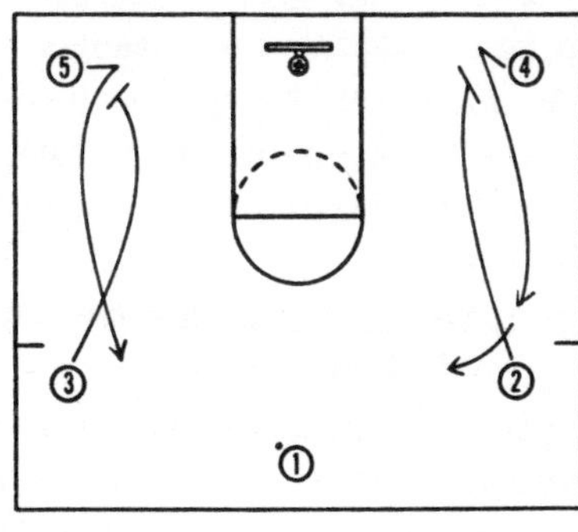

Diagram 5-16

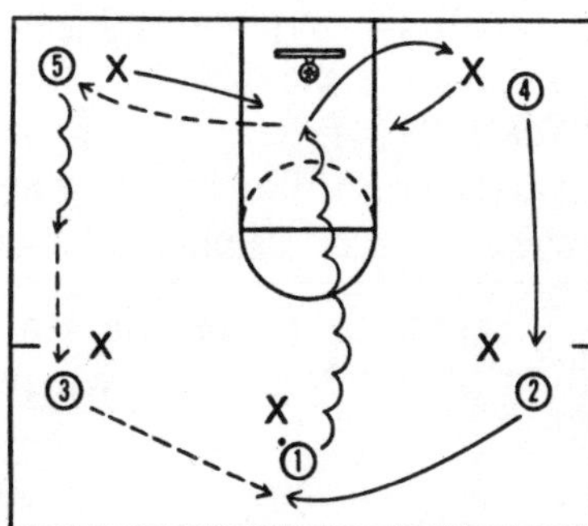

Diagram 5-17

beat a good defensive player. If a player decides to drive on his opponent, he, as a result, breaks the continuity of the pattern, and, of course, there is always the possibility of a defensive shift by the opposition. Diagram 5-17 shows the defensive man guarding No. 5 shifting to stop No. 1 on his drive to the basket. If this is done, No. 1 may execute a bounce pass to No. 5, who is stationed in the left corner of the court. After making the pass, No. 1 fades out to the opposite side of the court, and the usual rotation continues, with No. 4 moving to No. 2's wing position and No. 2 filling in No. 1's center position. No. 5 may attempt a drive to the basket, but, if this does not develop, he relays the ball out to No. 3 by using a dribble or a pass. No. 3, in turn, passes the ball to No. 2, who moves into the center position as shown in the diagram.

THE PIVOT-POST DELAY

Some of the early "delayed offenses" featured the pivot-post attack, whereby a player was positioned in a high post or in the outer half of the free throw lane just above the free throw circle. The ball was passed to this player, who functioned as a pivot, with the other players cutting off this player. These maneuvers entailed a great number of moving screens. Two-timing and jamming-of-the-middle maneuvers by the defense soon ended this practice, and, as a result, this brought about the more open and spread type of delay with more emphasis being placed on keeping the middle open, as has been previously explained in this chapter. However, many coaches still feature and favor a pivot-post type of "delayed offense," but the pivot-post player roams the free throw lane area from a position of well above the free-throw circle to the basket. The coaches who use this type of offense usually are favored with a fine pivot-post player with a lot of maneuverability. They also feel that the center area of the court must be penetrated, and this is the best way to do it. The idea of cutting players past the pivot-post player, who has the ball for purposes of freeing one of the cutters by screens, has been discarded. The following diagrams illustrate the chief features of a "delayed offense" using a pivot-post player.

Diagram 5-18. In the pivot-post delay offense, the players position themselves as shown in Diagram 5-18. Nos. 1 and 2, the

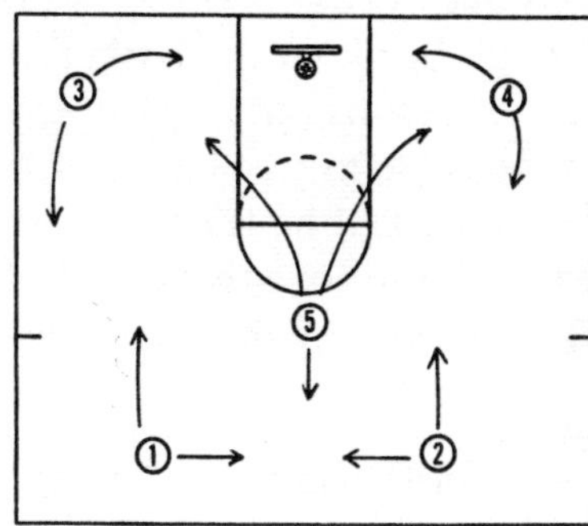

Diagram 5-18

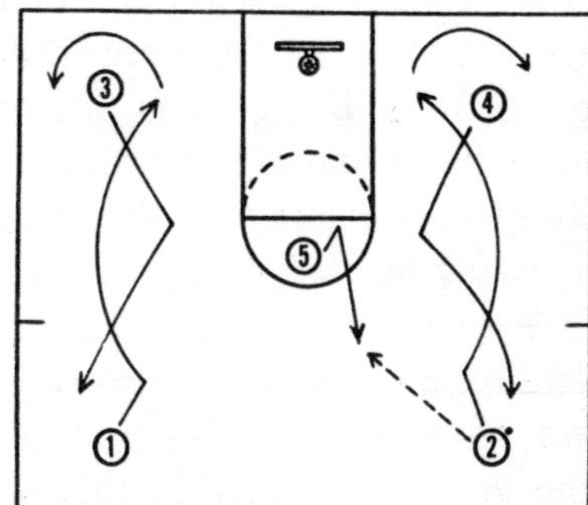

Diagram 5-19

guards, are stationed in the mid-court area, and they leave themselves plenty of room to maneuver and still not have their movements jeopardized by the presence of the center division line. No. 5, the pivot-post player, roams the free throw lane area, which can include an area two to three strides above the free throw circle. He can flash this area for possible passes, and he should also be ready to dribble the ball out to the mid-court area to relieve the offense of any defensive pressure which they may encounter. He should also be ready to fill the position of any of the other players when it is necessary to do so. The forwards, Nos. 3 and 4, are stationed wide, as shown in the diagram. They should keep well-spread out at all times, and never under any circumstances move into a teammate's area unless it is to retrieve the ball. The players should force the defense to play 1-on-1 as much as possible. They should not do any crossing, splitting or breaking over the top of the man with the ball.

Diagram 5-19. If either of the guards, No. 1 or 2, should pass the ball into the pivot-post position, then these two players exchange positions with Nos. 3 and 4, as shown in the diagram. This interchange of positions by the guards and forwards often results in one of them freeing himself for a quick break to the basket and a pass from No. 5. This maneuver often results in a good scoring opportunity. If one of these players is not able to free himself for the pass, then No. 5 may attempt to free himself. If he is not successful, he may pass the ball back out to the guard positions to No. 3 or 4, or dribble the ball out of danger and pass to one of the guards before returning to the pivot-post position.

Diagram 5-20. After the maneuvers in Diagram 5-19 have been completed, the players are stationed in the positions shown in Diagram 5-20. If No. 5 is not able to retain possession of the ball because he is closely guarded for over 5 seconds, he may either dribble the ball out to the mid-court area or pass it to No. 4. No. 4 then passes the ball to No. 2. Any time the ball is passed to one of the players who is stationed in the sideline position, No. 4 or 3, depending on which one has the ball, cuts hard and fast toward the basket, as shown in the diagram. No. 1 or 2 dribbles the ball back out to the guard positions. In this diagram, No. 2 dribbles the ball out. This maneuver brings about a change of position with No. 4. No. 2 should be ready at all times to take advantage of any opportunity to execute a pass to either No. 4 or 5 in the hope that this might result in a scoring opportunity. After No. 2 has dribbled the ball back out to the guard position as shown in the diagram, he may turn and pass the ball back to No. 4. After making this pass to No. 4 he should drive hard again for the basket, repeating the shuttle maneuver. If this should happen, Nos. 1 and 3 should exchange positions again.

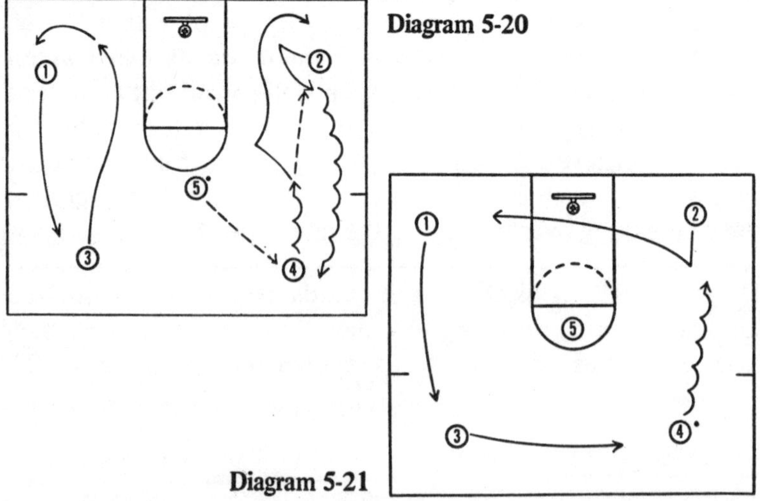

Diagram 5-20

Diagram 5-21

Diagram 5-21. Any time one of the players with the ball dribbles toward a player in another position and this player cannot free himself to receive a pass, he vacates his position, and the players then rotate and fill positions as shown in Diagram 5-21. This maintains good floor balance and keeps the players spread out. It also helps to maintain the 1-on-1 position and prevents two players from getting close to the ball. This is one of the most important aspects in executing the delayed offense. In Diagram 5-21, No. 4 dribbles toward the wing position, which is occupied by No. 2. No. 2 moves out of this position, as shown in the diagram, and the players rotate and fill the positions as they are vacated by their teammates.

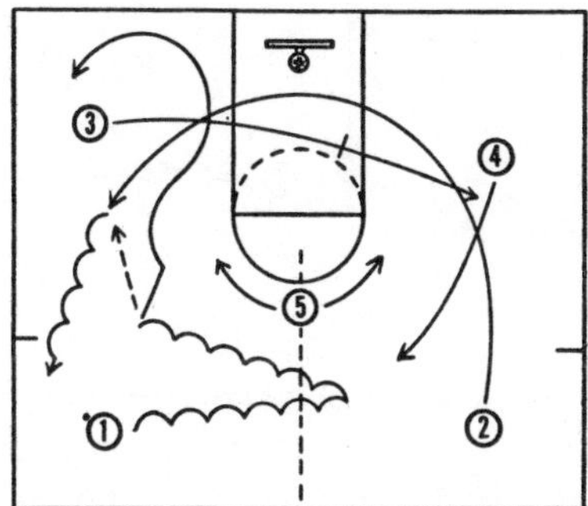

Diagram 5-22

Diagram 5-22. In the situation presented in Diagram 5-22, No. 1 should be careful and not dribble beyond the dotted line. If he is forced to do so, then No. 2 should move out of the position in which he is stationed. If No. 1 should double back and move in the direction from whence he came, then Nos. 3 and 2 execute a "screen and cross" as shown in Diagram 5-22. This maneuver allows all the positions to be filled and floor balance to be maintained, as shown in the diagram.

Diagram 5-23. When No. 4 passes to No. 2, as shown in Diagram 5-23, and makes his cut toward the basket, it results in an exchange of positions between these two players. No. 4 first fakes in the direction of the center of the court and toward No. 5. He makes his cut toward the basket and attempts to place himself between his defensive man and the ball if this is possible. The guard has a much

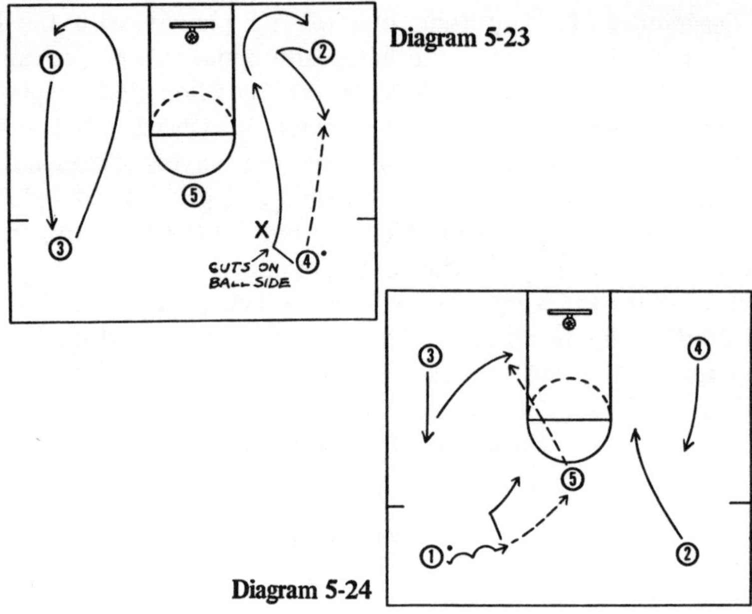

Diagram 5-23

Diagram 5-24

better chance of breaking free to receive the pass from No. 2 and making the drive to the basket, if he is able to cut to the inside of his guard. These two players can often coordinate their moves so that there is a good opportunity for the "give and go" type of maneuver, which can be used very effectively and successfully.

Diagram 5-24. Any time the ball is passed to the player stationed in the pivot-post position, regardless of where he is located, the play shown in Diagram 5-24 should be attempted as the first alternative. As soon as No. 5 has received the pass from No. 1, he should automatically turn to see if No. 3 is breaking behind him to the basket. This "back door" play is most effective in this type of situation, especially if No. 3's guard takes his eyes off of the offensive player to look at the ball. This is when the break should be made by No. 3. If No. 3 cannot shake loose from his guard, he then returns to his original position and follows the prescribed pattern of movement called for in this particular sequence.

Diagram 5-25. This final diagram shows a complete continuity pattern from the pivot-post delay, which eventually results in a scoring play if all the maneuvers are successful. This is, of course, dependent upon how well the play is defensed. Usually the pattern needs to be continued until the scoring play presents itself. No. 2 has the ball and dribbles over to the middle of the court. No. 1 moves in and screens for No. 3. No. 3 breaks out from the corner position and receives a pass from No. 2, as shown in the diagram. After making the pass, No. 2 moves back to his original position in order to maintain floor balance. Meanwhile, No. 5 who is stationed in the high post area, maneuvers for a pass by moving down to the lane and then back out in an attempt to free himself and position himself for the expected pass. No. 3 now turns and passes the ball to No. 1, who is stationed in the corner of the court. No. 3 then cuts toward the basket. No. 1 may pass to him, but, if he cannot, he dribbles out on the shuttle move with No. 3. As he gets out to the mid-court area, he passes the ball in to No. 5, who has done a reset and positioned himself near the top of the free throw circle. No. 4 has faked a move toward No. 2 and the mid-court area, and, as No. 5 receives the ball, No. 4 cuts behind him using the "back door" or "sucker" play for an easy two points as No. 5 passes to him for the lay-up.

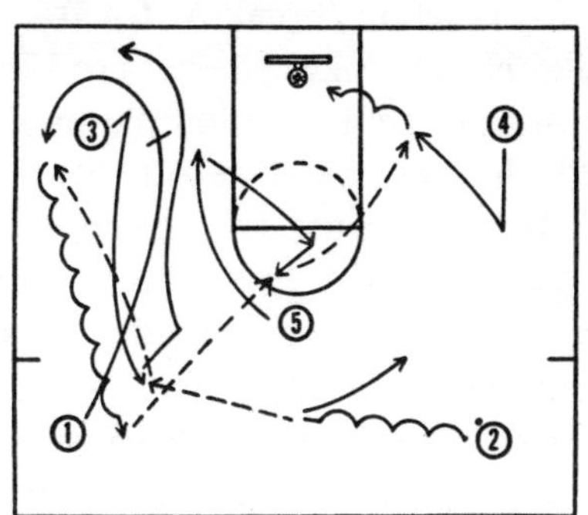

Diagram 5-25

THE SHUFFLE-CUT DELAY

Sometimes a team finds itself in a situation where one player is such a poor ball handler that when an attempt to use a delayed offense is made, it is advantageous to keep him away from the ball and use him as a decoy or for other purposes. A shuffle-cut pattern can use the pivot-post player, or for that matter, any other player, in this way—and to good advantage. The following diagrams will show how this can be done.

Diagram 5-26. The players take the positions shown in Diagram 5-26. By positioning themselves in this manner, they force the defense to spread out their players. No. 5 is the big, awkward player who must be kept away from the ball as much as possible. Nos. 1, 2, 3 and 4 will do most of the ball handling and interchanging of positions and makes the cuts off the double screen that will be provided for in the shuffle-cut offense. No. 5 will operate near the top of the circle and will shift from side to side in this area, dependent upon the movement of the ball. The diagram shows No. 2 passing the ball to No. 4, who shakes his defensive man and comes to meet the pass. After passing the ball to No. 4, No. 2 drives in a diagonal direction across the court to a position near No. 5, as shown in the diagram. At the same time, No. 1 fakes a move toward the base line and the left side of the court, but, just as No. 2 arrives at a position below No. 5, No. 1 cuts sharply to his right off the shoulder and hip of Nos. 5 and 2. No. 4 should maneuver so that he is in a position to receive the ball as deep and as near the base line as possible. As No. 4 executes a slow dribble toward the position previously occupied by No. 2, he looks for the possibility and the opportunity to pass to No. 1, who is breaking for the basket. If No. 1 is free to receive the pass, No. 4 makes the pass to him. There can be other scoring opportunities that could materialize from this maneuver, which could develop as a result of individual player initiative and ingenuity. No. 5 can use the screen set for him by No. 2 and follow the same path as No. 1 in his break to the basket. The ultimate purpose of the offense is eventually to score a basket. However, as has previously been stated, in using any delayed offense, ball possession is the first consideration, because that is why the offense is being used in the first place. However, it should be remembered that many games are lost because the team stopped trying to score and just tried to control the ball and run out the clock.

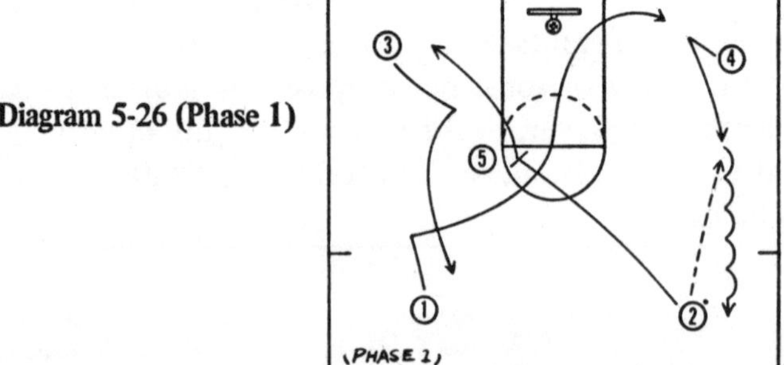

Diagram 5-26 (Phase 1)

If No. 4 does not have an opportunity to pass the ball, he dribbles to the position No. 2 just left. No. 1 cuts over the free throw circle area to the right corner of the court, where he takes the position just vacated by No. 4. No. 3 fakes a cut behind No. 5 and then moves out to the position left vacant by No. 1, as shown in the diagram. He could roll off the screen, move past Nos. 5 and 2 toward the basket and receive a release pass from No. 4. No. 2, after providing a screen for No. 1 on his shuffle cut, moves over to the corner position just vacated by No. 3. The interchange of positions brings the players to the positions shown in Diagram 5-27, Phase 2 of the series.

Diagram 5-27. As a result of the player movement shown in Diagram 5-26, the players are now stationed in the positions shown in Diagram 5-27, with No. 4 in possession of the ball. If No. 4 should pass the ball to No. 1 on his side of the floor, the pattern would be repeated again without movement or change of sides by No. 5. However, if No. 4 should pass the ball to No. 3 and No. 3 should pass to No. 2 in the left corner position, then No. 5 quickly moves over to the right side of the lane near the top of the free throw circle. This maneuver will enable him to provide a better screening position and angle for the shuffle cut to be made by No. 4. After No. 3 makes the pass to No. 2, he cuts sharply toward the basket area. If he sees that he is not going to free himself for the pass from No. 2, he sets a screen behind No. 5, as shown in the diagram. No. 4 now cuts straight down court and then veers to the left behind Nos. 5 and 3, using them as a double screen. He continues his drive straight toward the basket. If he does not receive a pass from No. 2, he moves to the left corner of the court and takes the position vacated by No. 2. If he is free to receive the pass, No. 2 passes the ball to him for an easy lay-up. If No. 2 is not able to make any of these passes, he dribbles

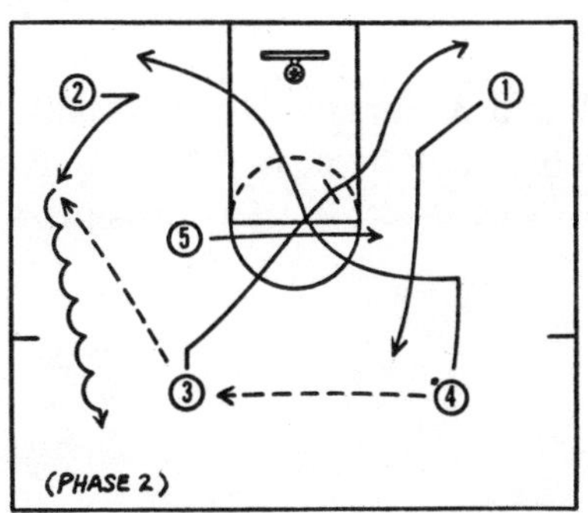

Diagram 5-27 (Phase 2)

the ball out toward the center line so that he may retain possession and continue the continuity of play. Now the players are all in positions where they will be able to continue the pattern, keep possession of the ball and still have an opportunity to score.

Diagram 5-28. After two complete changes of position by the players, as shown in the last two diagrams, they will find themselves stationed in the positions shown in Diagram 5-28. Actually, the players are in their beginning positions, except that they are on opposite sides of the court. Two more position changes would put the players back in their beginning positions and on the same side of the floor from which they started. Actually, the purpose of the offense is not to rotate the players but to control the ball and eventually score. If the defense should pressure the No. 3 and 4 offensive players to the degree that guards No. 1 and 2 may experience difficulty in making the pass to them, the maneuvers shown in Diagram 5-28 may be used. This maneuver can be accomplished by attempting an interchange of positions between players No. 3 and 4. After this exchange of positions is accomplished, the players will be stationed in positions from which the shuffle-cut delayed offense can be begun. Also, if No. 2 needs to pass to No. 1, as shown in the diagram, and is unable to do so, a change of

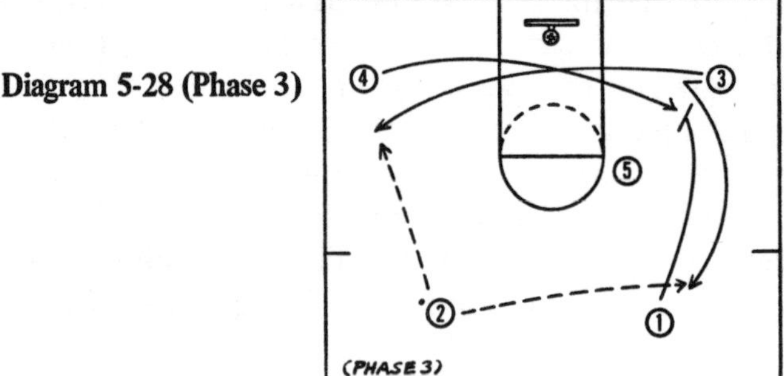

Diagram 5-28 (Phase 3)

positions between Nos. 1 and 3 can free No. 3 so that he can receive the pass from No. 2. The ball may be passed back to No. 2, as shown in the diagram, and, from this position, it is possible again to begin the shuffle-cut delayed offense.

THE FIVE AROUND PLAY (A DELAYED OFFENSE)

Diagram 5-29. Quite frequently a team may have two players who are not good ball handlers. This poses a problem, because, in any type of delayed offense, ball handling is of extreme importance. Great emphasis is placed on ball handling ability if ball possession is to be maintained. If there are any players that cannot handle the ball well, an offense must be used to take care of this deficiency. The "five around play" is such an offense. The players position themselves as shown in Diagram 5-29. Nos. 1, 2 and 3 are the active ball handlers and do the passing, cutting and most of the ball handling. Of course, Nos. 4 and 5 can be used as decoys and can occasionally be brought into the play for scoring situations, especially when the defense begins to neglect or forget them as prospective scorers. No. 1 brings the ball to the mid-court area to begin the play. Nos. 4 and 5 station themselves wide and just above the free throw line extended. They can adjust their positions as needed, but their main duty will be to screen the defensive players guarding Nos. 2 and 3. These players position themselves deeper down court and somewhat nearer to the free throw lane. After Nos. 4 and 5 perform their screens, Nos. 2 and 3 break to the outside of the screen and up court to receive the pass from No. 1. Players No. 4 and 5 move back to their wide positions as soon as possible. Their

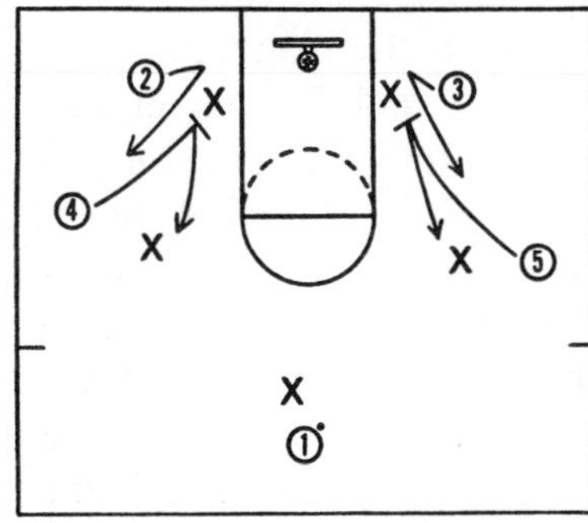

Diagram 5-29

principal function is to move in and out, as shown in the diagram, and to provide screens for the moving, passing and cutting players, Nos. 1, 2 and 3. Ball possession can be maintained using these maneuvers until a scoring opportunity presents itself.

Diagram 5-30. When No. 1 is challenged by the defense, Nos. 4 and 5 move down court and screen for Nos. 2 and 3. Nos. 2 and 3 fake a move to go deep toward the basket in what is meant to be a cooperative move, with the players doing the screening. They then cut back to the outside of the screens set by Nos. 4 and 5 in an attempt to free themselves to receive a pass from No. 1. In this diagram, No. 1 passes to No. 2 when he frees himself as a result of the screen set by No. 4. After the pass, No. 1 drives down the middle of the court toward the basket in an attempt to free himself for the return pass from No. 2. If he is free to receive the pass, then, of course, No. 2 passes the ball to him for what should be an easy lay-up. If No. 1 is not free to receive the pass, he continues his drive toward the basket and then veers toward the left side of the court, or to the same side to which he made the pass, and takes the position vacated by No. 2. The options that No. 2 may have from this position are shown in the following diagrams.

Diagram 5-31. After the player movement shown in Diagram 5-30 has been completed, No. 2 ends up with the ball and is situated in the position shown in Diagram 5-31. No. 2 could possibly pass the ball to No. 3 and begin the continuity of play from this point. He could possibly drive the middle himself if he felt he could do this successfully. If neither of these options are exploited, then No. 2 dribbles the ball out to the mid-court area and Nos. 4 and 5 return to their wide positions, as shown in the diagram. No. 3 moves back to where he started. With Nos. 1 and 3 now in the low and close positions and Nos. 4 and 5 in the wide positions, No. 2 is ready to start the play all over again. Nos. 3 and 4 repeat the screening movements used to free Nos. 1 and 3, which in turn will enable them to receive the pass from No. 2. Any one of these players may use his own initiative and break from the pattern for either a pass or a drive, should he feel that it will be successful. The next diagram will depict other options that would be possible if No. 2 should pass to No. 3.

Diagram 5-32. Diagram 5-32, Phase 3 shows the positions of the players after the maneuvers have been completed in Diagram 5-30. No. 2 now has the ball in the position shown at the beginning of Diagram 5-31. No. 3 waits for the screen from No. 5 and then breaks

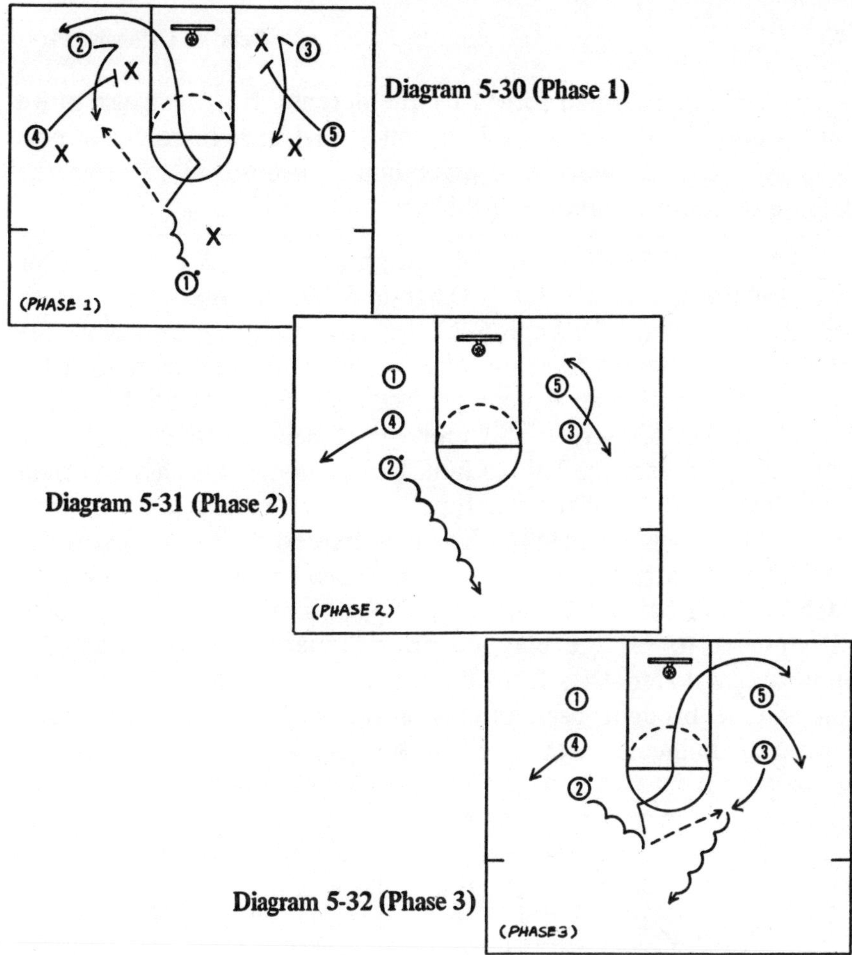

Diagram 5-30 (Phase 1)

Diagram 5-31 (Phase 2)

Diagram 5-32 (Phase 3)

out from his former position to the one shown in Diagram 5-32. As he moves around the screen set by No. 5, No. 3 could be free to receive a pass from No. 2. If No. 2 makes the pass to No. 3, he has two option possibilities. The first is as shown in this diagram. It shows No. 2 moving out with the ball and passing to No. 3, who has freed himself as a result of the screen set by No. 5. After passing to No. 3, No. 2 drives the middle lane and then floats out to the wide post position just vacated by No. 3. Nos. 4 and 5 move back to their wide positions, and, as No. 3 dribbles the ball out toward the mid-court area, they are now ready to start the play over again with Nos. 4 and 5 screening for Nos. 1 and 2, when No. 3 is pressured by the defense. No. 3 should not stop his dribble in this area but should save it for a move when forced by the defense. No. 3 can also move out around the screen toward the mid-court area to receive a pass from No. 2. This move will place him in a position to bring the defense out before making a dribble.

Diagram 5-33. The second option that No. 2 can use after receiving the ball as he did in Diagram 5-30 is to make the pass to No. 3, as shown in Diagram 5-33. Instead of cutting or driving the middle in an attempt to score, No. 2 follows in the direction of his pass to No. 3 and then screens off No. 3's defensive man. No. 3 has cut off of No. 5's screen and moved out near the mid-court area, where No. 2 passes the ball to him. No. 2 follows his pass and then moves over in front of the free throw circle where he sets up a screen on No. 3's defensive man. If No. 3 is free to do so, he drives the middle in an attempt to score. No. 1 must move out quickly to establish floor balance on this play. Nos. 4 and 5 can quickly make adjustments to set the play up again if necessary. If no scoring opportunity materializes from the moves made by Nos. 2 and 3, the ball can be brought back outside again, with No. 1 moving back toward the mid-court area to receive the pass.

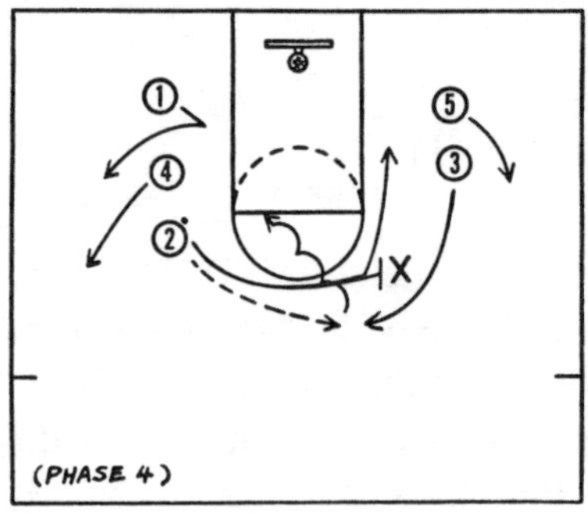

Diagram 5-33 (Phase 4)

Diagram 5-34. There are several option plays that can be used from the "five around formation." As a result, the "clear the side maneuver" makes it possible to take advantage of a weak defensive player. It is also possible, as a result of this maneuver, to capitalize upon the strong offensive player's ability, because he can beat most defensive players in a 1-on-1 situation. The play, as shown in Diagram 5-34, starts in the usual manner, and, as No. 3 moves around

Diagram 5-34 (Clear the Side)

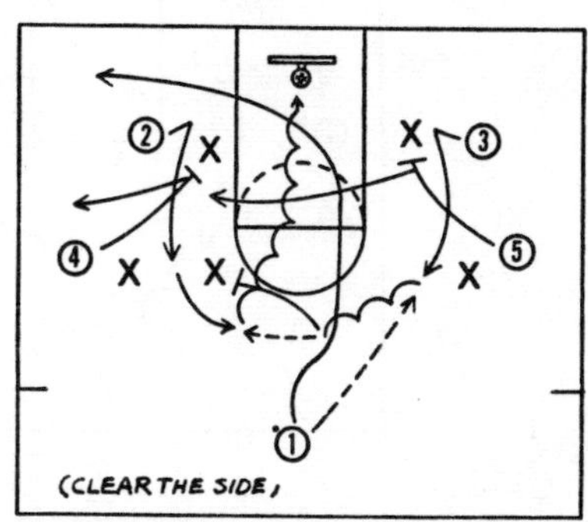

the screen set by No. 5, No. 1 passes the ball to him and then drives down the middle of the court toward the basket. No. 3 passes the ball to No. 2, who has made his cut after having received a screen from No. 4, as shown in the diagram. No. 3 can move in the direction of his pass, or drive down the middle toward the basket. In this diagram, he moves in the direction of his pass and then sets a screen on No. 2's defensive man. As No. 1 is making his move down the middle of the court in the direction of the basket, he calls to No. 5 "clear out." At this time, instead of swinging out to the position vacated by No. 3 on the right side of the court, No. 1, along with No. 5, suddenly breaks to the left side of the court. This move clears the entire right side of the floor, and as a result leaves No. 2 an open lane down which to drive after receiving the screen from No. 3. This same maneuver can be used on either side of the court, and, with practice and proper timing on the clearing move, it can be extremely successful.

Diagram 5-35. The complete cycle of the "five around delayed offense," showing the continuity of play in its entirety, is shown in Diagram 5-35. Nos. 1, 2 and 3 cut off the screens set by Nos. 4 and 5. Nos. 4 and 5 shuffle back and forth, using screening movements at every opportunity. At the same time Nos. 1, 2 and 3 drive the middle and break in and around the screens. Actually, the offense can be used very well as a delayed offense, without the necessity of pulling the defense all the way out to the mid-court area if this is desired. The "five around offense" can be utilized using ball control tactics and ball possession for almost the length of time desired. As a result

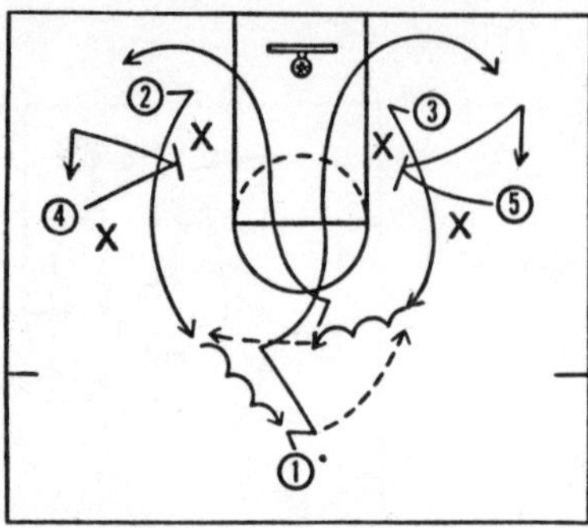

Diagram 5-35

of these maneuvers, scoring opportunities will present themselves and should be capitalized upon when they are available.

THE WHEEL DELAY

Diagram 5-36. The "wheel delay" is similar in many respects to the "five around" delayed offense, in that Nos. 1, 2 and 3 move in and around Nos. 4 and 5 while in the process of cutting, driving and maneuvering for screens. It differs from the "five around offense" in that the players are positioned closer to the free throw lane area, and players No. 4 and 5 do not move in and out to provide the screen, but instead remain in stationary positions. The other players, Nos. 1, 2 and 3, maneuver their opponents so that they can brush them off as they themselves move past these stationary screens. The players station themselves as shown in the diagram, with Nos. 2, 3, 4 and 5 positioned close to the free throw lane. However, they should purposely stay far enough away from the lane so that they will not violate the 3-second rule. No. 1 starts the play from the position shown in the diagram. Nos. 2 and 3 break forward and around Nos. 4 and 5 in such a manner as to obtain a screen and free themselves for a pass. In this diagram, No. 1 passes the ball to No. 3 on the left side of the free throw lane, and then breaks down the middle of the lane toward the basket in anticipation of receiving a return pass from No. 3. If No. 1 does not receive the pass, he then fans out to the side of the free throw lane away from the ball, as shown in the diagram. No. 3 may pass to No. 2 and drive toward the basket or he may execute a pick-and-roll option with No. 5. This maneuver will be explained in later diagrams.

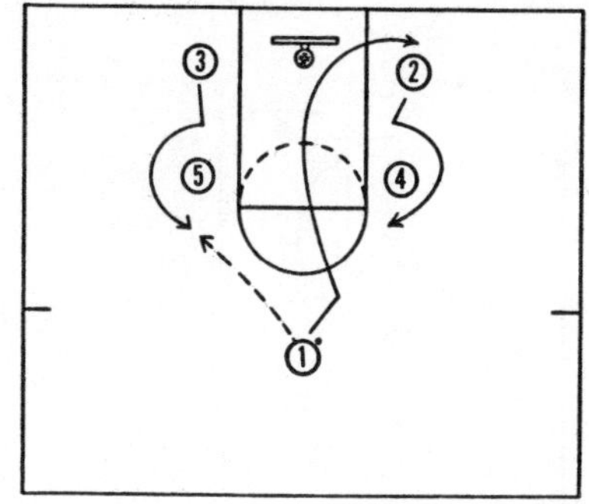

Diagram 5-36

Diagram 5-37. Following the action illustrated in Diagram 5-36, the ball is now in the position shown in Diagram 5-37. Player No. 3 has possession. No. 3 may dribble drive either to the left or right of No. 5, using him to obtain a screen if the defense moves up with him or succeeds in executing a defensive switch. If the dribble drive succeeds in bringing about another switch, No. 3 can then possibly pass to No. 5 on the roll-off during the "split" in the defense. The screen will force the defense to switch, which in turn will provide the pass opportunity during the interval of time the switch is being made.

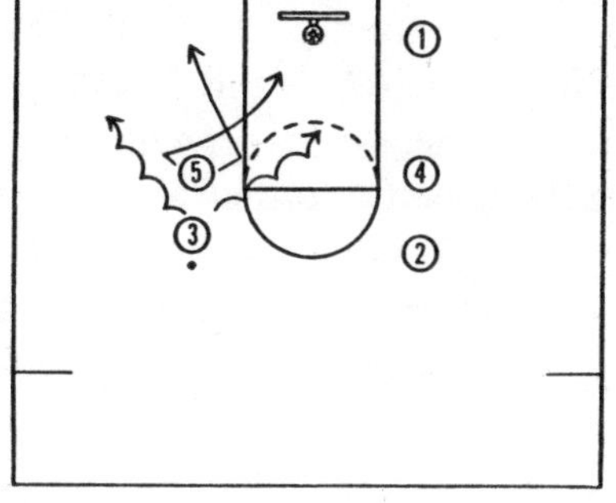

Diagram 5-37

Diagram 5-38. The second option that No. 3 can use after receiving the pass from No. 1 is shown in Diagram 5-38. No. 3 may pass the ball to No. 2, who drives off the screen provided him by No. 4 to a position just above the top of the free throw circle, where he receives the pass. After making the pass, No. 3 may now drive down the middle of the free throw lane toward the basket. He may receive a return pass from No. 2, but, if he does not, he swings to the left side of the court, as shown in the diagram. The offense is now set up

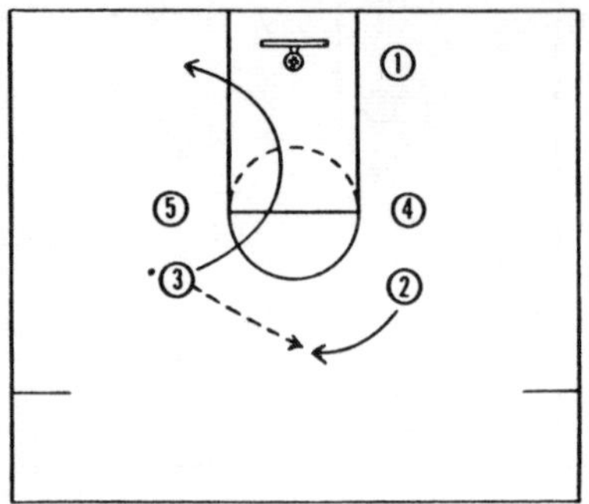

Diagram 5-38

and ready to start over again. Another option which is possible from this position is for No. 2 to drive down the middle after coming off the screen provided him by player No. 4. If the screen is executed properly, he could be free for a drive down the middle and a pass from No. 3. If he does not receive the pass, No. 2 would then swing out to the left side of the court, and No. 3 would dribble out to center court to set up the continuity of play once again.

Diagram 5-39. Another maneuver, very similar to the "wheel," is called the "circle round," and is shown in Diagram 5-39. The maneuver begins with Nos. 2 and 3 circling in and around Nos. 4 and 5, who provide the necessary screens. No. 1, who has the ball at the mid-court area, passes it to either No. 2 or 3 whenever one of them is free to receive it. After making the pass, No. 1 then breaks down the middle of the court toward the basket in anticipation of receiving a return pass. If No. 1 does not receive the pass, he swings back to the side of the court to which he passed the ball and enters into the circle play again. The players should be alert to reverse their directions and peel off for a break to the basket for scoring opportunities. After No. 1 passes the ball to No. 3, as shown in this diagram, No. 3 should be alert to the possibility of making a return pass to No. 1 as he breaks down the middle toward the basket. The pass can also be made to No. 2. If these opportunities do not materialize, No. 3 can always dribble out toward the mid-court area to a position where he can pass the ball to one of the other players coming off a screen. He can also dribble down the middle himself should the opportunity present itself.

Diagram 5-39

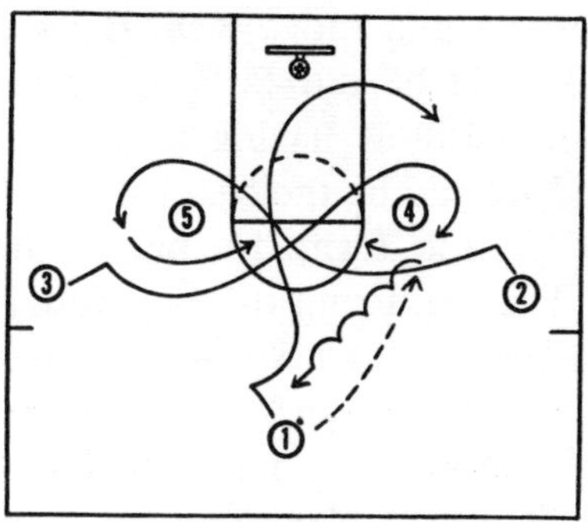

SPECIAL DELAYS

Occasionally, a team will have only two players who can really handle the ball and drive well. With a delayed offense being used, this team may want to keep the ball away from the players who are lacking in ability and compel the opposition to defense the better players. This can be done by "banking" or "stacking" the poorer players in areas that will leave the court clear for the "two that can play." The opposition may try to "float" or "zone" a defense to cope with this situation. However, if they do, they will always leave a player open for an outlet pass. Almost any player can fill this outlet pass position and help the "delayed offense" accomplish its purpose. It must always be kept in mind that the purpose of the "delayed offense" is two-fold: to beat the clock, and to score two points if possible.

Such a "banking" procedure can also be used if a team has a good, strong pivot-post player who can move well, a guard who is good in a 1-on-1 situation and a third player who is versatile in all areas of play. This player should be one to whom the ball can be passed when extreme defensive pressure is being applied by the opposition.

Diagram 5-40. Diagram 5-40 shows how the players are "banked" just inside the mid-court area, away from the main area of play. It is evident that this arrangement of players permits the removal of some players who are not as capable as others, and allows those players who are capable enough room to maneuver successfully. No. 4 should be the rugged type of player who can play the pivot-post position and move well. He is stationed in the high post position and should be out far enough so that he can maneuver in either direction without having to worry about the 3-second lane violation. No. 1 should be the best ball handler and the best offensive 1-on-1 player on the team. He begins the play from the position shown in the diagram. From this position, he can either maneuver on his own or pass the ball to No. 4 stationed in the pivot. If he passes to No. 4, he should cut and move to the open area behind No. 4. Seldom, if ever, should No. 1 pass to No. 4 and cut off of him for a rub-off play. Of all the players in the "bank," No. 5 should be the slowest player on the team. No. 2 should be the second best ball handler and be able to relieve No. 1 when he is needed. No. 3 should be the poorest ball handler and the man least likely to handle the ball. However, both Nos. 3 and 5 should be alert for opportunities to lose their defensive players. This opportunity often occurs when there is a two-timing situation. Nos. 2 and 5 can often move away from the players guarding them unnoticed, and move under the basket unmolested for an easy lay-up shot.

Diagram 5-41. As stated previously, if No. 1 can beat his defensive man in a drive to the basket, he should do so. He has the entire side of the court in which to maneuver. If he passes the ball to No. 4, No. 1 should drive the open area. No. 4 should always be alert to the possibility of making a pass-back to No. 1, both on the drive in and on his move out from the basket area. While this maneuver is being carried out, No. 5 screens for No. 2. After the screen, No. 2 breaks out to the mid-court area in an effort to take any pressure off of No. 4 or 1, should they be tied up with no one to pass to. No. 5 should be alert for an opportunity to execute a roll-off to the basket.

Diagram 5-40

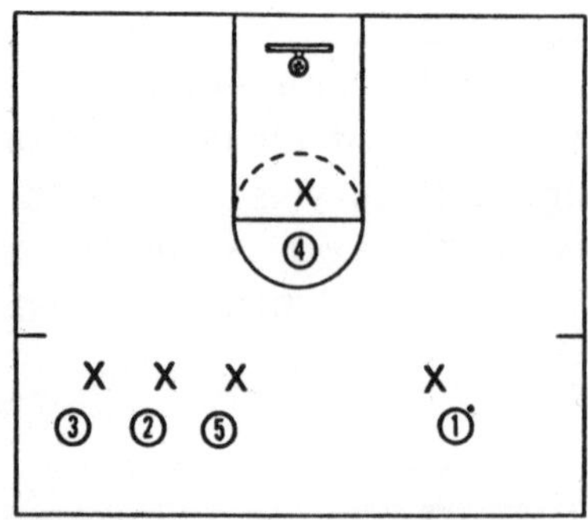

Diagram 5-41

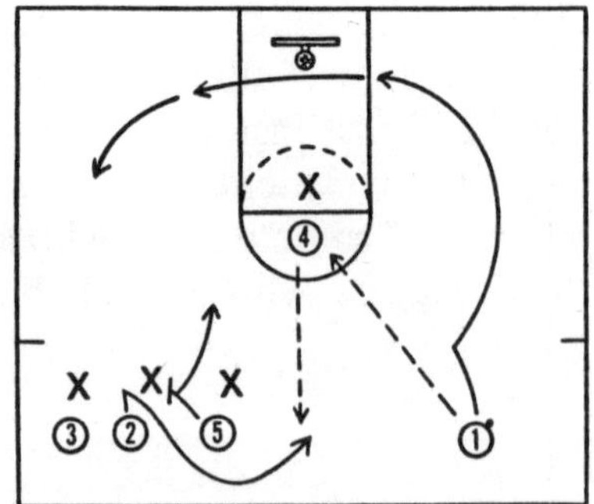

If the defense resorts to two-timing tactics on either No. 4 or 1, then all the other players should be alert to the possibility of slipping in behind the defense for the easy basket. If the ball is passed to No. 2, and if he is a good enough player to maneuver as did No. 1, then he should do so. No. 1 will then take No. 2's position in the "bank." If No. 2 cannot perform in this capacity, or if No. 1 is a player who can perform better in this situation, then No. 2 can pass the ball back to him and move back to the position he formerly occupied in the "bank."

Diagram 5-42. Players No. 5, 2 and 3 can be "banked" or stationed in another area on the court, as shown in Diagram 5-42. It is important, however, that they be banked on the side opposite to which No. 1 is stationed in order to provide him with a large enough area in which to maneuver in a 1-on-1 situation. This diagram shows No. 5 screening for No. 2 so that he might move "out court" and help Nos. 1 and 4 should they need it. No. 5 should be alert for opportunities to execute the roll-off from the screen that he sets for No. 2.

Diagram 5-43. This diagram shows Nos. 2, 3 and 5 "banked" in the left front court area. Players No. 1 and 4 are stationed in their usual positions. No. 1, being the best dribbler, starts his dribbling drive in an attempt to move the ball toward the basket. If he is unable to continue his drive and encounters any difficulty on the dribble, then Nos. 2, 3 and 5 start moving across court, as shown in the diagram. No. 2 cuts sharply up toward the mid-court, off the tails of Nos. 3 and 5, and takes the outlet pass from No. 1. No. 4 takes a deep move toward the basket area and then doubles back off the tails of Nos. 3 and 5 to arrive at a high post position. No. 2, who has just

Diagram 5-42

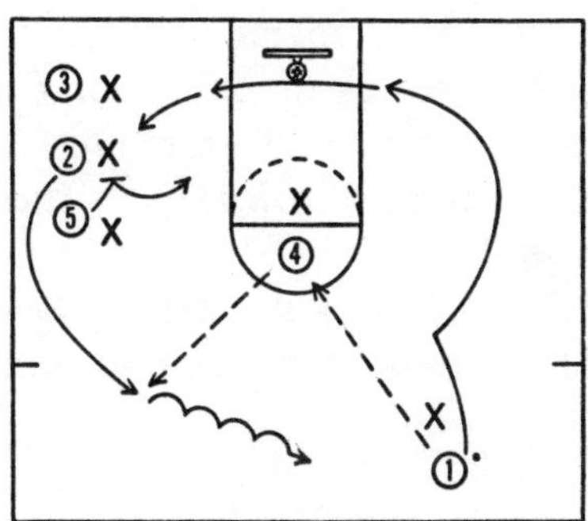

Diagram 5-43

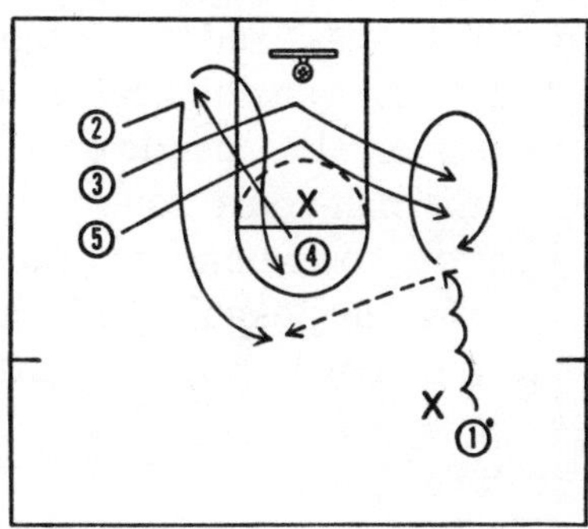

received a release pass from No. 1 may play the entire left side of the floor because it has been cleared for him, or he may flip the ball to No. 4 and drive toward the basket for a return pass from No. 4 and a possible lay-up shot. After passing the ball to No. 2, No. 1 drives toward the basket, and, as he approaches the basket area, doubles back using No. 3 and 5 as a possible screen, as shown in the diagram. As a result of this maneuver, he may be open for a pass from either No. 2 or 4. Nos. 3 and 5 have moved all the way across court and lined up in a "bank" position on the right side of the court. As a result of this maneuver, No. 1 may now take the position formerly occupied by No. 2, only it will be on the opposite side of the court. No. 2 may now perform the same maneuvers as did No. 1 on the opposite side of the court.

THE HI-LO DELAYED OFFENSE (1-3-1)

The hi-lo or the 1-3-1 offense can provide an excellently balanced attack, and one which can be successfully used as a delayed offense. It provides excellent offensive spreading of the players, which in turn demands full and excellent defensive coverage by the opposition. Using one player who is stationed in the top or point position near the mid-court area, two players wide and even with the free throw line extended, one player in the high post and one in the low post position, will allow penetration at all points.

Coaches using the 1-3-1 offense can go into a "delayed offense" by attempting only to draw the defense out a little farther from the basket area. They then proceed to play a more cautious type of game, but still use the same offensive patterns they employ in their regular offense. Many patterns and options are possible in this offense, but the low post man roaming the base line makes deep penetration possible, while the high post man makes center penetration possible. The wing men and the top man fill in the other possible areas, and the offense is now well prepared to "kill the clock" and possibly get a score in the process of doing so. This offense can also operate equally well against the man-to-man pressure and the half-court zone presses that might be thrown up in these situations to combat the delayed offense.

Not all possible options for a 1-3-1 offense will be given here, but one good, popular pattern will be presented. As previously mentioned, if the team is already using the 1-3-1 as its regular offense, then their best delayed offense would probably be their regular offense, operating on a more drawn-out scale, with more caution then usual, to capitalize on the high percentage shot after a certain period of ball control has allowed a player to free himself to take the easy shot.

Diagram 5-44. The offense presented in the following diagrams as a "delayed offense" will have Nos. 1, 2 and 3 rotating positions, and Nos. 4 and 5 interchanging positions. This assumes that Nos. 1, 2 and 3 are capable ball handlers and can play equally well at the top or point position and the wing or side court positions. It assumes also that Nos. 4 and 5 are the pivot-post type players and can operate equally well in these positions. To start the "delay," the players spread out into the positions shown in the diagram. In the first move, No. 1 passes the ball to No. 2, who is stationed in the right wing position. No. 2 makes a strong fake and moves toward the basket to free himself for the pass from No. 1. If the fake does not free No. 2, he should continue his drive to the basket. If No. 1 decides that he can pass to No. 3 instead of No. 2, then No. 5 will have to hurriedly cross over to the other side of the lane. After passing to No. 2, No. 1 fakes as if he intends to follow the pass, but instead breaks toward the basket off the back side of No. 4. Using No. 4 as a screen, he continues his drive down the lane and swings out to the right corner of the court. If he is open, No. 2 should pass the ball to him. If he is not open, then No. 1 should move on out toward the corner and take his defensive man out of the area.

Diagram 5-44 (Phase 1)

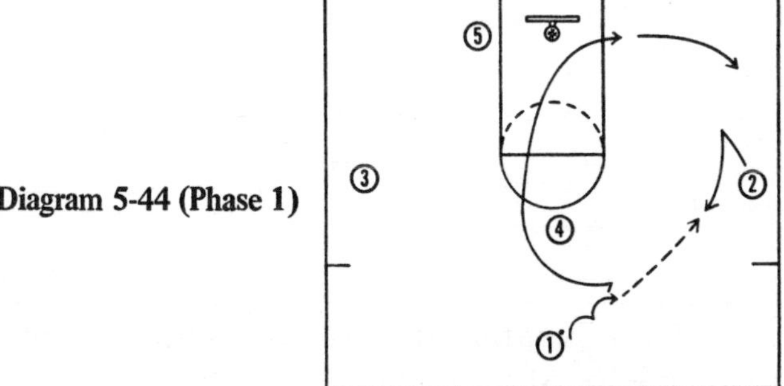

Diagram 5-45. If No. 2 is unable to pass to No. 1, he may be able to pass to No. 4 or back out to the top or point position, as shown in Diagram 5-45. If he is unable to pass to No. 4 at the high post position, he should be alert to the possibility of passing the ball to No. 3. If No. 4 finds that he is not in a position to receive the pass, he immediately moves to his left, as shown in the diagram, and sets a screen for No. 3. No. 3 fakes a cut toward the basket, and then, taking advantage of the screen set by No. 4, breaks out to the point position to receive the pass from No. 2. As soon as No. 3 clears the screen set by No. 4, No. 4 rolls toward the basket as shown in the diagram. No. 2 can pass to No. 4 on the roll-off if he is open. However, if this option does not materialize, then the pass is made from No. 2 to No. 3 at the top or point position. As soon as No. 4 executes the roll-off, drives to the basket and does not receive the ball, No. 5 moves out quickly to the high post position. No. 4 is now in the low post position on the opposite side of the lane. This has brought about an interchange on the low post and the high post position. No. 3 has moved out to the top or point position. No. 2 moves over to the position formerly occupied by No. 3, and No. 1 moves up to the position formerly occupied by No. 2. This exchange of positions will set up the 1-3-1 formation and enable the continuity of movement to continue.

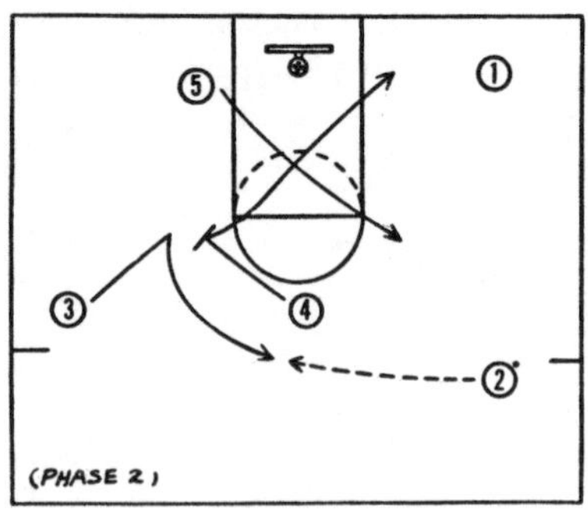

Diagram 5-45 (Phase 2)

Diagram 5-46. A continuation of the continuity of play is shown in Diagram 5-46. After passing the ball to No. 3, No. 2 drives toward the basket, but, as he approaches the free throw lane area, he angles to his left and moves to the position formerly occupied by No.

Diagram 5-46 (Phase 3)

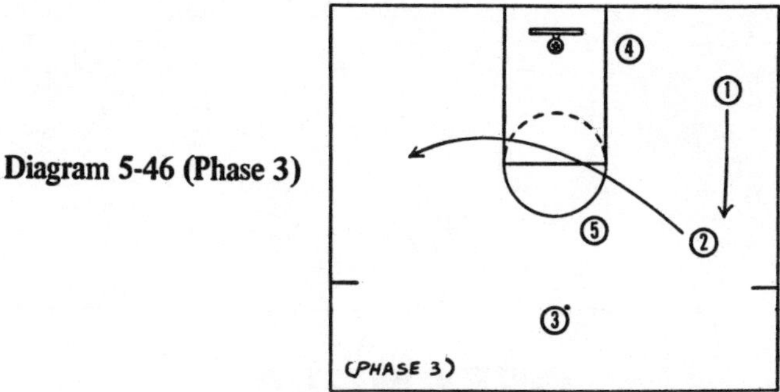

3. No. 1 moves up the sideline and takes the wing position vacated by No. 2. The play is now ready to start over again. No. 3 may move the ball to either side of the court. His best move is to pass to No. 2 because No. 4 is on the proper side of the lane for this move. If No. 3 should pass to No. 1, then No. 4 should hurriedly move across to the other side of the lane.

Diagram 5-47. The offense can be executed on the opposite, and, in this case, the left side of the court, as shown in Diagram 5-47. No. 3 passes to No. 2 and cuts off No. 5's hip down the free throw lane and toward the basket. If not free to receive a pass, he drifts to the left corner of the court. No. 1 fakes deep toward the basket and then pops off the screen that No. 5 sets for him as he moves out to the top spot to receive the ball from No. 2. In the meantime, No. 5, after executing his screen on No. 1, rolls down the lane. No. 4 breaks out to the high post position. The pattern is now all set to run over again.

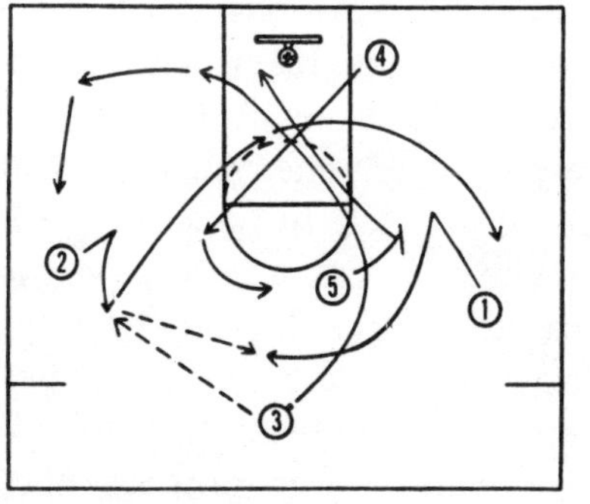

Diagram 5-47

SIX

OFFENSES AGAINST PRESSING DEFENSES

Any successful offensive basketball team today must be prepared to cope with the many types of pressure defenses that may be used during the course of a game. Basketball offenses and offensive maneuvers have developed and changed rapidly over the years. The defensive techniques and tactics which are now being used are attempts to keep pace with the offensive game. Multiple defenses that are constantly changing have been one of these developments. As a result, defensive basketball today presents many problems to the offensive-minded team. The offensive team today must be prepared to meet and successfully cope with the situations brought about by these changes. The offensive team must *never* be caught unprepared, or allow itself to be surprised by any defensive attack or maneuver by the opposition at any position on the court. Many defensive teams no longer retreat to a point within the shooting range area near the basket and there await the offensive attack. Instead, the defenses often begin their attack at any point on the court. The defense, upon losing possession of the ball, may immediately instigate a full-court, a three-fourths court, half-court or mid-court attack. In addition to these different attacking points, the defenses may also use man-to-man pressures, zone pressures or combinations of man-to-man and zone, as well as match-up defenses. This poses many offensive problems which must be dealt with. Various defensive trap-play situations can also be effective and constantly used against the offense as it advances the ball down court toward the offensive basket.

As a result of these defensive tactics which have been developed, the coach today must design an offense that can successfully operate from base line to base line (end line to end line). The coach can no longer rely entirely on an offense that moves down court and sets up its offensive operation within the confines of the front court playing area. If he allows this to happen, he could find that the defense may not allow the offensive players to move into this area. The offense must, therefore, be prepared to cope with the defensive pressure at any position on the court and be ready to react accordingly. The element of surprise many times confuses the offense and allows the defense to be effective in causing turnovers that oftentimes give them possession of the ball. In order to combat these various defensive pressure situations, the offense must have at its command many so-called escape routes available for immediate use. It still must provide, however, the opportunity to use the quick break or the fast escape. The various escape routes provide a safety measure in preventing turnovers, while the quick break always provides the opportunity of moving quickly up court before the defense can organize and set up its pressure defense in the back-court area. Both factors must be present in the offense in order that it may effectively combat the varying, combative, multiple pressure defenses that are used in basketball today.

Many of the situations that result from these defensive pressures could be considered "special situation" plays, and this chapter will present offenses to meet some of these very "*special situations.*"

OFFENSE AGAINST MAN-TO-MAN FULL-COURT PRESSURE DEFENSES

The most common full-court pressure defense in use at the present time is the man-to-man. Usually the defensive team applies this defense immediately after a basket or a free throw has been scored, or when the opponents have the ball out-of-bounds along the end line.

Diagram 6-1. This diagram shows the defensive players applying the pressure in a full-court, 1-on-1 situation. The offensive team players, always on the alert and always expecting the defensive pressure to be applied, advance to the positions shown in the diagram. No. 1 takes the ball out-of-bounds, and the defensive team aggressively moves in to guard either a previously assigned or the nearest offensive player. The defensive player, X1, guarding No. 1, plays him very aggressively in an effort to thwart a throw-in. The other offensive players take the positions shown in the diagram and advance cautiously down court, always prepared to come back and help if needed. Also, if the opportunity presents itself, they can make a quick dash for the basket. They are always alert for this opportunity to present itself, as this maneuver offers a definite threat to a pressing defense. No. 2, the best ball handler and the one who has the most ability to advance the ball down court against a 1-on-1 situation, takes a position near the free throw lane, as shown in the diagram. Nos. 3 and 4 advance to their positions as shown. They should, from these positions, be able to move down court easily and quickly or come back up court if their help is needed. No. 5, the pivot-post player, moves far down the court just as soon as possible, and always past the division line and into the front court. Probably the best way for the offensive team to bring the ball down court in this situation is to get the ball to No. 2, have the other players clear out the area and let No. 2 bring the ball down court by himself if he is able to do so.

As shown in Diagram 6-1, No. 2 shakes himself loose from his defensive man and No. 1 passes him the ball. No. 1 now moves down court, taking his defensive man as far away from No. 2 as possible. If No. 2 should get into trouble, No. 1 should be ready at all times to come back to help him. Nos. 3 and 4 fake their defensive men as if to receive the ball and then proceed down court, keeping the middle area open. No. 5 also clears out of the middle to one side and moves deep down court. No. 2 pits his offensive ability against his defensive man, and, assuming that a good offensive man can beat the defensive man every time, he should have no trouble bringing the ball down court. Opportunities may present themselves which may make it possible for No. 2 to go all the way for a lay-up. If this is not possible, he can pass off to a teammate who has caught a defensive man turning away. If none of these maneuvers materializes, No. 2

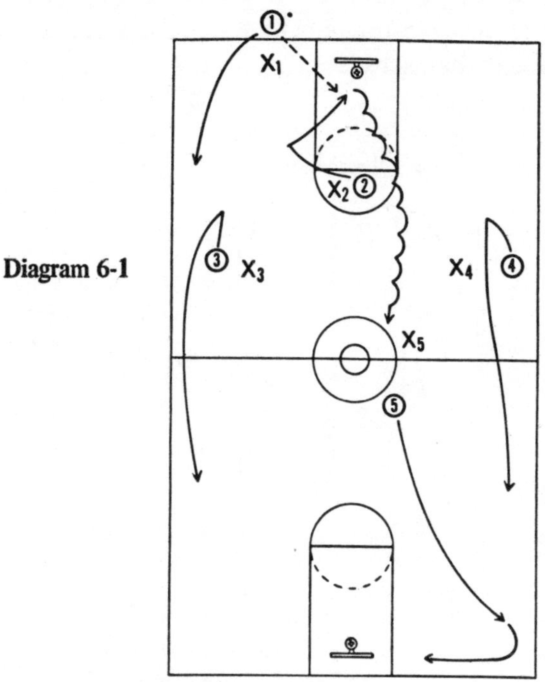

Diagram 6-1

can bring the ball down court, and the team can then go into its regular offensive pattern.

Diagram 6-2. In Diagram 6-2, only one change has been made. Sometimes No. 1 may be the most reliable player to throw the ball in-bounds in this particular situation. He may also be the most reliable in bringing the ball down court against a 1-on-1 pressure defense. If this is true, then the ball may be thrown in to No. 2. No. 1 immedately breaks to a position as shown in the diagram so that he may receive a return pass from No. 2. No. 2 passes the ball right back to No. 1 as soon as possible after he steps in-bounds and is free to receive the pass without fear of interception. This is a dangerous pass because it is made in front of the basket and interception could be disastrous. No. 2 now clears the area, first making sure that he can come back to help No. 1 if he is needed. No. 1 brings the ball down court. There is one advantage this situation has for the offensive team over the one shown in Diagram 6-1. This advantage is: When No. 1 receives the ball, he is facing down court, and consequently is in a much better position to see what is taking place down court. As a result, it is possible for him to take advantage of openings as soon as they present themselves.

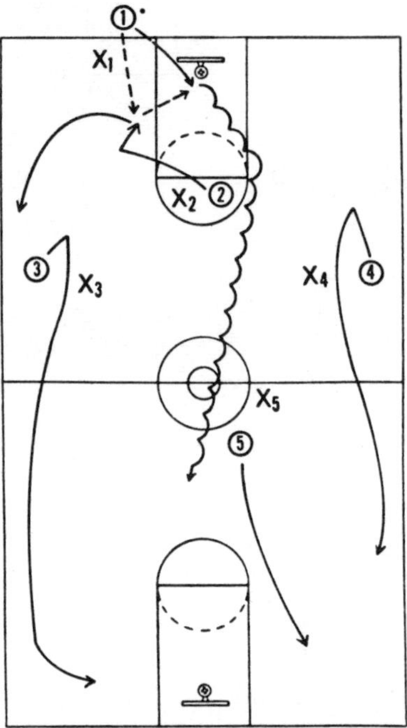

Diagram 6-2

Diagram 6-3. Sometimes in the man-to-man full-court pressure defense, the defense will leave the player taking the ball out-of-bounds free and double team one player in-bounds, as shown in Diagram 6-3. Here, X1 and X2 double team on No. 2, the most logical recipient of the pass from No. 1. If this should happen, then No. 2 should take the defensive players as far away from the ball as possible. As shown in Diagram 6-3, No. 2 fakes toward No. 1 as if to receive the ball and then breaks sharply to the right side of the court, taking both defensive players as far away from the ball as possible. Now Nos. 3 and 4 make concerted efforts to free themselves in order to receive the in-bounds pass from No. 1. Here No. 3 is shown shaking his defensive man, and No. 1 passes the ball to him. After the pass is made to No. 3, No. 1 steps in-bounds and moves sharply down the middle of the court, being alert for a return pass from No. 3. No.

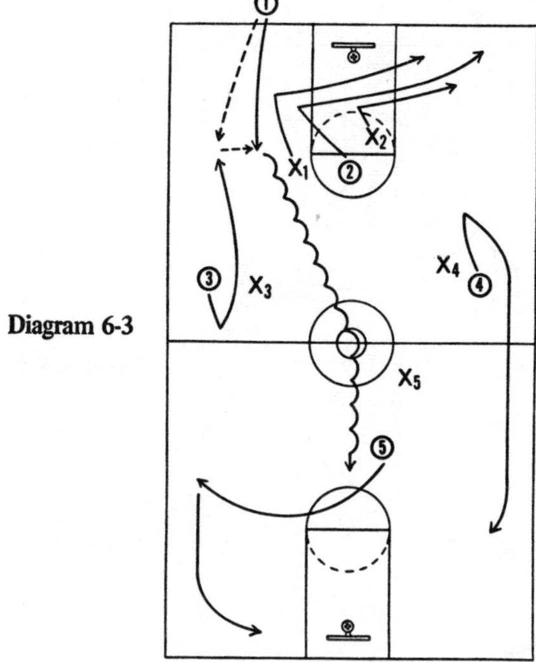

Diagram 6-3

2 has pulled two defensive men away from the play, and, unless one of the defensive players guarding No. 3 or No. 4 shifts to guard No. 1, he should be free for an open drive all the way to the basket. Here he is shown dribbling down the middle of the court. He goes as far as possible, and, if defensive players shift to guard him, then he should be alert for opportunities to pass off to the teammate who would be left open by such a shift in defensive alignment. Other possibilities that may be used when this two-timing defensive maneuver is employed, are shown in Diagram 6-4.

Diagram 6-4. When the defense two-times the logical in-bounds pass receiver, the options shown in Diagram 6-4 may be used. No. 2 fakes toward the out-of-bounds player who has the ball. He then takes the two defensive players away from the ball by breaking to the right and stepping out-of-bounds along the end line on the opposite side of the floor. If the throw-in situation is the result of a scored basket or free throw, No. 1 may pass the ball to No. 2 along

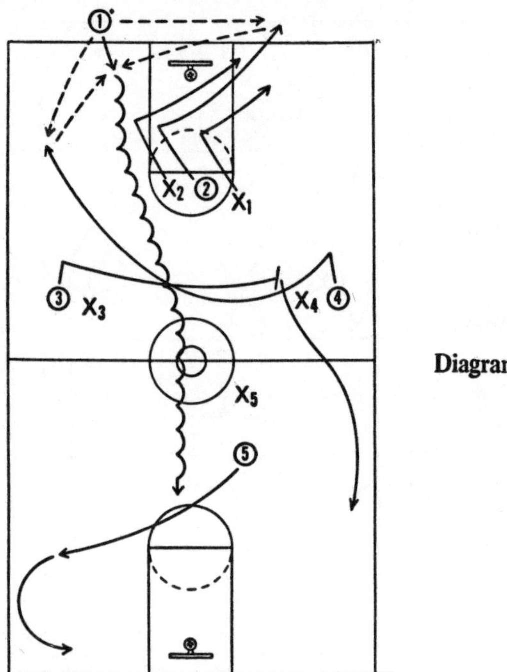

Diagram 6-4

the base line out-of-bounds. No. 1 may then step in-bounds and receive a return pass from No. 2. No. 1 now is free to dribble down court. He may dribble all the way to the basket if he is free to do so, or he may pass off to a teammate. However, to make sure that an outlet pass can be made, Nos. 3 and 4 execute a screening move, as shown in the diagram. No. 3 screens No. 4's defensive player as No. 4 breaks across the court in an attempt to position himself for a possible outlet pass from No. 1. No. 1 can now pass the ball to No. 4 and then quickly step in-bounds to receive a return pass and be in a position to drive down court as previously described. Note also that No. 5 usually breaks deep to the same side of the court from whence the first pass-in is made. This places him in a position for a possible long pass down court which could result in a quick two points if it is properly executed.

Diagram 6-5. Sometimes a team will find that it can facilitate bringing the ball down court against the tight man-to-man pressure defense by executing screens in the back court. Such maneuvers can lead to quick scoring opportunities. This technique, however, does

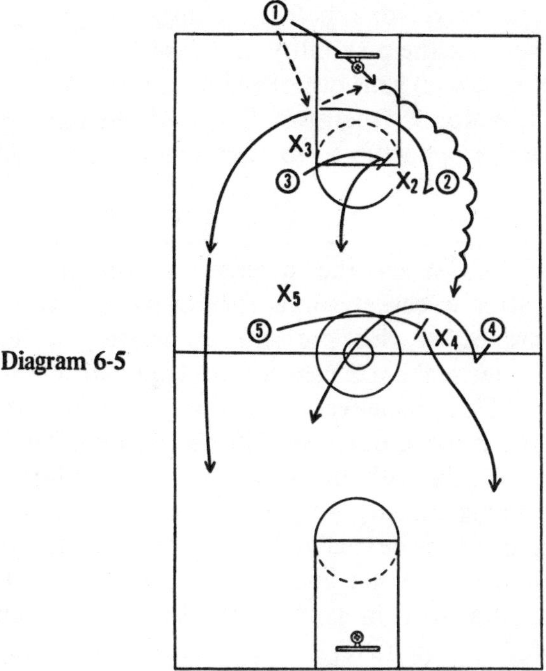

Diagram 6-5

have the disadvantage of sometimes cluttering up the area of activity, thereby enabling the defensive team to quickly double team the dribbler or the man with the ball. As shown in Diagram 6-5, the players go to the positions indicated. No. 1 is the best player to throw the ball in-bounds besides being the best ball handler and the most adept player at bringing the ball down court against the pressing defenses. Nos. 2 and 3 are the next best ball handlers. When No. 1 is ready to throw the ball in-bounds, Nos. 2 and 3 execute a cross screening move, with No. 3 screening No. 2's defensive player so that No. 2 may break free and be in a position to receive the out-of-bounds pass. No. 3 rolls out of the screen and moves down court. Nos. 5 and 4, if the situation warrants such a maneuver and in their estimation it is desirable, may execute a cross screening move, with No. 5 screening No. 4's defensive man, as shown in the diagram. No. 5 rolls off this screen after its execution and moves down court. No. 4 breaks out toward the area shown in the diagram for a possible outlet pass from either No. 1 or 2. If the pass is not forthcoming, he moves on down court. As shown in this diagram, No. 1 passes the ball in-bounds to No. 2 as he comes off the screen set by No. 3. No.

2 immediately returns the ball to No. 1, who then brings the ball down court. However, No. 2, before making the return pass to No. 1, should not overlook the possibility of a pass down court to No. 4, or possibly to No. 3, who rolls out of the screen and down court. No. 2 may also pass to No. 5. When No. 1 receives the ball from No. 2, he may also have the opportunity to pass down court for quick scoring plays.

Diagram 6-6. When the defense applies full-court pressure immediately after a basket, or a free throw is made, the offense oftentimes can offset this pressure by moving a second player out-of-bounds and making a pass to him from No. 1 behind or along the end line. This maneuver can often confuse the opposition temporarily and provide quick pass-in possibilities. The team should always try to take the ball out of the nets before it hits the floor and step out-of-bounds quickly to get the ball in play. If the defense applies strong pressure immediately, as shown in Diagram 6-6, No. 1 takes the ball from the net and steps out-of-bounds in preparation for throwing the ball in-bounds. If the defense fails to apply immediate pressure, then No. 2 could just step in-bounds and receive the pass from No. 1. If No. 1 passes the ball to No. 3, then No. 1 penetrates deep down the middle of the court and moves in back of

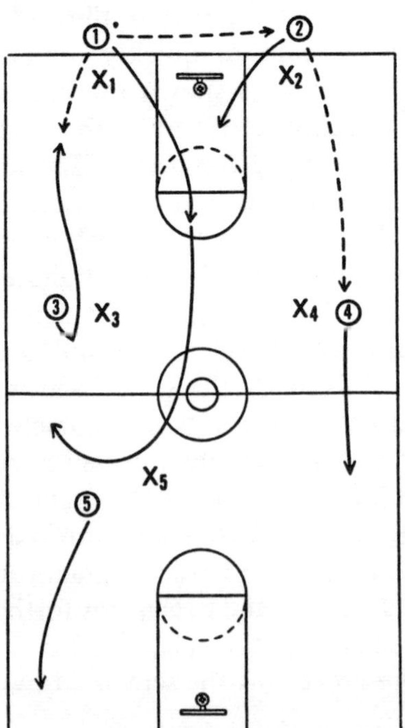

Diagram 6-6

No. 3 in the front court. No. 5 goes deep down the sideline for a possible long pass and a quick scoring opportunity, and, in this case, No. 2 would step in-bounds and trail the play.

If the ball is passed to No. 3, then No. 4, the other forward, penetrates deep down court for quick scoring possibilities. If No. 1 should pass the ball to No. 2 along the base line, and No. 2 should pass to No. 4, then No. 2 would penetrate deep down the middle of the court. No. 3 would then move down court, with No. 5 going deep to the side of the court where the pass-in is made. With No. 2 making the pass-in and penetrating down the middle, No. 1 steps in-bounds, and, by so doing, places himself in a position to take a pass from No. 4 if a pass cannot be made down the floor to Nos. 2, 3 and 5. The only limitation on passing the ball out-of-bounds outside along the end line is that the rules state the ball must be put in play and become alive within the 5-second time limit specified by the rules.

Diagram 6-7. To avoid a trap and to relieve the pressure applied by the defense when it is a tight man-to-man all the way to the end line, the offensive team will find it advantageous at times to run three players out-of-bounds behind the end line. In Diagram 6-7, No. 1 takes the ball out of the net and steps out-of-bounds in preparation

Diagram 6-7

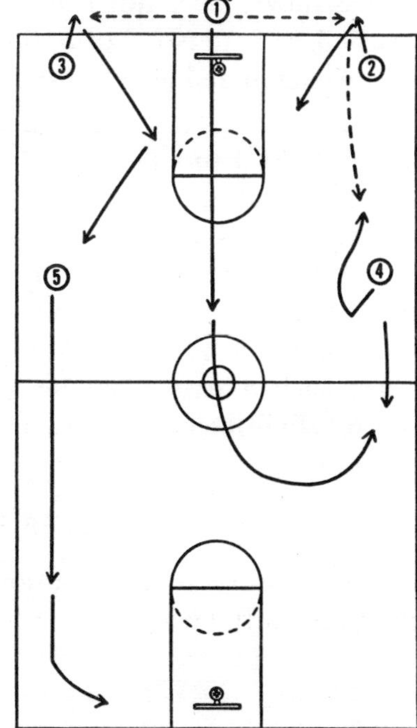

for the throw-in. When Nos. 2 and 3 see that the defensive pressure is tight and the defense is attempting to intercept the first pass-in, they both step out-of-bounds behind the end line, as shown in the diagram. No. 1 can now pass to either No. 2 or 3 behind the line, either of whom may pass the ball in-bounds. Nos. 4 and 5 move to the positions shown in the diagram and then reverse back toward the end line for possible outlet passes. After passing the ball to No. 2 or 3, No. 1 immediately steps in-bounds for a possible return pass from them. If the pass-in is made to either No. 4 or 5, then No. 1 penetrates deep down court through the middle area, and then later tails out to the side of the court where the ball is. As shown in Diagram 6-7, No. 2 passes the ball in-bounds to No. 4. No. 1 penetrates deep down the middle of the court. No. 5 goes deep down court to the opposite side of the court. No. 2 steps in-bounds for a possible return pass from No. 4, if it is necessary for him to make the pass because of defensive pressure. No. 3 moves in-bounds, first to an area near the top of the free throw circle in the back court and then later on down the right side of the court. From these positions, the team can advance the ball down court by making use of the opportunities as they arise. No. 4 may pass to No. 1 as he moves down the center of the court, or back to No. 2 or 3, who are stationed in the positions shown in the diagram . No. 4 even has the option of passing long to No. 5, who is driving for the basket, or to No. 1 after he has moved deep down along the left side of the court. If the ball is passed back to No. 2 or 3, there would also be the same possibilities of movement and penetration down court.

Diagram 6-8. If No. 1 should step in-bounds for a return pass (as shown in Diagram 6-8) after passing to No. 2 or 3 along the base line out-of-bounds, then Nos. 4 and 5 should penetrate deep down court. Nos. 2 and 3 would then move to the areas shown in the diagram to help in bringing the ball down court. No. 5 could first move toward the center of the court to receive a possible pass from No. 1. If he does not receive such a pass, then he would move down court. Several passing possibilities could present themselves as the ball is brought down court.

THE SPIN-OUT SERIES

Diagram 6-9. This offensive formation is presented as one that could be used against a full-court, man-to-man press, and at times it

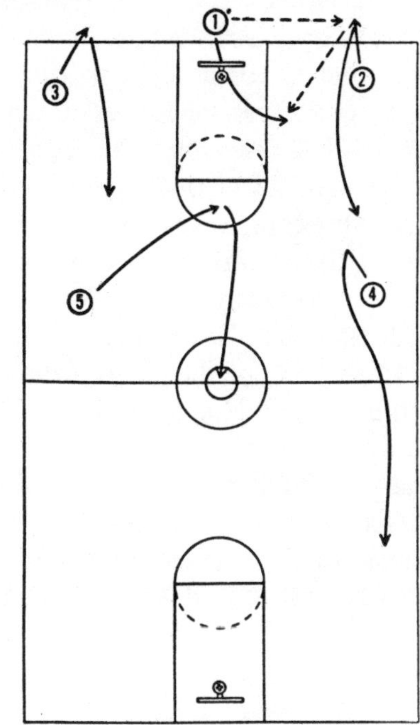

Diagram 6-8

could function against the *zone press*, especially when such a defense exerts pressure on the first pass-in or tries to intercept the first pass. No. 1, the best ball handler, takes the ball out-of-bounds. No. 2, the other guard and second best ball handler, takes a position (as shown in Diagram 6-9) in the left outer half of the free throw circle or just outside the circle to the left side. Nos. 3 and 4 line up to start their movements about two strides in-bounds and about even with the free throw line extended. No. 5, the pivot-player, and the player least likely to handle the ball, goes to a position near the center circle or deeper into the front court. To begin the play, Nos. 2 and 3 start a maneuver as if they are about to execute a cross screening move. To do this, No. 2 moves about two strides in to his left and toward the base line. He then stops and sets a screen for No. 3. No. 3 moves quickly as if to break toward No. 1 off the screen set by No. 2. Instead, just as No. 3 gets there, he changes direction by quickly turning or executing a pivot turn, and cuts down toward the middle of the court. At the same time, No. 2 executes a "pivot roll" off of the screen or fake screen he has set for No. 3 and moves toward No. 1 with the expectation of receiving a pass from him. If No. 2 is free to receive the ball, No. 1 passes it to him, as shown in the diagram. However, if No. 3 is open as he moves down court, then No. 1 should pass to him for quicker down court scoring possibilities. No. 3 may veer to the right or left as he moves down court for possible pass openings. While Nos. 2 and 3 are executing their moves, No. 4 also fakes toward the ball. After making a good, hard move toward the ball, No. 4 suddenly stops, fakes and then reverse pivots and moves either down court for openings, or, if No. 2 is not open for the pass, No. 4 may move in to receive a pass from No. 1. Diagram 6-9 shows No. 4 moving down court. In the meantime, No. 5 moves deep down court, usually to the side of the pass-in which is made by No. 1. This maneuver on the part of No. 5 usually will pull a defensive player deep down court and help open up the middle of the playing area. No. 5 should always be alert to the possibility of moving to the side court area to receive a direct pass from No. 1. This pass should always be a threat to the defense, and No. 1 must be able to throw the baseball pass at least to mid-court. Such a pass would make quick penetration possible. Diagram 6-10 gives the subsequent phases of this play.

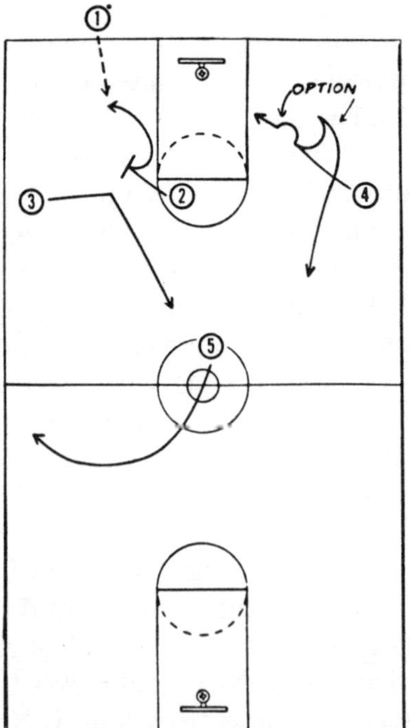

Diagram 6-9

Diagram 6-10. This diagram depicts the movements shown previously in Diagram 6-9, along with some of the follow-up possibilities. After passing in-bounds to No. 2, No. 1 steps in-bounds for a return pass from No. 2. However, do not rule out the possibility of No. 2 passing down court to No. 3, 4 or 5. After passing back to No. 1, No. 2 clears out of the area and moves down the right side of the court. He should always be alert to the possibility of doubling back to help No. 1 if help is needed. When No. 1 receives the ball, he is in a clear position to see the entire down court area, and, as he advances the ball, he takes advantage of any opportunities that might develop. He could pass to No. 3, 4 or 5 if they are open and free to receive a pass.

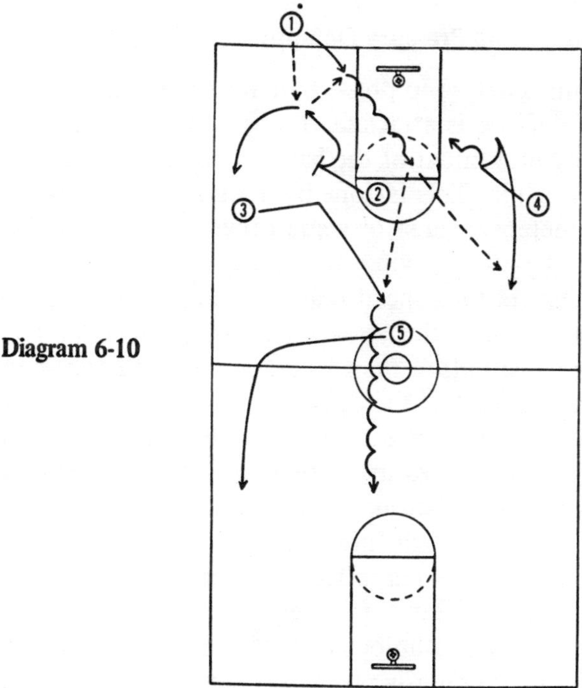

Diagram 6-10

OFFENSES AGAINST FULL-COURT ZONE PRESSING DEFENSES

The full-court pressing zone defenses present special situations that the offensive team must be prepared to meet and cope with at all times. The full-court zone press defenses include many formations and various patterns.

Kinds of Zone Press Patterns

The zone pattern may be a 1-2-1-1, a 2-2-1, a 1-2-2, a 2-1-2, a 3-2 or a 2-1-1-1, plus other formation variations. Moreover, the zones may be combined with man-to-man defenses, or they may include both man-to-man and zone principles in a combined pressure defense. It would be impossible for a team to have a different offense for every type of zone press that might be used against them in one game. Rather, the team should use an offense against the zone defense that applies certain principles, and one that, with certain slight automatic adjustments, could be effective against most zone pressure and combination defenses.

Attacking the Zone Pressure Defenses

The full-court zone pressure defense should be attacked as any other zone defense is attacked. To beat any zone defense, the team must employ movement of the ball, movement of the players and the overload principle. This is done by jamming three offensive men into a two-man defensive area or some other overload combination. This is accomplished by having the offensive players outnumber the defensive players in a specific area. Actually, the offense should be better able to apply the abovementioned principles to a full-court zone defensive situation than to a zone defense confined to the area near the basket. Part of the difficulty in defeating the full-court zone pressure defenses is brought about by the surprise that comes to the offense when the two- or three-man defensive trap on the ball handler is sprung. This usually causes the offense to make hurried or haphazard passes which are thrown into lanes covered by the defense. The defense plays for interceptions and quick turnovers, which many times result in a quick two points. The element of surprise presents a psychological dilemma for the offense. This makes it difficult for the offensive team to recover their "cool" and thereby proceed in their attack in a manner that will enable them to beat such defenses.

Another factor that causes the full-court zone pressure defenses to be so effective is the 10-second rule. Most players feel that 10 seconds is a very short time in which to move the ball across the division line, and when confronted with defensive pressure in the back court, they tend to panic, and as a result, throw passes into lanes where they are easily intercepted by the defensive players.

THE USE OF FUNDAMENTAL PRINCIPLES IN ATTACKING THE ZONE PRESS

If a team is drilled in a few fundamental principles, it should always be able to withstand the onslaughts of the zone pressure defenses—even penetrate them quickly and beat them. Every player, therefore, must be thoroughly drilled in these fundamental principles and imbued with definite ideas that are to be used in attacking the zone pressure defenses. Here are a few of the principles that must be adhered to in successfully attacking the zone press:

PRINCIPLES USED IN ATTACKING THE FULL-COURT ZONE PRESSES

1. The players should never be surprised by the defense's tactics. They should know when to expect such attacks and be ready for them.
2. A player should never begin any maneuver or movement until he turns and looks to find who is near, both offensively and defensively.
3. A player should protect the ball on all turns and at all times.
4. Every player should *eat the ball* before losing it.
5. If possession of the ball is given to a team by the official along the end line, *walk to it*. If the ball is loose, wait for the official to get it.
6. Let the official force the ball upon the player. The player in possession of the ball out-of-bounds should make sure his teammates are ready for the pass action.
7. The player in possession of the ball out-of-bounds should move along the base line (end line), if necessary to do so, in order to make a successful pass to a teammate.
8. If the surprise is complete, *call a time out*.
9. Once having crossed the division line, continue to penetrate.
10. Make the defense move. More movement is more work for the defense, and it will more likely bring about an error on their part that will make escape easier and a solution quicker.

11. If the defense provides a quick escape, take advantage of it immediately.

12. If the defense does not advance or move to meet the offense, then the offense should fake moves or get just enough movement to obtain a declaration from the defense. The offense will then know what lanes to move into for penetration or escape.

13. Make passes up and down court and avoid cross court passes.

A few important "don'ts" which can be used to good advantage in these defensive pressure situations are as follows:

1. Don't criss-cross or dribble into corners or near the sidelines.
2. Don't forget that 10 seconds is a long time.
3. Don't dribble unnecessarily.
4. Don't throw long or lob passes.
5. Don't rush–in any situation.
6. Don't become surprised, confused, excited or flustered.

TEACHING THE PLAYERS TO ATTACK THE ZONE PRESS

The players must be drilled, coached and taught to attack all zone press situations calmly, methodically and analytically. They should be conditioned to meet the zone press joyously and take great pride in beating it. Practice sessions which are conducted with this in mind will pay rich dividends by making a shambles of the pressure defenses.

Diagram 6-11. This offensive formation is being presented as the one best offensive formation to use against *all* zone press defenses. It is in reality a full-court, 1-3-1 formation and can be utilized to move the ball, to get the overload against the zone and to provide the method of escape quickly when the defense errs. This formation, with slight adjustments, can be used against all zone press defenses. As soon as it is known that the zone press is on, the offensive players move to the positions shown in the diagram. No. 1, the best ball handler, takes the ball out-of-bounds. He moves along the base line as much as necessary to throw the ball in-bounds. However, if he is right handed, his first move should be to the left side of the basket to enhance his right-handedness. No. 2, who is the other guard, should be the best player at penetrating the defense and possibly as good as No. 1 at bringing the ball down court. Nos. 3 and 4 are the forwards, and their adeptness at ball handling should be second only to Nos. 1 and 2. No. 5, the pivot player, goes to the center circle area and executes his moves from there, although his position in this particular area is optional. No. 5 may begin his moves near the center of the court, but, at times, he should take a deep court position near the offensive basket. The optional position depends upon what the defense does. If the defense is a 1-2-1-1 or a 2-1-2, perhaps his being stationed in a center position would be better, because sometimes a quick move by No. 5 to the side of the court can free him for a pass direct from No. 1. Such a pass would provide deep penetration opportunities at once and almost assure success in beating the defense in this particular situation. However, if the defense is more bunched in the back court, No. 5 should probably take the deep court position to pull at least one defensive player back as far as possible. This, in turn, would open up the middle court more and possibly make movement and penetration by Nos. 1, 2, 3 and 4 easier. If No. 5 is left open down court, the fly-pattern pass could be thrown to him for an easy two points. If No. 5 takes the position near the center of the court, he is in a position to move quickly in

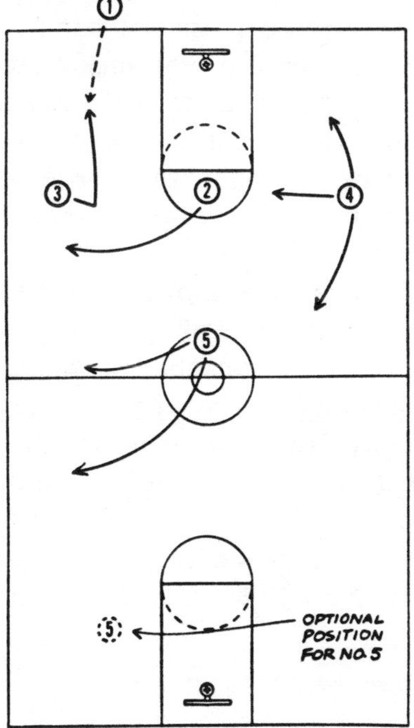

Diagram 6-11

either direction as the floor play develops. From this position, he can move to either side of the court, deep down court or even up court to provide outlet pass possibilities if they are needed. However, it usually is not expected that No. 5 would be thrust into this particular situation very often. Rather, he should try for side court or deep penetration and possibly confine his movements to the mid-court area. Diagram 5-11 depicts breaking and cutting possibilities for all the players. Later diagrams will show other possibilities in more detail.

Diagram 6-12. As explained in Diagram 6-11, as soon as it is apparent that the press is being used, the players move to the positions shown in Diagram 6-12. No. 2 takes a position near the top of the circle, with Nos. 3 and 4 near the sideline and in an area of about the free throw line extended. No. 5 goes to mid-court or to a deep position near the basket. Usually most zone presses will not contest the first pass. Therefore, No. 1 can possibly pass the ball to either one of the side position players, which in this case is No. 3 or 4. He may also pass to the middle player, No. 2. After passing the ball to No. 3, No. 1 steps in-bounds for a possible return pass. The return pass to No. 1, although not the most desirable pass, is always a possibility, and should be used when the other passing lanes are cut off by the defense. The return pass may also be used when a two-timing maneuver by the defense on the ball handler threatens to throw a tight umbrella defense around him, making it difficult for him to complete the pass. The pass-back to No. 1 can always relieve the pressure. After No. 1 passes the ball in-bounds to either player No. 2, 3 or 4, and then steps in-bounds, the plan of attack can be pretty much the free-lance type. The offense from this point on should function just like it would against any zone defense. This would be accomplished by passing and moving the ball, working for the overload situation, eliminating the prolonged dribble and penetrating quickly and as far as possible at the first available opportunity. In this particular diagram, No. 1 passes the ball to No. 3 on the right side of the court. No. 3 moves up for the release pass. No. 2 moves in behind No. 3 for a possible opening on the side of the court. After faking down court, No. 4 moves to the center area near the top of the free throw circle in the back court. No. 3 now has option pass possibilities to No. 2, 4 or 1, and even a deep pass

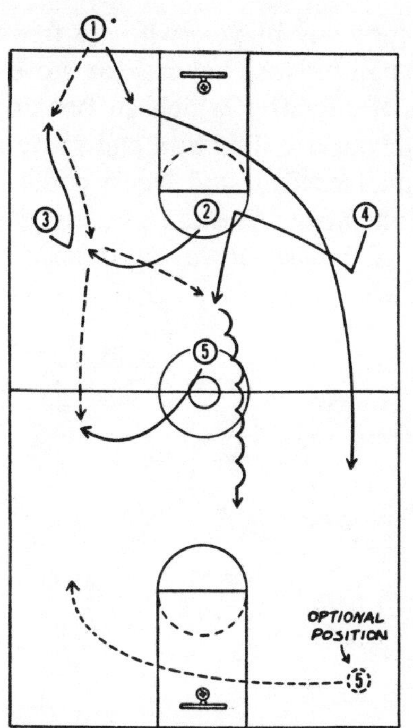

Diagram 6-12

possibility to No. 5. As soon as the pass has been made to No. 3 on the side of the court, No. 5 cuts deep down court on that side of the floor. In Diagram 6-12, No. 3 is shown passing to No. 2. No. 2 may pass to No. 5 or 4, or he may bring the ball down court himself. As soon as the second pass is made to No. 2, No. 1 breaks down court in the outside lane on the left side of the court to become part of the penetration and fast break possibility.

Diagram 6-13. One of the options always available is for No. 1 to pass in-bounds to No. 2, the player in the middle position of the front line. In this diagram, No. 1 is shown passing in-bounds to No. 2, who moves up to meet the pass. No. 2 may turn and look down court for possible passing opportunities. He may find that he can pass down court to No. 3 or 4, who are positioned on the side of the court, or to No. 5, who is stationed still deeper down court. No. 2 may also start just enough movement with a dribble to get a declaration from the defense, after which he may be able to pass off and make penetration. In Diagram 6-13, No. 2 is shown passing back to No. 1 after No. 1 steps in-bounds. No. 1 is facing down court and is in a good position to spot any players who are free to receive a pass. No. 1 could pass the ball to Nos. 3, 4 or 5, or move down court until the defense declares itself, after which an opening should be available. No. 3 or 4 could reverse direction and move back to the back-court area to help out if needed, and No. 5 could break down court in a deep penetration move. As soon as penetration is made with the second pass, No. 2 breaks down the outside lane for fast break penetration possibilities.

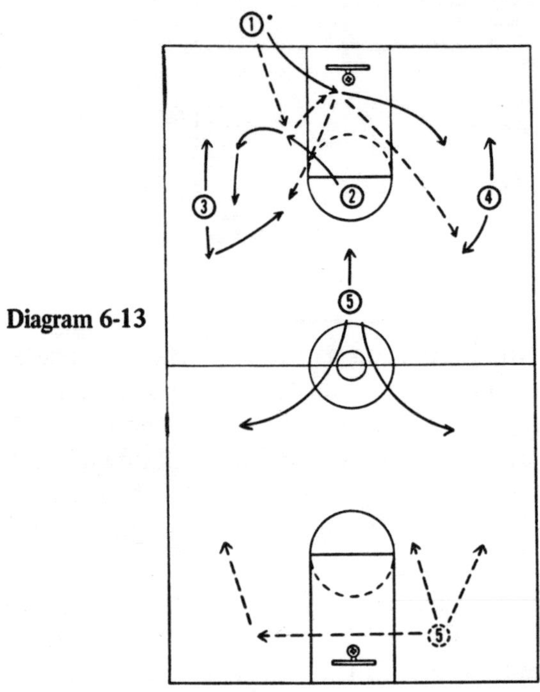

Diagram 6-13

Diagram 6-14. Many times the players using the zone press defense will position themselves and then wait for the offense to move into areas where the defense is able to two-time them. The defense will then pressure the ball handler and force him into making a turnover or a hurried pass into an interception lane. The 10-second rule is on the side of the defense, so they wait for the offensive advance. Diagram 6-14 shows the defense in a 1-2-1-1 zone defense. No. 1 passes the ball to No. 3 with a minimum of defensive pressure. The defense does not advance or declare itself but awaits offensive movement. To combat this waiting game, the offense should execute fake movements, or actually start movements to force a declaration from the defense. In Diagram 6-14, No. 3 has possession of the ball, and, being aware that the defense is waiting for the offense to commit itself, he executes a "fake" dribble move down court. As a result of this move, the defense must also declare itself and make its move.

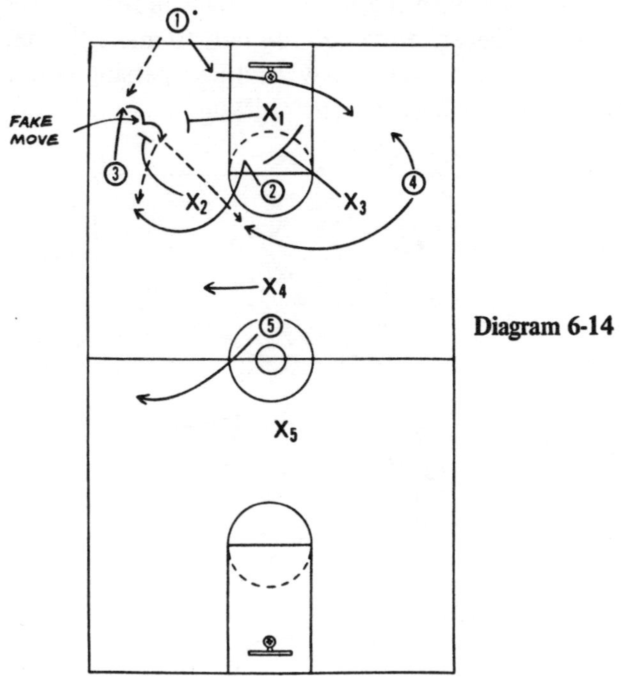

Diagram 6-14

As No. 3 moves forward using the dribble, X1 and X2 move to two-time him and X3 moves up to cut off any passes which are made near the free throw area. Dribbling, but actually faking a prolonged dribble movement, No. 3 must be careful not to allow defensive players X1 and X2 to "put a defensive umbrella over him" before he can pass the ball to a teammate. As soon as No. 3 is aware of the movement and declaration by the defense, he should be alert to any passing opportunities which he might be able to make to No. 2, who has moved to the right side, as shown in the diagram. No. 3 might also pass to No. 4, who has made penetration to the middle of the court and has positioned himself behind the defensive players. No. 3 can always pass the ball back to No. 1 for other escape routes, or possibly a deep pass to No. 5. However, it should be remembered that No. 2 must be careful not to throw or pass the ball into the lanes which are being guarded by the defense. He must analyze the defensive shifts and pass where the defense has left the open lanes. If X3 cuts off the pass to No. 4, and X4 cuts off the pass to No. 2, while X5 is coyly waiting to intercept the long pass which is to be made to No. 5, then No. 3's only alternative is to pass back to No. 1, who can then maneuver with the ball or perhaps move it to the other side of the court. However, if the defense fails to make the necessary defensive moves needed to cover any of these passing lanes, No. 3 should quickly pass the ball to the open player.

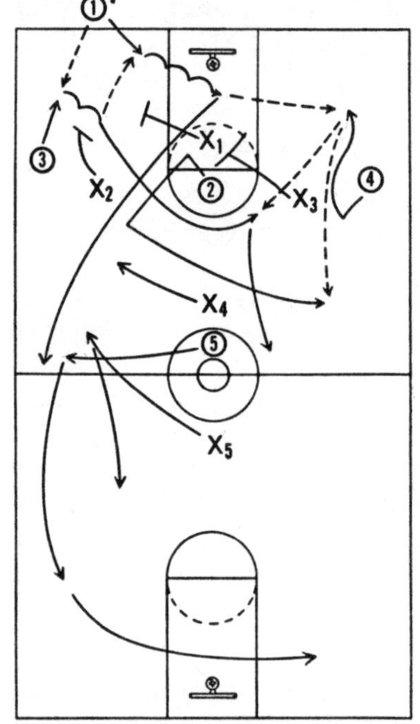

Diagram 6-15

Diagram 6-15. Diagram 6-15 illustrates some of the possibilities of the pass-back option to No. 1. No. 1 passes the ball in-bounds to No. 3 on the side of the court and then steps in-bounds for a possible return pass which might be made to him from No. 3. No. 3 executes a fake dribble drive just enough to force a declaration of movement from defensive players X1 and X2. As these two players move to double team No. 3, he notes that X4 is in position to cut off a pass to No. 2, and that X5 has moved up to cut off a pass to No. 5. Also, defensive player X3 is firmly established in the middle court area near the free throw circle and can cut off passes to that position. No. 3, after forcing some movement from X1 and X2, passes the ball back to No. 1, as shown in the diagram. No. 1 starts a short dribble move to the opposite side of the floor at this time, and attempts, if possible, to force a defensive move from X1 and X3; also, he allows No. 4 to adjust his position so that he may receive a possible outlet pass to the left side of the court. No. 1 should not delay his actions very long. He should attempt to pass the ball to No. 4 or 3, both of whom have now moved into the middle area behind the defensive players. At this point, No. 1 passes to No. 4. No. 2, as soon as he realizes that there was a pass-back to No. 1 and a possible movement to the opposite side of the court, quickly adjusts his position. When the ball is passed to No. 4, No. 2 breaks to the side of the court near the division line behind No. 4. No. 4 could possibly pass the ball to No. 2 or 3, both of whom could be in good receiving positions. No. 5, in the meantime, has gone down court and then across to the ball side of the court. When the ball is passed to No. 2 or 3, it is well on the way down court. No. 1 swings down court to the outside and opposite side of the court as quickly as possible. From this point, the players on the offensive team can penetrate with the regular fast break patterns or offense. Naturally, they will move the ball down court and work it to the middle for fast break opportunities.

Diagram 6-16. The offensive team should have no hesitation about throwing the ball all the way to the division line or farther than this if the opportunity presents itself. This means that No. 1 must be able to throw the ball with adeptness, force, speed and accuracy. In some defensive formations, the defensive players are slow to move and cover the side position near the mid-court area. If this is true, oftentimes a good baseball pass will immediately nullify the effectiveness of the press, and, as a result, will enable the offense to quickly outnumber the defense down court, and do so very easily.

In this diagram, X4 hesitates to move to the side of the court to cover No. 5 as No. 5 pulls over to the side of the court and near the division line. The reason for this hesitation is that the movement of No. 2 has caught X4's attention, and he must guard the area of the

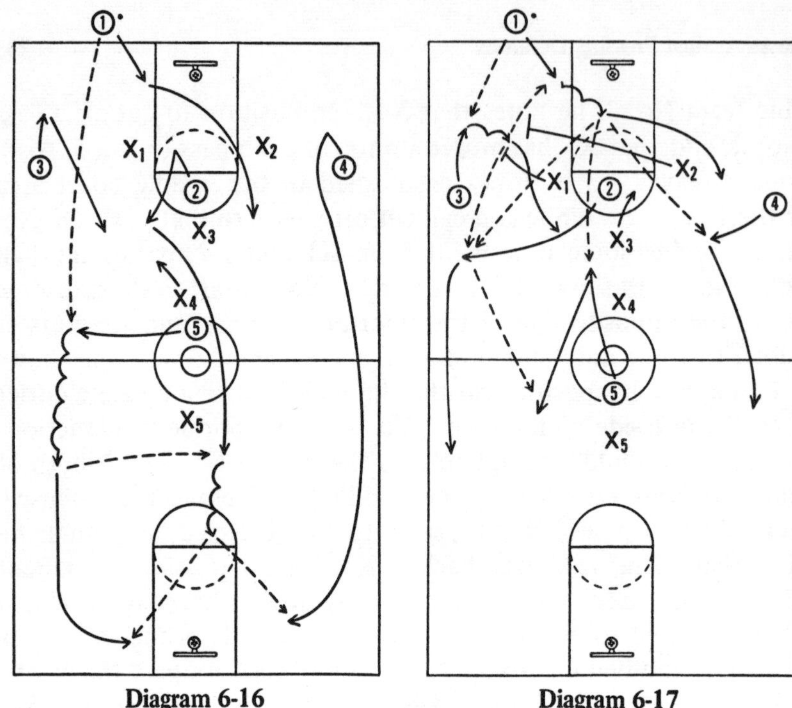

Diagram 6-16

Diagram 6-17

court in which No. 2 has positioned himself. Also, X5 has been slow to move up to cover the area. This leaves No. 5 wide open for a good pass from No. 1. From here it is an easy matter to quickly outnumber the defensive players down court as Nos. 2, 4 and 5 move into this area. If No. 5 wishes to take an optional position deep down court and near the basket, as is advised sometimes and previously mentioned, it is still possible. No. 5 can, from a deep position, move up into areas near the division line to receive passes such as those illustrated in Diagram 6-16. A pass by No. 1 even one-half to three-fourths the length of the court is always a possibility, and should be exploited if the defense shifts to make such a play possible.

Diagram 6-17. This diagram shows the multiple possibilities of bringing the ball down court using the 1-3-1 offense against a full-court zone press. In this case, the zone press is a 2-1-1-1, full-court press that concedes the first pass in-bounds. No. 1 passes the ball in-bounds to No. 3 on the side of the court. No. 3 moves or dribbles just enough to get movement and declaration from the defense. In this case, X1 and X2 move to two-time No. 3. No. 2 cuts to the side of the court behind No. 3, and now No. 3 may pass to No. 2, or back to No. 1, who has stepped in-bounds. Now No. 1 may pass to No. 4, or possibly to No. 5, or to No. 2. As a result of the pass to either No. 2 or 4, the down court possibilities are unlimited. The team can fill the fast break lanes and penetrate as far as possible. Thus, deep penetration has been accomplished quickly and the full court zone press has immediately lost its effectiveness.

THE "OFFENSE OF TRIANGLES" AGAINST THE FULL-COURT ZONE PRESSES

The "offense of triangles" is a slight variation of the previously presented 1-3-1 offense, and it is presented as an offense that can be used effectively against all types of full-court zone presses. This formation provides for a series of "triangles" which results in establishing the overload principle. It is very effective against the full-court zone press, and, at the same time, it provides for quick escape avenues for the offensive team.

Diagram 6-18. This diagram illustrates the basic alignment of the players for this formation. Nos. 1 and 2 would ordinarily be the guards, Nos. 3 and 4 the forwards and No. 5 the pivot man. If No. 1 takes the ball to the left side of the basket (his own right), the players line up as shown in the diagram. If No. 1 should take the ball out-of-bounds on the right side of the basket, then the dotted numbers show the basic player alignment, with No. 2 lined up on the

Diagram 6-18.

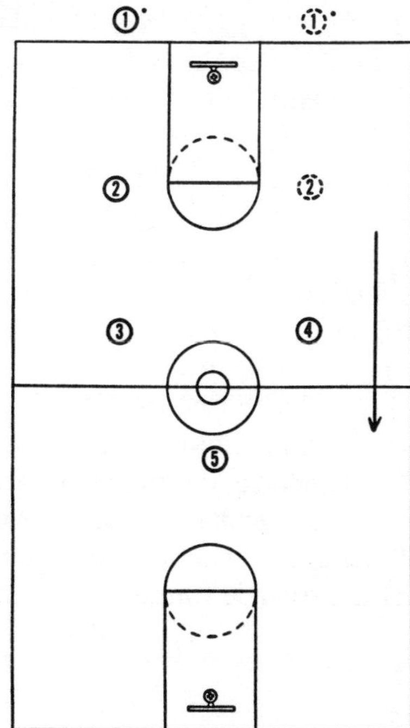

right side of the free throw lane. Actually, No. 2 could line up in the outer half of the free throw lane, and then his movement would depend upon the move made for the throw-in by No. 1.

The first pass is made from No. 1 to No. 2. Against a zone press, such a pass is usually uncontested. After making the pass-in from out-of-bounds, No. 1 immediately steps in-bounds. The following diagrams show the different moves and maneuvers which can be used by the offensive team in bringing the ball down court after the first pass-in is made from out-of-bounds by No. 1.

Diagram 6-19. In Diagram 6-19, No. 1 moves to the left side of the basket as a preliminary move before making the throw-in pass. No. 2 breaks to his left and prepares to receive the pass from No. 1. Against zone press defenses, usually a pass to this particular area is uncontested. No. 1 passes to No. 2 and then moves in-bounds for a possible return pass from No. 2. By observing the position of the players in the diagram, it is easy to discern the triangular positions formed by the players. These triangle positions are made possible by using players Nos. 1, 2 and 4 for one triangle, Nos. 2, 3 and 4 for another and Nos. 3, 4 and 5 for the third triangle. Such positioning of the players makes it possible to use overload principles against the zone presses. When No. 2 receives the ball from No. 1, he passes it to No. 3, the left wing man, if it is possible to do so. No. 3 adjusts his position as shown in the diagram to make the pass to him possible. When the pass to No. 3 is made, No. 1 breaks to the opposite side of the court and fills the outside fast break lane. No. 4 breaks to the center court area towards No. 3, so that he may receive a pass from No. 3 if it is feasible and possible to make such a pass.

No. 5 always breaks to the side of the wing player receiving the ball from No. 2, which, in this case, is No. 3. Now No. 3 has passing possibilities to No. 4 or 5. If the pass is made to No. 4, he could pass to No. 5 or 1, and the down court escape possibilities are now present. A return or safety valve pass can always be made back to No. 2 by either No. 3 or 4, if it is necessary to make such a pass. If the movement should be started on No. 4's side of the court, which is the left side, and No. 2 should pass to No. 4, then Nos. 1, 3 and 5 would move accordingly to the opposite side of the court, and the same formation and triangular movement would be situated on the opposite side of the court. The next diagram shows the down court possibilities using the triangle formations for moving the ball.

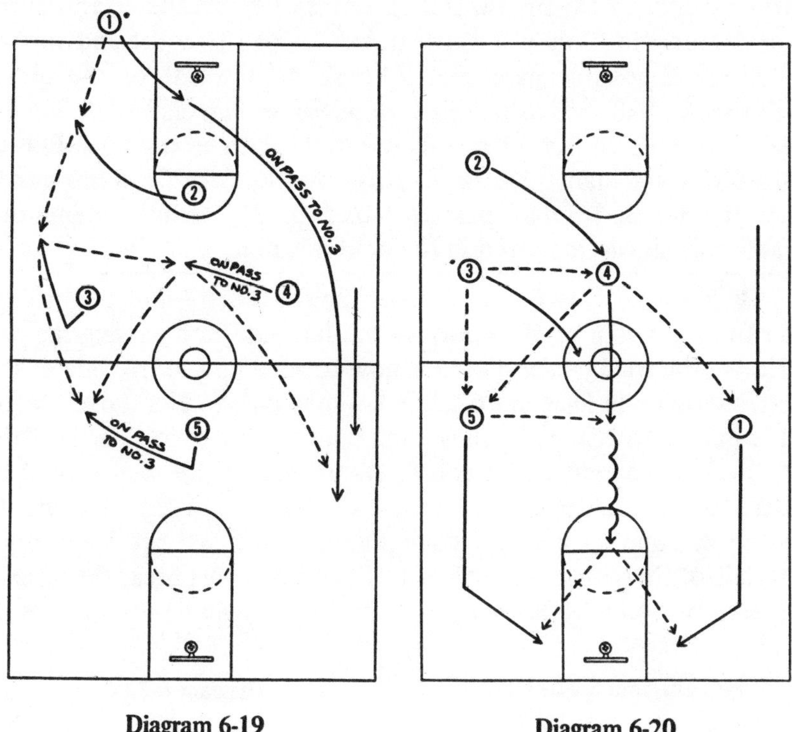

Diagram 6-19

Diagram 6-20

Diagram 6-20. Diagram 6-20 shows how No. 3, once he receives the pass from No. 2, may pass the ball to No. 4 or 5. With a pass to this position and the movement of the players as shown in the diagram, an overload situation should result which can be used against the defense. If the pass is made to No. 4, he may pass to No. 5 or 1. On the movement down court, the ball should be passed to the center lane position as soon as possible, with Nos. 4, 5 and 1 filling the fast break lanes. No. 3 trails the fast break and No. 2 provides the safety valve on defense in case of interception.

Diagram 6-21. When the pass-in is made to No. 2, as shown in Diagram 6-21, and he cannot immediately pass the ball to the wing player on his side of the court (in this case, No. 3), No. 2 makes a pass-back to No. 1. No. 1 reverses the movement of the play quickly to the other side of the court. This is done by executing a quick pass or a fast dribble and a pass to the other wing player, in this case No. 4, as shown in the diagram. When No. 4 receives the pass, No. 2

moves quickly to fill the outside fast break lane on the opposite side of the court. No. 3 cuts toward the center of the court and toward No. 4 for a possible pass. No. 5 breaks to the side of the player receiving the ball, which in this case is No. 4. Players No. 4, 3 and 5 have now formed an overload situation with a triangle. Passing possibilities are many. No. 4 may pass to No. 3 or 5. If the pass is made to No. 3, he may pass to No. 5 or 2. Possible passing and breaking situations are given in the next diagram.

Diagram 6-22. With No. 1 reversing the direction of the offense from the right side of the court to the left side, and passing the ball to No. 4, the triangle formation is now formed on the left side of the court, as shown in Diagram 6-22. No. 4 may pass to No. 3 or 5. If the ball is passed to No. 3, he may then pass to either No. 5 or 2. If the fast break movement down court gets underway, the ball should be moved to the middle lane as soon as possible, and the play should proceed as soon as possible from there. If the fast break does not materialize, then once the ball is in the front court area, the normal offensive half-court offense against the defense can be set up. Nos. 3,

Diagram 6-21

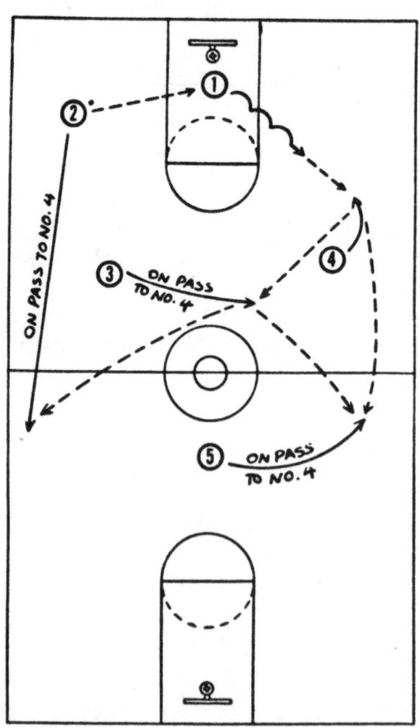

Diagram 6-22

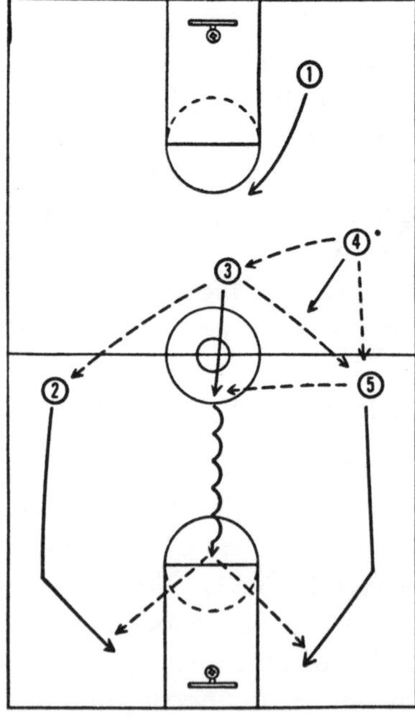

5 and 2 lead the fast break, with No. 4 trailing the play and No. 1 being used as the safety valve for defensive protection.

OPTIONAL MOVEMENT OF PLAYERS IN THE "OFFENSE OF TRIANGLES"

There are many player movements that are automatic in nature that can be learned and used for this offense. They will not only make the offense more effective, but they will also help the players to know what to do at all times. These movements take into consideration most of the passing situations not shown in the diagrams previously described. If No. 1 (who is taking the ball out-of-bounds) should pass directly in-bounds to one of the wing players (who in this case would be either No. 3 or 4) instead of passing to No. 2 as is shown in the diagrams, the following principles would dictate the movement of his teammates.

For Nos. 1 and 2

1. The player passing the ball to the wing player (either No. 3 or 4), now becomes the safety man.
2. The nonpasser to the wing player (either No. 3 or 4) breaks to the outside lane opposite the ball for fast break possibilities.

For Nos. 3 and 4

1. These players should hold their respective original positions until the direction of movement is decided by Nos. 1 and 2. The players should then break for openings on the same side of the court in which the movement is made.
2. The weak-side wing player should break toward the center of the court and toward his wing teammate who is receiving the ball.
3. The wing player receiving the pass from either No. 1 or 2 becomes the trailer on the fast break, once he passes off to another player.
4. The wing player who moves to the center of the court in forming the triangle always fills the center lane on the fast break pattern down court.

For No. 5

1. No. 5 should always hold his original position until one of the wing players (No. 3 or 4) has received the ball. Then he breaks to

the side of the court where the ball is, so that a passing triangle can be formed using the two wing players, Nos. 3 and 4.

2. On the fast break, No. 5 always fills the outside lane on his side of the court.

The "offense of triangles" can be an effective automatic overload offense that will provide safety features and quick escape routes against all types of zone pressing defenses. It is simple, effective, easy to learn and, by applying and learning the principles and rules established for its use, it should become so automatic to the players that they should never be surprised or upset by the pressure of having to cope with "pressing defenses."

OFFENSES AGAINST HALF-COURT PRESSING DEFENSES

The half-court pressing defenses may be man-to-man, zone, combinations or special trap plays. Whatever they are, the offense must be prepared to meet this special situation as they approach the division or center court line.

POINTS OF ATTACK BY THE HALF-COURT PRESSING DEFENSES

Some of the half-court pressing defenses meet the offense just behind the division line or right on the line. Other defenses meet the offense at the court division line and then advance two to three strides into the back-court area to begin their attack. Still others advance to a point in the back court which makes the defense more of a three-fourths court press than anything else. Regardless of the point of first attack, the offense must never allow itself to be caught unprepared for this eventuality and never be without the necessary plays to combat it and nullify its effectiveness.

There is a psychological advantage that the defense has in its favor by waiting to attack at mid-court or near the division line as the offensive team approaches this area. The defense, waiting here, allows the offense to consume time—part of the 10-second time limit imposed upon the offense in bringing the ball into the front court. Now the moment of truth has arrived. They must advance across the division line within the 10-second time limit. Part of the time has gone. The defensive attack at this particular time gives them the feeling that they cannot get the ball into the front court in the required 10 seconds. As a result they panic. A pass is made into defensive lanes and it is intercepted–thus the primary reason for so much success with the half-court presses.

Diagram 6-23. If a straight man-to-man defense is used as the half-court pressure defense, it would be much easier to use the regular offense and attack it in the usual offensive style, except that the offense advances up court to meet the attack. As shown in Diagram 6-23, the center, No. 5, or the forwards, Nos. 3 and 4, move up court for release passes, timed, of course, to coincide with the attacking pressure of the defense. If the center moves to a point near the mid-court area to receive a release pass, as shown in Diagram 6-23, then one of the forwards should reverse his direction and do a base-line cut, as shown in the diagram by No. 3. This type of reverse move will provide opportunities for the cutter to receive a pass, and it will help to keep the defense honest. If a release pass can be made to either the center or one of the forwards, the pressure exerted by the defense at the division or center line will be minimized.

Diagram 6-23

Diagram 6-24. There are two types of traps applied by half-court pressure defenses that the offensive team must learn to avoid. One is the center trap, whereby the defense drives the player advancing the ball into the middle lane and then double teams or quickly traps him, causing him to commit a turnover. The other trap is the sideline trap. Diagram 6-24 shows a type of center trap. No. 1, the player bringing the ball up court, is forced by X1 to dribble into the middle lane. No. 2's defensive player, X2, is nearby, and, knowing that No. 1 is to be forced into the middle lane, quickly shifts with X1 to trap and two-time No. 1. No. 1 will now be in trouble if he delays his release pass to a teammate too long. Usually his best release pass is to No. 2, who in this case has held back a little when he saw his defensive player, X2, making an overshift to the inside to help X1 in his efforts to set the trap on No. 1. This type of pass to No. 2 in this particular situation should enable No. 2 to advance quickly across the division line. It would be better, however, if No. 3 or 5 could advance quickly up court to receive a release pass from No. 1 before the trap can be applied. If at all possible, No. 1 should pass the ball to either of them because this provides for a quicker release pass. If No. 3 comes up for the release pass, No. 5

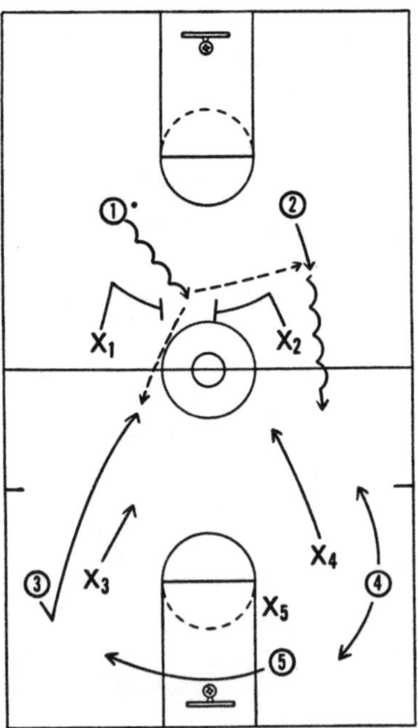

Diagram 6-24

should drive the base line. If No. 5 should move up court to receive the release pass, then No. 3 should drive the base line. In this type of situation No. 4 should free-lance, but he should always be prepared to clear out of the area if No. 1 executes a release pass to No. 2, so that the ball can be brought up on the same side of the court.

Diagram 6-25. Diagram 6-25 shows another way to avoid the center trap. It also depicts several offensive moves which the players should try and avoid. For example, as No. 1 is forced to the middle, No. 2 should *never* cross in behind him for a release pass. Such a cross movement would present an ideal situation for the two defensive players, X1 and X2, to move in and use a two-timing attack on No. 2 as he receives a pass from No. 1. A quick two-timing situation could cause real trouble for the offensive team at this particular point of attack. An escape possibility is shown, however. As soon as No. 2 notes X2 moving toward No. 1 to help X1 in a trap move on No. 1, he quickly moves in behind and down court from X2. No. 1 should be able to give No. 2 a release pass in the area shown in the diagram and thus solve the pressure placed on No. 1 by X1 and X2. It will help a great deal for either No. 5 or 3, or both, to move to the mid-court area at this same time to help Nos. 2 and 1,

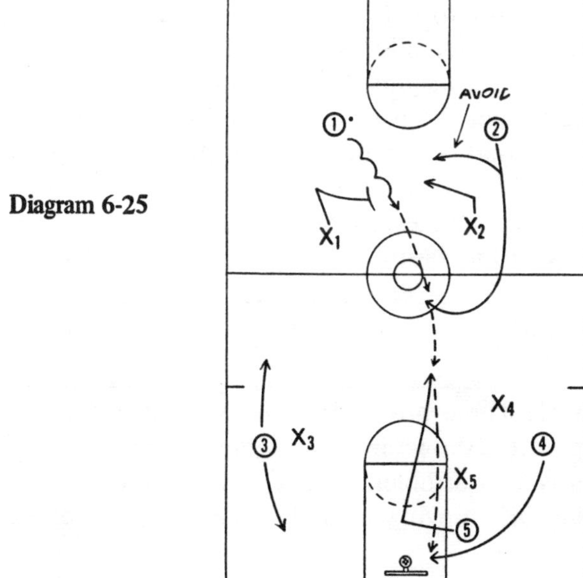

Diagram 6-25

by being available for release passes from them. If No. 2 receives the pass from No. 1, then No. 4 should drive the base line. A pass from No. 2 to No. 5 to No. 4 could bring an easy two points and a complete solution to the defense.

Diagram 6-26. Diagram 6-26 shows the sideline trap play that is frequently used by half-court pressing defenses. Strong zone principles are brought into play in the use of this defense. The defense may start out looking very much like a straight man-to-man, and then suddenly a switch is made and the zone press principles are applied. As No. 1 approaches the division line, X1 advances to meet him and turns him to the outside with an attempt to trap him near the division line and the sideline. As soon as X1 forces No. 1 to move in the direction desired, X1 then hustles to head off his advance and force No. 1 to stop his dribble near the sideline, as shown in the diagram. Once No. 1 starts for the sideline, X2 and X4 act together and in unison. X2 moves over quickly to help X1 two-time and trap No. 1. X4 leaves his guarding position on No. 4 and moves up quickly to the mid-court area in an attempt to intercept any cross court passes that might be made by No. 1 to No. 2. X4 will also be alert to intercept any other passes which might be made to players in this area by No. 1 in his frantic efforts to get rid of the ball. While this maneuver is taking place, X3 is playing for interception of all passes that might be made to No. 3. X5 is playing the area shown in the diagram in an effort to cut off any passes that might be made to No. 5. The defense has actually two-timed No. 1 in a trap move, and while covering the other players, has left No. 4 open. However, he is the player farthest from the ball; to get the ball to him from No. 1 requires a long pass that X5 could intercept. If X5 plays his position correctly, he should be able to move in either direction for this interception. Such a long pass by No. 1 while he is being pressured and trapped quite often results in a bad pass which can easily be intercepted.

The next diagram will give some possible solutions to this outside trap.

Diagram 6-27. Three possibilities are suggested for combating the outside trap as it is shown in this diagram. The first one is that as soon as X1 turns the dribbler, No. 1, to the outside, No. 2, his teammate, seeing X2 moving in and attempting to set the trap, quickly drops back and to his right for a quick release pass from No. 1 (see Option A). With X2 out of position, No. 2 can now advance quickly across the division line. If X4 has made his move simultaneously with X2 to the division line area, this would provide a good opportunity for No. 2 to pass the ball to No. 4, who is cutting toward the basket.

The second possibility is one in which No. 2, as soon as he realizes this move is being made, quickly circles in behind the intended trap on No. 1 to place himself in an excellent position for a release pass from No. 1 (see Option B). This same type of move which illustrates the center trap is shown in Diagram 6-25. This move must be made quickly, before No. 1 is pressured in the umbrella of a two-timing trap. (Then it can be too late to make the pass. He can make his release pass much easier before the full pressure of the trap is applied.) Receiving a pass here, No. 2 could possibly pass to No. 4 on a base-line move or pass in to No. 5 or 3.

The third possibility is one in which a pass by No. 1 is made to either No. 3 or 5. If No. 3 or 5 can beat his defensive man up court and position himself to receive a release pass from No. 1, then this

Diagram 6-26

Diagram 6-27

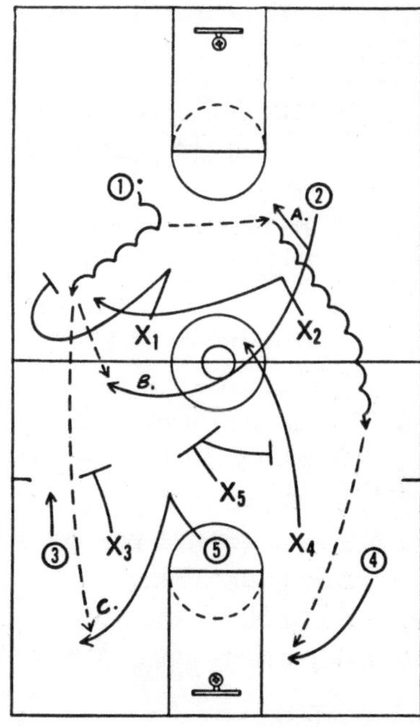

should be done. However, if Nos. 3 and 5 both fake toward the ball and draw defensive players X3 and X5 into high court positions, either one of them could then reverse the area shown in the diagram (see Option C). Such a pass would penetrate and solve the defense at once.

Diagram 6-28. The offense can expect to meet the half-court zone presses at any time and must be prepared to meet them successfully. The defense may position itself in any of the various floor formations. In Diagram 6-28, a half-floor, 1-2-2 defense is set up, and it is a common one. Against these various floor defenses, penetration in the mid-court area, just past the division line, is important. This diagram shows No. 1 bringing the ball down court. As the defense moves to two-time the ball handler, No. 5 breaks out to the mid-court area near the sideline on the dribbler's right. No. 4 fakes in toward the center of the court. He then breaks up court to a high post position in the mid-court area and near the division line circle. No. 5 or 4 should be open for a pass, and the best pass option is to No. 4. When No. 1 passes the ball to No. 4, No. 2 should break down the left side of the court, which would place No. 4 on his right as he moves toward the basket. A "sucker" option pass to No. 2 from No. 4 can then be made, and No. 2 might be able to drive all the way to the basket for a score. A pass could also be made to No. 3 or 5, depending upon the defensive shift.

Diagram 6-29. By playing the pivot-post man deep along the base line against the half-court zone presses, some additional scoring opportunities may be realized. At least one of the defensive players will have to play deeper to cover No. 5, thus making it easier to get penetration in the mid-court area near the division line. In Diagram 6-29, No. 5 plays deep near the basket. As No. 2 brings the ball down court to his left, No. 3 breaks in from the opposite side of the court to the mid-court area. As this move is made, Nos. 1 and 4 also move as shown in the diagram. No. 2 should be able to pass to No. 3, 1 or 4. If X2 moves in to cut off the pass to No. 3, No. 2 could pass to No. 1, as shown in the diagram. If No. 3 is open and the pass is not cut off by defensive players X2 or X4, then No. 2 should pass to him. He, in turn, has passing possibilities to No. 1 on the "sucker" move, or to Nos. 4 and 5, if they are available to him. If the defense cuts off passing lanes to Nos. 3 and 1, certainly No. 4 should be open. A pass to No. 4 could bring a quick opening to No. 5 along the base line, as could a pass to either No. 1 or 3. If passing lanes to Nos. 1, 3 and 4 are all blocked, then certainly No. 5 should have the area near the basket all to himself, and a pass to him from No. 2 in this situation is not impossible. This could bring a quick and certain two-point conversion. The defense by necessity must hold back a player to cover this area, and by so doing will leave openings that make penetration in the mid-court area possible.

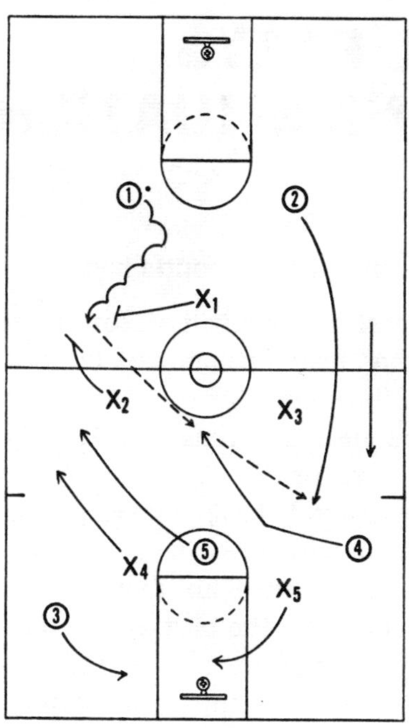

Diagram 6-28

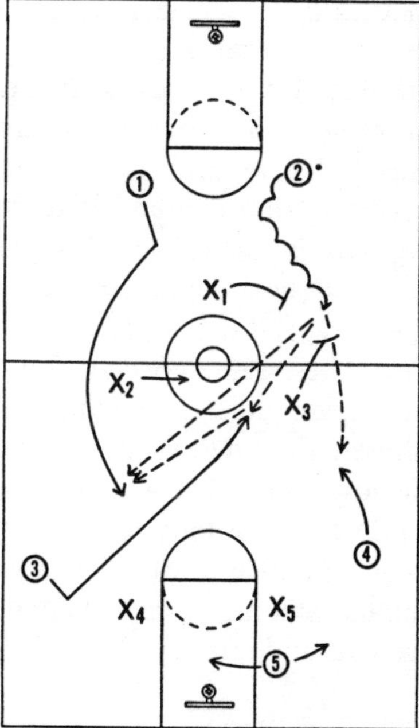

Diagram 6-29

SEVEN

SPECIAL PLAYS FOR LAST SECOND SITUATIONS

The Coach's Attitude Toward the Use of Last Second Plays

During the course of a basketball season, there are many games that are decided in the closing seconds of the contest. This, of course, results in many thrilling contests that are exciting to players and spectators alike. There are many times, however, when the games that go down to the wire or to the final gun can be decided by the coach if he has provided his players with the necessary plays or maneuvers which will give them "the winning edge." There are those coaches, however, who feel this is not necessary and contend that extra effort on the part of the players is all that is needed in this particular situation and in this type of circumstance. These coaches can explain their losses by stating that the players did not give that extra effort, and as a consequence they lost. These same coaches can then shrug off the loss using this type of explanation. The truth may be, however, that such a coach is himself floundering in a sea of uncertainty and lacks the knowledge of how to combat and solve such a problem He does not know what to do and is totally unprepared to meet this type of situation. It has been said that football is a game of inches, feet and yards. Using a similar axiom, it can then be said that "basketball is a game of seconds and minutes."

The Players' Preparation for Last Second Plays

The battle against time available for practice is always a serious coaching problem. How can the coach prepare the team for the execution of the fundamental aspects of the game as well as teach them the regular offenses and defenses they must learn and master, and yet still have enough time to practice all the special play situations that might occur during the course of a game. In reality, it can be part of the total learning process which the players are subjected to so that they can understand the total game procedure. With the coach performing a total teaching process, he will of necessity have to plan his practices and scrimmages carefully to include these special play situations. They are of tremendous importance to the outcome of the closely contested game which can be won by a timely basket in the last second of play.

Purpose of Special Last Second Plays

The special situations that arise during a game are numerous. To discuss and illustrate all these situations would be impossible and impractical. Therefore, the purpose of this chapter is to present some proven scoring plays that will provide the team with the offensive punch needed to meet and combat some of the most frequently occurring special offensive situations arising in the closing seconds and minutes of a game when points are needed.

There are also many defensive situations that arise during the waning moments of the game which require special plays. When the team is behind, with the score close in the crucial final phases of the game, and the opponents have possession of the ball, the team's defense literally becomes the offense. They must be able to go after the ball and gain possession of it. This is a part of the defensive coaching of the game and is not to be included as a part of "special plays for last second situations."

The Coach's Responsibility in Preparing for Last Second Plays

The coach should install fundamental guidelines and principles to be used in preparing special plays for last second situations. The plays selected should be simple and not be those which are beyond the comprehension of the players or their ability to execute them. The plays selected not only should be simple but also few in number. They should, however, be those which will prepare the team for the special situations that may arise during a game.

Selection of Last Second Plays

Plays should be selected for use in those situations which will utilize the talents of the players as much as possible. If the players possess unusual talents, then this ability should be utilized in every way possible. The plays which are to be selected should have options and provide for team balance so as to not be "one-shot affairs." Some special identity in the use of the plays selected for these situations should be used. These identities could be names, numbers, color calls, verbal calls, signals, etc. This would help bring about the identification and recognition of the play which would be associated with a given situation. Each team can usually work out a personalized system which would be most advantageous to it. This identification will vary with each team.

PLAYS FOR LAST 1- TO 3- SECOND SITUATIONS

Invariably at one time or another during the course of the game, a team will find itself placed in a situation whereby the clock shows from 1 to 3 seconds left in the game. The team has possession of the ball and needs one successful shot that will result in a victory or tie the score. Can this be accomplished? It can not only be done, but with as much as 3 seconds left on the clock, a team can many times obtain more than one shot–sometimes two or three shots, if the time is used properly and the correct plays and tactics are utilized.

Getting the shot is one thing. Converting it into a score is another. It is important to realize, therefore, that before a conversion can be made, the shot must be obtained. Any basketball team that is well coached will make every effort to approach the final moments of the game with two or more time outs left at their disposal. Regardless of how well the players know and have rehearsed the play to be used, each player's assignment should be gone over again at this time so that everything is absolutely clear to the players, and everyone is sure of his particular part in the execution of play and the specific assignment he is expected to perform.

The players should be coached to take these time outs when the ball can be awarded out-of-bounds at a point that will be to their advantage when play resumes.

Some of the plays given elsewhere in this book may be used for 1- to 3- second situations when a basket is needed for the tie or win. For instance, in Chapter 1 some of the out-of-bounds plays along the offensive end line could be used as scoring plays. The reader can review and select plays which will best serve his needs and adequately fit the situation. There are several such plays presented in previous chapters. These plays may be used in situations where the ball is awarded to the team out-of-bounds after a time out at a specific position on the court. For example, moving the ball the length of the court in 1 to 3 seconds is very difficult. Therefore, in this type of situation, the team should try to take the time out so that the ball will be awarded out-of-bounds in the front court, or at least no farther away than the "center division line" when play is resumed. By so doing, valuable seconds will be saved at a time when they are desperately needed.

Diagram 7-1. Diagram 7-1 shows a play that is designed primarily to get the "one shot" which the offensive team might find necessary to obtain in a very short time. The team has taken their "time out" and will have the ball awarded out-of-bounds for the resumption of play. The play will be more successful if the ball is in the front court area long the sideline. It could, however, be awarded out-of-bounds at mid-court or even in the back court. An accurate, long pass could be successful from this position. The players line up as shown in the diagram with No. 1 taking the ball out-of-bounds. No. 2 lines up in the mid-court area. No. 5, the pivot-post player, positions himself in the outer half of the free throw circle. Nos. 3 and 4, the forwards, line up as shown in the diagram. No. 4 is the best "one-shot" situation player on the team. When the play starts, No. 5 moves down the right side of the free throw lane and over three or four strides to set a screen for No. 4. No. 4 fakes out toward the ball and then breaks in behind No. 5 to take advantage of the screen. At the same time that No. 5 starts his move, No. 2 fakes toward the ball and then breaks toward the basket and sets a screen just below the free throw line, as shown in the diagram. No. 4, after cutting past the screen set by No. 5, now cuts over the screen set by No. 2. This should free No. 4 for a pass from No. 1, right at and just to the side of the free throw line extended. No. 4 should be free to take the shot and make the much needed conversion. No. 3 fakes a move toward the ball as if to receive a pass from No. 1. He then reverses and moves to a rebound position on the left side of the basket. Nos. 2 and 5 also move quickly to rebound positions for possible second and third rebound shots. No. 4 should be able to get off a shot in 1 second. Three seconds gives him plenty of time, and, in fact, a good possibility for a second and third attempt off the rebound if he should miss the first shot attempt.

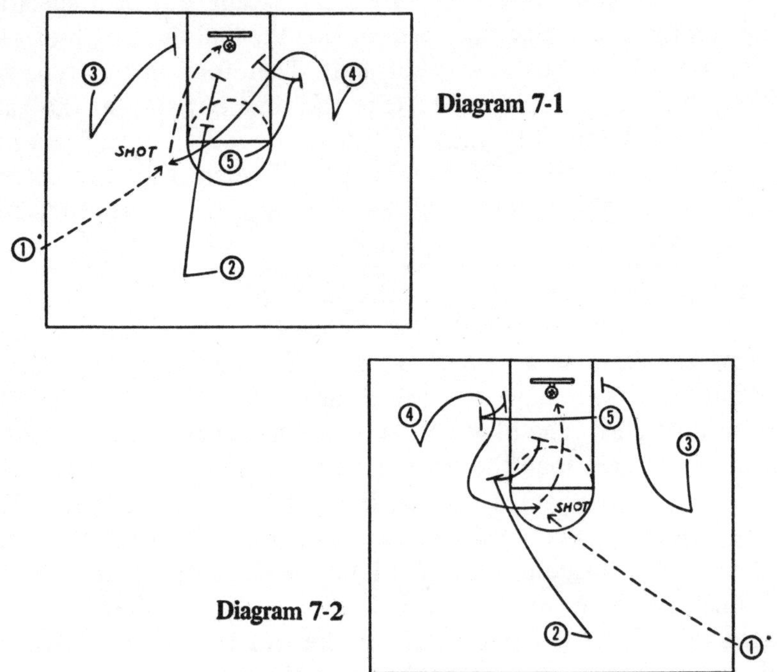

Diagram 7-1

Diagram 7-2

In this play, if executed properly, No. 4 will nearly always be open to receive a pass near the free throw line area. However, where more than 1 second of time is left and No. 4 is not open, it is entirely possible for No. 1 to pass the ball to No. 3, who may in turn relay the ball to No. 4 or attempt the shot himself. For this reason, No. 3 should be the second best shooter. If the defense should "scramble" and rush No. 4 on his shot, he may fake as to shoot and then relay the ball to No. 5, 2 or even 3 for easier shots in situations where enough time is left to execute this maneuver.

Diagram 7-2. The play shown in Diagram 7-2 is very much the same as in Diagram 7-1. The play can be executed from both sides of the court. However, the positioning of No. 5 and the screening of Nos. 2 and 5 are slightly different. Also, No. 1 is shown taking the ball out-of-bounds at mid-court.

To begin the play, No. 5 stations himself lower and nearer the basket, as shown in the diagram. To set the screen for No. 4, No. 5 moves across the free throw lane. No. 2 also moves toward the basket and to the left side of the free throw lane to set his screen for No. 4. With No. 4 cutting behind and below No. 5 and over and behind No. 2, it gives him a quick double screen and definitely should free him right at the free throw line area for a good shot attempt. The pass from No. 1 should be accurate and timed just as No. 4 comes off the screen set by No. 2. Again, Nos. 5, 2 and 3 follow for rebound possibilities. From this play, it is possible for a team to obtain as many as four shots within a 3-second time limit.

Diagram 7-3. A slightly different version of the play presented in Diagrams 7-1 and 7-2 is shown in Diagram 7-3. The players line up as shown in the diagram, just as they did in Diagram 7-1. When the play is ready to begin, Nos. 3, 5 and 2 all move to the left side of the free throw lane to form a shoulder-to-shoulder triple screen. No. 4 fakes deep underneath the basket and behind the screen, but then quickly reverses his direction and moves up and over the top of the screen to receive the ball from No. 1 on a long pass. No. 4 should receive this pass at the free throw line or in that immediate area. Nos. 2, 3 and 5 roll out of the screen to be in position for rebounds, as shown in the diagram. If the defense scrambles, No. 4 can execute other options which are available to him, if he has time and it is feasible for him to do so. One option to the play which can be executed effectively is to have No. 4 fake a move high over the triple screen and then reverse his direction and move just underneath the basket and receive a long pass from No. 1, which will provide him with an easier shot near the basket. If, in the defensive scramble, the pass to No. 4 should be cut off, then Nos. 2, 5 and 3 can quickly roll out of the screen toward No. 1 and be in a position for a possible pass and a quick shot at the basket. It should be remembered that the time on the clock does not start until the ball touches a player in-bounds; No. 1 then has 5 seconds before he needs to pass the ball in-bounds.

Diagram 7-4. The play shown in Diagram 7-4 has been devised to utilize the special talents of players on the team and to take advantage of extreme height if such players are available. This play could be used as a good out-of-bounds play at any time during the game, but, with a time situation of from 1 to 3 seconds left in the game, and with the ball awarded out-of-bounds at this particular location, it could pay handsome dividends. Nos. 4 and 5 line up in a V position with the inside feet together. They face away from the basket and partially face each other, with their backs to No. 1. They hold up their outside hands as a target for No. 1. (If the defense demands a position between them, they must comply.) No. 1 can toss a high lob pass to either one of them, and they can move immediately toward the basket or execute a jump shot from this position. No. 1 can also toss the ball against the back of one of them and then quickly step in-bounds to retrieve it for a shot. He will need at least 3 seconds for this maneuver, however, since the time will start as soon as the ball touches a player in-bounds. Nos. 2 and 3 line

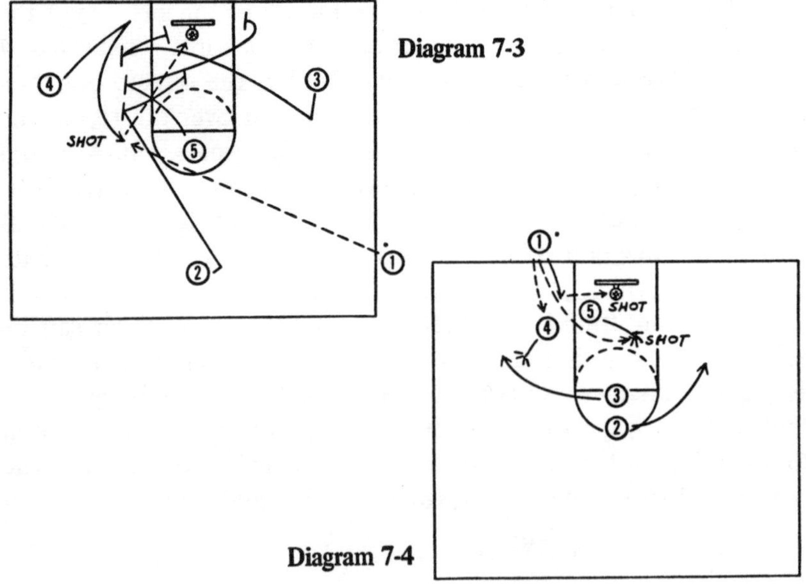

Diagram 7-3

Diagram 7-4

up in a vertical position as shown in the diagram, and, on the signal, one breaks to the right and the other to the left. The ball can be passed to either one of them if the other passing opportunities do not materialize.

PLAYS FOR 3- TO 5- SECOND SITUATIONS

If there are 3 to 5 seconds left in the game and the team is 1 or 2 points behind, then the situation is not quite as desperate as when there is only 1 to 3 seconds left. If there are from 3 to 5 seconds left in the game, then there is ample time for a pass, or perhaps even a screening maneuver, before the shot needs to be taken. In this length of time, it is possible to move the ball the full length of the court and obtain a shot before time runs out. It will take about 1 second for each pass or maneuver in this type of situation. However, it is difficult to ascertain how much time it will take because much will depend upon the defensive tactics of the opposition. Even though the same play may be used repeatedly, it will be impossible to use the same amount of time on each occasion. It is necessary, therefore, that every player know every move he has to make and exactly how it is to be made.

Diagram 7-5. Two passes and a maneuver consume just about the 3- to 5-second time limit. The players line up as shown in Diagram 7-5, with No. 1 taking the ball out-of-bounds. As the play starts, No. 2 fakes toward the basket to shake his defensive man, and then moves toward No. 1 to receive the pass from him in the mid-court area. After passing the ball to No. 2, No. 1 moves in-bounds and toward No. 5, who is stationed in the top half of the free throw circle. When he reaches his area alongside of No. 5, they both move quickly and simultaneously to the area just to the left of the free throw lane where they stop shoulder-to-shoulder to set a double screen for No. 4. When the play starts, No. 4 moves along the base line toward the basket, timing his move to coincide with the moves of Nos. 1 and 5. Just as Nos. 1 and 5 set the double screen, No. 4 reverses his direction and moves back around the screen to receive a pass from No. 2. No. 2, after receiving the pass-in from No. 1, begins a dribble toward the left side of the court so as to be able to pass the ball to No. 4 as No. 4 comes off the double screen set by Nos. 1 and 5. No. 3 fakes toward No. 1 in an attempt to receive the ball, and then reverses his direction and moves back toward the basket where he stations himself in a favorable rebound position. When No. 4 receives the pass from No. 2, he should be able to get off a good percentage shot. Nos. 1, 5 and 3 should also place themselves in good rebound positions. They should be able to obtain excellent positions for follow-up or rebound shots. If the defense should "scramble" to stop No. 4 on his shot attempt, then No. 4 may pass the ball off to either No. 1, 3 or 5. No. 4 may even have time to dribble away from the screen, and as a result obtain a better shot.

Diagram 7-6. Diagram 7-6 shows another play which can be used within the time limit of 3 to 5 seconds. The players line up as shown in the diagram. The play starts much the same as the one shown in Diagram 7-5. No. 2 shakes loose from his defender for the pass-in from No. 1. Nos. 4 and 5 move simultaneously to set a shoulder-to-shoulder double screen just to the right side of the lane, as shown in the diagram. No. 1 fakes a cut to the basket after he has passed the ball to No. 2 and then drives close behind the double screen set by Nos. 4 and 5. No. 3, after faking a deep drive along the base line and toward the basket, moves back toward the sideline to receive a pass from No. 2, who has executed a dribble to be in a position to execute a pass to No. 3. No. 3 now passes the ball to No. 1 just as he comes off the double screen. No. 1 should be able to move in for a good shot. If the defense "scrambles" in an attempt to stop No. 1 from shooting, then No. 3 may be able to pass the ball to either No. 4 or 5, both of whom might be left open as a result of the defensive scramble. This would enable either one of them to obtain a good shot. If these maneuvers do not result in No. 1, 4 or 5 getting a good percentage shot, then No. 3 could always take the shot, since he is within excellent shooting range.

Diagram 7-7. Diagram 7-7 describes a play that can be executed well within the 3-second time limit. However, it could be safer to use this play within the 3- to 5-second time limit. No. 1 has the ball out-of-bounds at the center court division line. Nos. 2, 5 and 3 move to form a triple screen near the top or outer half of the free-throw circle, as shown in the diagram. No. 4 breaks toward the ball and then swings around the screening players, Nos. 2, 3 and 5. He should cut as close to them as possible. As No. 4 clears the screens, he should be free to receive a pass near the basket area. No. 1 can now pass him the ball deep underneath the basket for an easy two pointer. An option to the play is possible by having No. 2, as soon as No. 4 cuts past him on the drive, break toward No. 1 and the ball.

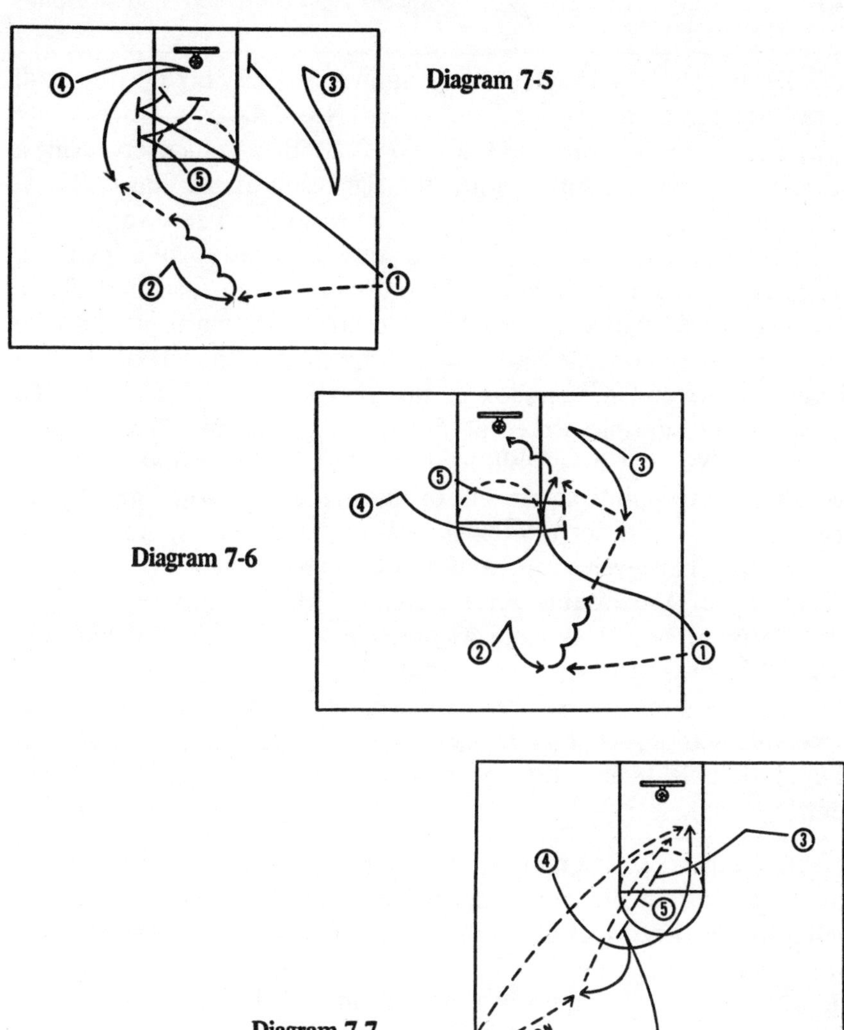

Diagram 7-5

Diagram 7-6

Diagram 7-7

No. 2 should be open as a result of this maneuver. No. 1 now has the option of passing the ball to No. 2. If the pass is made to No. 2, then he in turn can pass the ball to No. 4, who by this time has positioned himself underneath the basket. This option requires a little more time to execute, but it has the advantage of being more accurate and perhaps more successful. The pass, if made from No. 1 direct to No. 4, must be long and accurate. The relay pass from No. 2 to No. 4 is perhaps the better play, especially if No. 1 is not strong and accurate in executing the half-court baseball type of pass which is necessary for this type of play.

Diagram 7-8. Diagram 7-8 shows No. 1 taking the ball out-of-bounds at the side of the court. No. 2 fakes a move to get open and then takes the pass from No. 1. He then maneuvers, using a dribble to move the ball toward the right side of the court. No. 5, after faking a cut toward the basket, moves out to receive the pass from No. 2. Nos. 4 and 3 move simultaneously to a position indicated in the diagram and form a double screen for No. 1. They should leave enough space for No. 1 to drive between them and take advantage of the double screen set for him just to the left of the free throw line extended. As soon as No. 1 passes the ball to No. 2, he drives off the double screen as shown in the diagram. No. 5 passes the ball to No. 1 if he is able to do so, and No. 1 should be able to score two easy points as a result of this maneuver. Nos. 3 and 4 may start the play, and their original movements, from any position on the court. However, the timing of their movements and the placement of the double screen are of extreme importance. This screen should be set as close as possible to the area shown in the diagram in order to make the play more effective. Correct timing in the execution of the entire maneuver is of extreme importance. However, with a few practice sessions and frequent reviews, the team should be able to execute the play well within the specified time limit.

Diagram 7-9. Diagram 7-9 shows a play which will provide the shot easily within the 3- to 5-second time limit. It will work equally well against all types of defenses–zone, combination or man-to-man. Nos. 3 and 5 break toward the basket to form a double shoulder-to-shoulder screen, as shown in the diagram. No. 1 quickly passes the ball in-bounds to No. 2 who has eluded his defensive man. After passing the ball in-bounds to No. 2, No. 1 quickly breaks past No. 2 for a return pass. After receiving the pass, he executes a quick dribble maneuver toward the right sideline. No. 4, who is the best shot on the team, after moving out toward No. 1, as if to receive a pass from him, reverses his direction and drives along the base line toward the basket, and then around the double screen set by Nos. 3 and 5. No. 1 passes No. 4 the ball as he moves out behind the screen, and from this position he should obtain a high percentage shot. No. 3, meanwhile, moves quickly to a rebound position on the left side of the basket. No. 5 rebounds on the right side of the basket, and No. 4, the shooter, rebounds the center area after he shoots. Follow-up shots should be possible within the prescribed time limit. Practicing this play will bear this out.

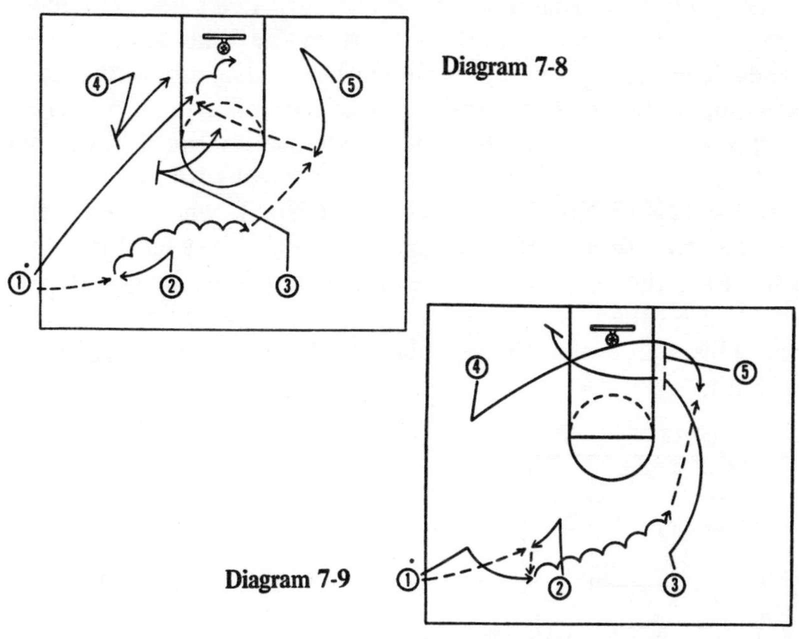

Diagram 7-8

Diagram 7-9

Diagram 7-10. Can the ball be advanced the length of the basketball court within the specified 3- to 5-second time limit? It certainly can. If a time out is taken after a basket or a free throw has been scored by the opponents, the ball may be dribbled or passed along the end line or base line out-of-bounds, so long as the team gets the ball in play within the 5-second time limit prescribed by the rules. The clock does not start until the ball touches a player in-bounds. Diagram 7-10 shows No. 5 taking the ball out-of-bounds and passing it to No. 4 along the base line outside the court. Nos. 1 and 2 set a double screen for No. 3, who breaks near the mid-court area where No. 4 passes him the ball. As soon as No. 5 passes the ball while out-of-bounds along the base line to No. 4, as shown in the diagram, he drives hard and fast down court. He also can take advantage of the screen set by No. 1. The play will have a better chance of success, of course, if No. 5 is fast, because he must get down court quickly so that No. 3 can pass him the ball within the required time limit. He may move to dribble the ball in for the shot depending on where he receives the pass from No. 3, but he will have time to do this.

Diagram 7-11. Diagram 7-11 shows how two passes can be used to move the ball down court well within the time limit of 3 to 5 seconds. The players line up as shown in the diagram, with No. 5 in possession of the ball after taking time out following a basket or a free throw. No. 5 passes the ball to No. 4 after No. 4 has stepped out-of-bounds along the base line. No. 3 screens for No. 5, and, as the action begins, No. 2 sets a screen for No. 1, who breaks behind the screen to lose his defensive man. He then drives far down court. No 4 passes the ball to No. 5 near the mid-court line, and No. 5 quickly passes the ball down the court to No. 1, who drives in for the score. This action can all take place well within the 3- to 5-second time limit.

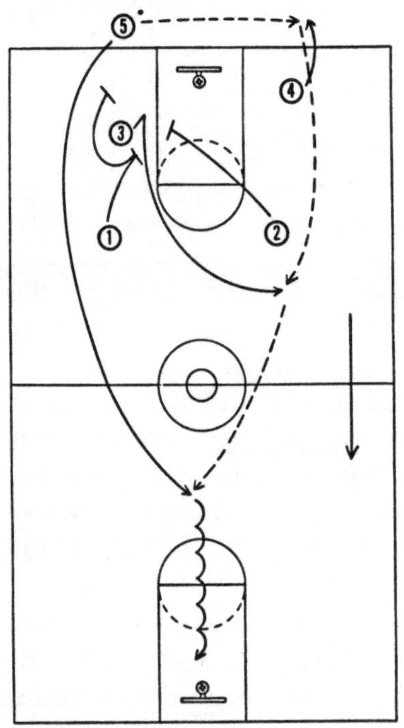

Diagram 7-10

Diagram 7-11

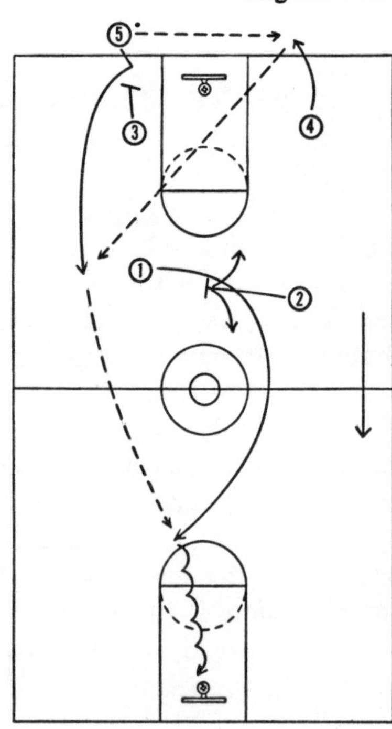

OTHER PLAYS FOR 3- TO 5-SECOND SITUATIONS

The reader is advised to review some of the other out-of-bounds plays described earlier in this book which could be used as quick-scoring plays with only a short time left in the game. Chapter 1 presents out-of-bounds plays to be used at the offensive end line. If the team has the ball out-of-bounds at this spot and needs to score quickly because of a limited amount of time left in the game, then a review of these plays will reveal that several are appropriate for use in this type of a situation.

Chapter 2 also describes some out-of-bounds plays for use in the front court sidelines, the mid-court and division line situations. A review of Diagrams 2-12, 2-13, 2-14, 2-17, 2-18, 2-19 and 2-20 will reveal plays that could result in scoring plays which can be executed within a short time limit period. The trap plays shown in Diagrams 2-22, 2-25, 2-28 and 2-31 in Chapter 2 are all examples of plays that can be used for quick-scoring plays when a short time is left in the game and a score is needed.

The full-court plays, which can be used for advancing the ball down court against pressure defense, given in Chapter 3, could also be applicable for use when there is a time limit in which to execute a play. Diagrams 3-7, 3-8 and 3-9 describe these plays. The "out play" and the "keep play" versions of moving the ball down court quickly are also good examples of quick scoring plays which can be carried out within a short period of time.

PLAYS FOR 6- TO 12-SECOND SITUATIONS

This type of situation demands specific and rigid guidelines. The score determines to a large extent just what type of action needs to be taken and the kinds of plays which will be used in this type of situation.

Some situations require that the team delay taking a shot, so that it will be taken late enough in the contest to prevent the opponents from recovering the rebound if the basket is missed and moving the ball the length of the court for a shot that could prove disastrous. The 6- to 12-second time remaining situation could result in this occurrence. A little maneuvering and a little timing may be required to get the shot off with just the right amount of time left on the clock. To the team that is coached to meet this kind of situation, and thereby acquire "the winning edge," it means victory.

Diagram 7-12. Diagram 7-12 shows a play that is a good one to use to get the shot off in the 6- to 12-second time limit. It has several good options. The play can go in either direction, but, in this diagram, No. 1 is shown taking the ball out-of-bounds at mid-court near the left sideline. Guard No. 2 is stationed at the mid-court area. Nos. 4 and 5 line up as shown in the diagram just below the free throw line extended and on the sides of the lane. No. 3 lines up to the forward position on the right side of the court. When the signal is given for the play to begin, No. 2 eludes his defensive man and moves out to receive the pass from No. 1. No. 2 now dribbles to the right side of the court, as shown in the diagram. Immediately after passing the ball in-bounds, No. 1 drives hard and fast toward the top of the free throw circle and off the left shoulder of No. 5. No. 3 has made a jamming move toward the basket and then comes back to receive the ball from No. 2. This should take place just about the time No. 1 comes around the screen provided by No. 5. No. 1 could be free to receive a pass from No. 3 at this point and at this time. If he is not free to receive the pass, he quickly circles back and comes off the triple screen that is formed for him at the free throw lanes, as shown in the diagram. This screening action is accomplished by Nos. 5 and 4 moving in to a position along the free throw line and in the outer half of the circle. They make their move as soon as No. 1 has cleared this first drive by No. 5. As soon as No. 2 passed the ball to No. 3, he moved quickly to the outer half of the free throw circle along the free throw line. In making their moves, No. 5 will move in alongside the right shoulder of No. 2, and No. 4 will set his screen alongside the left shoulder of No. 2. Nos. 4, 2 and 5 now have formed a shoulder-to-shoulder screen, and No. 1, circling back, comes off the screen in his second drive past No. 5 to receive a pass from No. 3. After receiving the ball from No. 2, No. 3 makes an adjustment dribble, which will consume enough time to allow No. 1 to make his cut off the triple screen afforded him by Nos. 5, 4 and 2. If he is able to do so, No. 1 may dribble all the way in for the score. If the defense should shift and prevent him from doing this, he could pass the ball to No. 5, who moves toward the basket from a roll-off maneuver after the screen.

Other options are possible from the play. No. 1 could stop behind the triple screen and receive a pass from No. 3 at that point. This could result in a possible shot. If No. 1 should drive around the

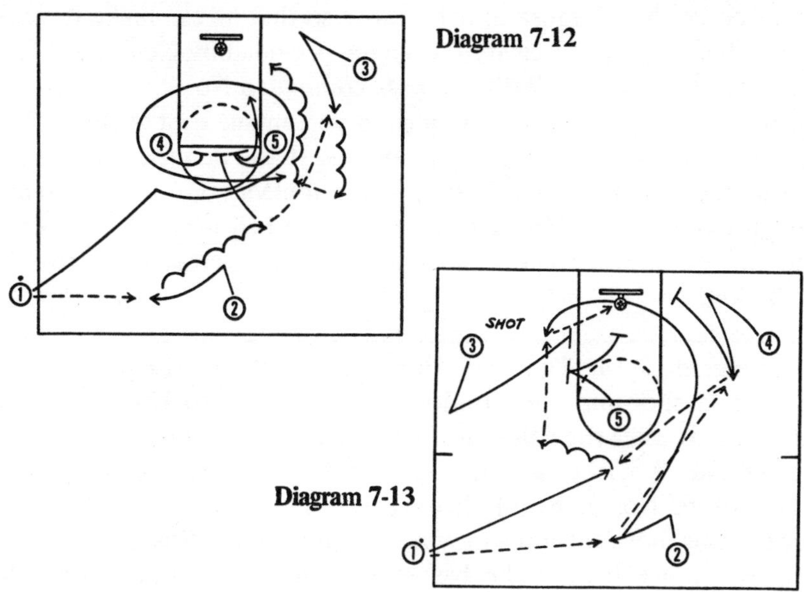

Diagram 7-12

Diagram 7-13

screen and the defense scrambles, possible roll-off options could be made by either No. 5, 2 or 4—all of which could result in good scoring opportunities.

Diagram 7-13. Another play that can be used within the required time limit is shown in Diagram 7-13. The timing on this play can be set at a certain tempo so it is possible to get a shot off sooner, or delay the shot so that it can be taken in the final few seconds. To begin the play, No. 1 passes the ball in-bounds to No. 2, who has freed himself for the pass. No. 2 is the player best suited to take the shot when using this play. As the play begins, No. 4 takes a deep move toward the basket and then comes back to receive a quick pass from No. 2. After passing to No. 4, No. 2 drives for the basket area as shown in the diagram. When No. 1 passes the ball in-bounds to No. 2, he drives to the area about halfway between the mid-court area and the top of the circle. As No. 1 arrives at this point, No. 4 quickly passes the ball to him. No. 3 first fakes toward No. 1 as if to receive a pass from him, and then reverses his direction and moves to the area shown in the diagram along with No. 5. Players No. 3 and 5 set shoulder-to-shoulder screens low and along the left side of the free throw lane near the basket. No. 2 now circles around the screen. No.

1, after receiving the ball from No. 4, starts a dribble to the left side of the court. No. 1 must time his move so that he can make the pass to No. 2 just as No. 2 clears the screen provided by Nos. 3 and 5, as shown in the diagram. With the pass coming to No. 2 from No. 1 in this position, No. 2 should have a good percentage shot at the basket. Nos. 3, 5 and 4 follow for the rebounds. If the defense shifts and is able to spoil his shot, No. 2 could still dribble around the screen and drive for the basket. He might also pass the ball off to Nos. 3 or 5, who can execute a roll-off maneuver after the screen and drive for the basket.

Diagram 7-14. The play shown in Diagram 7-14 can provide some good shooting opportunities within the 6- to 12-second time limit. No. 1 takes the ball out-of-bounds and passes in-bounds to No. 2 after No. 2 has positioned himself for the pass. After passing in-bounds to No. 2, No. 1 drives across the court toward the right corner. This move sets up a moving screen for both Nos. 3 and 5. No. 4 fakes a move toward the basket and then comes out to take the pass from No. 2, who has made a time adjustment dribble maneuver (if necessary). No. 3 first fakes a drive or drifts toward his right, and then, as No. 1 arrives in the area just to the right of the free throw line extended, No. 3 veers sharply to his left behind No. 1, using him as a moving screen. If No. 3 is open, No. 4, who is adjusting the timing of the play by using a dribble, passes the ball to him. If No. 3 is not open, then No. 5 may be open. After screening for No. 3, No. 1 continues his move toward No. 5. No. 5 has first faked a drive to the basket, then moved out to his regular operational area, as shown in the diagram. As No. 1 arrives in this area, No. 5 drives hard past him toward the basket for a possible opening in case No. 3 has not received the pass. No. 5 should be open for a pass from No. 4. If No. 3 is not open on his first cut, he fans out to the left of the area and prepares to come back for rebounding possibilities if needed. Nos. 3, 4 and 5 should move to the basket area for rebounding purposes. Nos. 1 and 2 should move back to provide defensive balance. However, if defensive splits are created in either one of the screens set by No. 1, there could be good openings for No. 1 rolling back off the screens on a drive down the middle, which could result in good scoring opportunities.

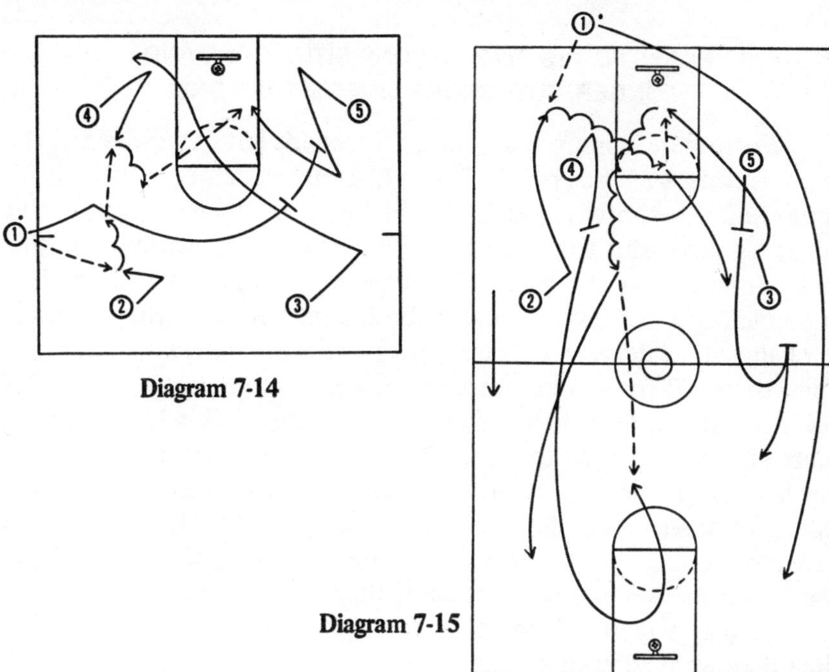

Diagram 7-14

Diagram 7-15

Diagram 7-15. Sometimes it may be necessary to move the ball the length of the court in the time limit under discussion against extreme defensive pressure. The play shown in Diagram 7-15 will get the job done in the required time limit if executed properly. The players position themselves as shown in the diagram. Nos. 4 and 5 "fake move" toward the ball and then set moving screens for Nos. 2 and 3. After this screen has been executed, No. 4 moves down court and then hooks back to the area near the top of the free throw circle. No. 5 moves down court to set another screen near mid-court for No. 1, who will move to this area after passing the ball in-bounds. No. 1 passes the ball in-bounds to No. 2 and then drives hard down court, as shown in the diagram. No. 2 dribbles toward the middle of the court and then passes the ball to No. 3, who has just come off the moving screen set by No. 5. No. 3 now dribbles down the right side of the court toward the division line and passes the ball to No. 4, who has hooked back for a possible opening. With Nos. 1, 3 and 2 all moving down court, possible openings could present themselves which would result in scoring opportunities.

PLAYS FOR 13- TO 20-SECOND SITUATIONS AND LONGER, BUT "SHORT TIME" SITUATIONS

When there is more than 12 to 15 seconds left in a game and the team is one or two points behind, it is extremely difficult to determine the strategy which should be used or what specific play might be successful from the out-of-bounds area. Actually, with this much time left in the game, the team may wish to throw the ball in-bounds and use their regular offensive pattern, or perhaps control the ball with a delayed offense until there is only a few seconds left. They then call for a time out and determine their strategy from this point on. If the team is in a "catch-up" position, in which they are short of time and need to score quick baskets to "catch up" and gain the lead from the opponent, they naturally will want to use plays that give them good shots as quickly as possible. However, if the situation is such that they are only one or two points behind and want to maneuver for one last shot, they will want to use a control type of play which will finally give them the shot they want at the time they want to take it.

There are many such plays that can be used in this type of situation. Many are run from the regular offensive pattern with perhaps some slight changes for a very special occasion or opponent. The following plays fall under this category:

Diagram 7-16. Diagram 7-16 shows a play that has been a favorite of coaches for a long time. This play can fit into any offensive formation and is often referred to as the "sucker" play. It can be worked from a 3-out and 2-in formation or a 2-out and 3-in formation, in fact from just about any formation. If the team has as much as 13 to 20 seconds or longer to use, they could, if they have the ball out-of-bounds, or after taking their assignments over during a time out, throw the ball in-bounds. They then could use as much time as they wish until the time is right for them to use the play they have prepared. The play shown in Diagram 7-16 is set up from the 2-out and 3-in formation. The players line up as shown in Diagram 7-16. No. 2 quickly passes the ball to No. 1 and then drifts to his right. No. 1 starts a dribble toward his left and toward No. 3, as if the action is to go in this direction. No. 4, making his initial move before or no later than No. 2's pass to No. 1, makes a deep jabbing move toward the basket and base line. He then suddenly veers to his left and moves out to the top of the free throw circle. No. 1 passes him the ball at this high post position. No. 4, as soon as he gets the ball, looks for No. 2. After passing the ball to No. 1, No. 2 then moves to his right and toward the sideline. As soon as No. 4 receives the ball from No. 1, No. 2 breaks sharply toward the basket, as shown in the diagram. If his defensive man has turned his head to watch the movement on the other side of the court or has slipped up in his defensive assignment for one fraction of a second, No. 2 will be wide open for a pass from No. 4 and a good scoring opportunity. If No. 2 is not open to receive the pass, No. 4 has two other options available to him. As the play is developing, No. 5 moves off his deep post position, as shown in the diagram, to set a screen for forward No. 3, who has been busy maneuvering himself into a position for a pass from No. 1. However, No. 3 now cuts down the back side of the court off No. 5's screen for a possible opening and a pass from No. 4. If none of these options develop, No. 1 can fake and drive hard off the screen provided by No. 4 for a possible opening and scoring opportunity.

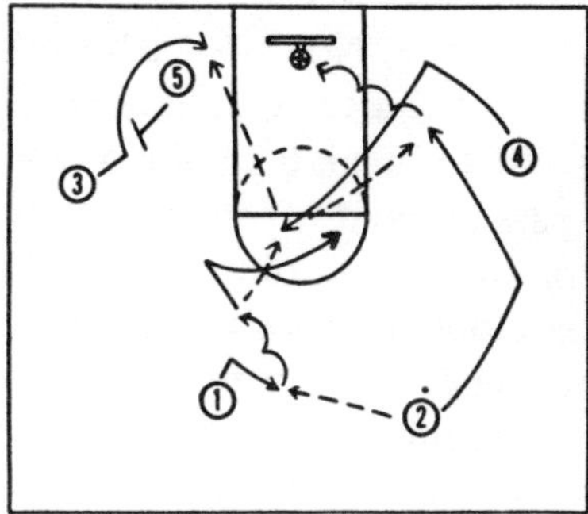

Diagram 7-16

Diagram 7-17. Diagram 7-17 shows a play often referred to as a revolve or a "circle-round" play that can be used in the closing seconds of any part of the game to get off a good shot. It is given here in two phases. Phase 1 of Diagram 7-17 illustrates the first movement. No. 1 starts the play with a dribble to his right. He passes off to No. 2 as No. 2 breaks behind No. 1 or off his outside shoulder. After passing or handing the ball off to No. 2, No. 1 moves to a position along the right side of the free throw lane and deep toward the basket, where, along with No. 4, they position themselves

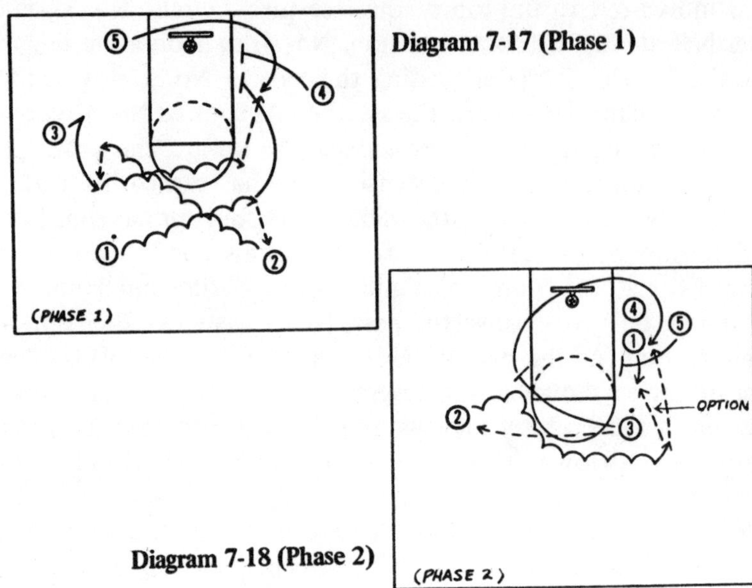

Diagram 7-17 (Phase 1)

Diagram 7-18 (Phase 2)

shoulder-to-shoulder to form a double screen. No. 2 dribbles to the left side of the court and toward No. 3. No. 3 holds his position until No. 2 moves close to him, and then, after taking his defensive man toward the basket, he comes out to break behind No. 2, as shown in the diagram. No. 2 can now pass or hand-off the ball to No. 3. No. 3 dribbles the ball toward the top of the free throw circle. At this time, No. 5, the pivot player, breaks along the base line close to the basket and comes out sharply behind the double screen set by Nos. 1 and 4. No. 3 passes him the ball at this point, from where he should have an unmolested shot at the basket. Nos. 1, 4 and 5 are all in good rebounding positions.

Diagram 7-18 (Phase 2). In the previous diagram, if No. 5 is not open for a pass from No. 3 as he comes around the double screen set by Nos. 1 and 4, he moves up into a position with them and sets up a shoulder-to-shoulder triple screen. At this time, No. 3 passes the ball to No. 2 and then follows the pass and sets a screen for No. 2 as he dribbles out to the top of the circle. No. 3 rolls out of the screen and then cuts in behind the triple screen, as shown in the diagram. No. 2 now passes him the ball for an unmolested shot from behind the screen. If the defense "scrambles" as it often does, No. 3 may pass to

No. 5, who can move on around the screen. No. 3 could go up for a shot, and, if pressed, he could pass off to Nos. 1, 4 or 5, or possibly pass back to No. 2. If No. 2 should find that No. 3 is not open as he comes around the screen, he could possibly pass to No. 5, 1 or 4 as they roll out of the screen. Nos. 1, 4 and 5 should all play for the rebound if and when a shot is taken.

PLAYS TO INCREASE A LEAD

Many times a team has a small lead late in the ball game and is being subjected to intense defensive pressure. The well-coached team will exploit this situation by turning the tables on the pressing defense, and as a result increase their lead. A few well-chosen plays can make this possible.

Diagram 7-19. The play presented in Diagram 7-19 will do it! The opponents have just scored a basket. The defense is pressing and making a desperate effort to gain possession of the ball. The team calls for a time out. The entire pattern of play is reviewed at this time. The coach and players all have a vital part in the success of this play. Play is resumed by having the players line up as shown in the diagram. Just as the signal to begin the play is given or just prior to this signal, the coach jumps up and yells, "Line up, line up." Nos. 3, 4 and 5 quickly position themselves in a straight line, standing

Diagram 7-19

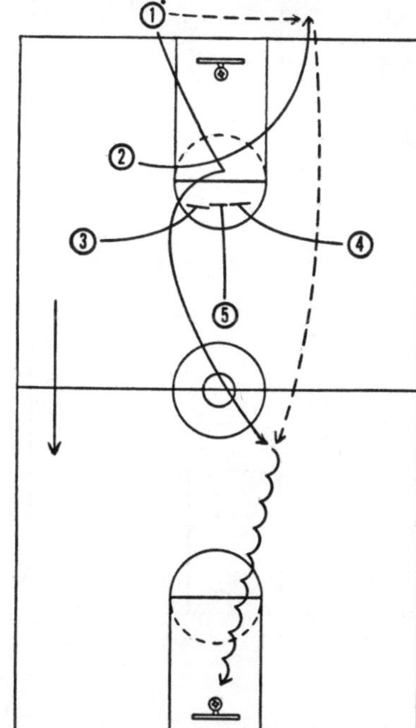

shoulder-to-shoulder just back of the free throw line and facing No. 1, who has the ball out-of-bounds. No. 2 fakes a move toward the free throw line, but then suddenly cuts sharply to a position out-of-bounds on the opposite side of the free throw lane from No. 1, as shown in the diagram. No. 1 passes the ball to No. 2 behind and along the base line. Immediately after passing to No. 2, No. 1 drives straight at the three teammates lined up at the free throw lane, then suddenly veers to his right and moves around them in such a way as to brush off his defensive man in the pocket formed by the triple shoulder-to-shoulder screen of Nos. 3, 4 and 5. No. 1 should now be free as he cuts deep toward his basket at the opposite end of the court. No. 2 passes a long "butterfly" type of pass to the mid-court area or beyond, and No. 1 dribbles in toward the basket unmolested, to score a certain two points. This scoring play can also be used for short time situations of 4 seconds or more any time the defense is pressing. The entire play can be executed in less than 5 seconds if the timing is perfect.

Diagram 7-20. The play shown in Diagram 7-20 was previously diagrammed in Chapter 2 (Diagram 2-29) under "Mid-Court Plays." The play needs to be reviewed and repeated here, however, because it

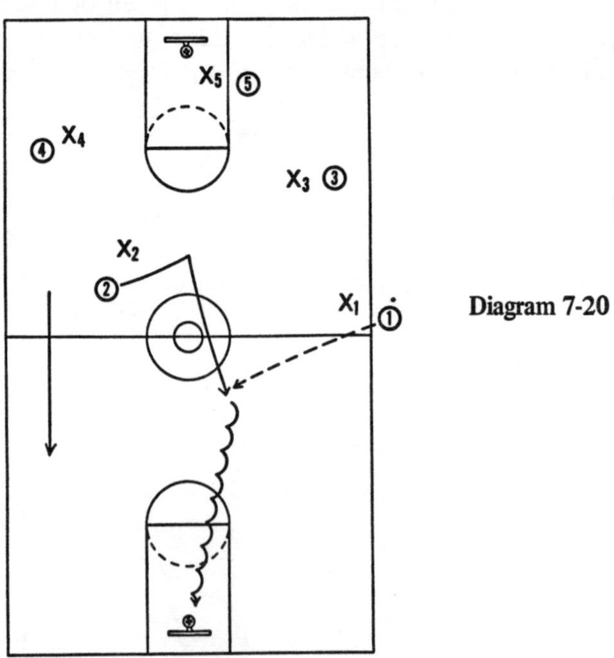

Diagram 7-20

can be adapted to this particular situation very well. The defensive team is exerting pressure, the lead is very slim and the team is attempting to control the ball and run out the clock. The ball is out-of-bounds at mid-court, or along the sideline near this area. When play is to resume after the time out, the players line up as shown in the diagram as if they are going for the wrong basket. If this happens (and it has happened many times), all No. 2 has to do is elude his defensive man, using a fake, and then dash for his own basket to receive a pass from No. 1. He can then dribble to his basket for an easy two points. All players have to be good actors on this particular play. If the defense is playing tight, only one defensive man needs to make an error to give the offensive player a chance to dash for his own basket. If it works, it not only is an easy two points but can also be a morale-breaking factor which will be difficult for the opposition to overcome.

EIGHT

SCORING PLAYS FROM MISSED FREE THROW SITUATIONS

Player Positions on Free Throw Attempts

The positioning of the players along the lanes on free throw attempts lends itself well to special situation plays from missed free throws. The fact that two defensive players are stationed on both sides of the lane next to the basket practically assures the defensive team possession of the ball a good share of the time if the free throw is missed. The team should take advantage of this situation, and special plays should be used that will give the defensive team the opportunity to capitalize on this opportunity.

Reasons for Using a Scoring Play After a Missed Free Throw

There are two conditions that must be considered if a team is going to be able to take advantage of this particular stiuation: (1) Does the defensive team wish to attempt to score after gaining possession of the ball from the missed free throw? (2) Does it wish to gain ball possession and then use ball control tactics only? If the latter is true, it means that the team may want to protect a lead late in the game, and therefore will attempt ball control type maneuvers which will assure them of ball possession. They also may be the type of team that does not wish to use fast break tactics, which is the characteristic maneuver used in bringing the ball down court from the missed free throw. It is possible, also, that a team may wish to bring the ball to the front court area slowly and use a deliberate style of attack to move the ball into scoring position. One of the reasons for this type of action is of course the personnel makeup of the team. If the players cannot perform the skills necessary in the fast break maneuvers, it would be foolhardy for any coach to insist on its use. He would, in this case, be destroying its usefulness and defeating its purpose. It should be remembered, however, that players need not necessarily be fast to move the ball down court quickly. It is the ability of the players to judge when ball possession is going to be obtained that determines the success of this maneuver. The players should have the ability to start their movement down court in a systematic and organized fashion, as soon as possible after they realize they have gained or are about to gain possession of the ball from the missed free throw.

Movement of the Ball After Missed Free Throws

In modern day basketball, with its all court presses, it is to the advantage of the team that has gained possession of the ball from the missed free throw to move the ball away from the basket area and toward the front court area as quickly as possible. As a result of this maneuver, the defensive team will not be able to use their pressing tactics nearly as easily and effectively, because they will be out of position and will not be able to recover in time to use the press if the ball is moved out of the back-court area quickly.

In moving the ball down court quickly from the missed free throw, it is best to incorporate the movements and maneuvers that are necessary to perform these skills into the regular pattern of play which is used in the fast break. The fast breaking type of maneuver can work to advantage after a missed free throw, even though the team may not employ the fast break as part of their regular offense. The reason for this is that the players can be aligned in a certain way each time there is a free throw attempt.

Fast Break Patterns Used After the Missed Free Throw

There are many and varied fast break patterns which will move the ball down court quickly, and most of them are fundamentally sound. Some coaches deplore the use of the dribble at any time, believing that the ball should never touch the floor on any fast break.

Other coaches believe that the use of the dribble will enhance the chances of the fast break succeeding. While present day basketball is still a passing game, the dribble continues to play an important role. The reasons for this of course are numerous, with perhaps the biggest one being that of enabling players to operate on their own so that they are able to remove themselves from a particularly vulnerable situation. Dribbling also provides an opportunity whereby the talented player may use his skills in an individual effort, such as would be true in a 1-on-1 situation.

It should be remembered, however, that the most important reason for the use of special plays from missed free throws is to move the ball into the front court quickly, so as to offset any pressing tactics that might be employed by the opposition. If they are able to score by the use of such tactics, so much the better.

Player Alignment During Free Throws

The player alignment on all free throw situations will vary, depending upon personnel and the desire of the coach to place his players in positions which will enhance the successful use of specific plays or formations. Because of the usual 4-on-3 player ratio used in placing the players along the free thow line, on all free throw situations it is possible to station at least one player off to the side of the court so that he will be in an excellent position to receive the outlet pass. Many teams will place two players away from the free throw area. Usually these two are fast and good ball handlers. They usually are stationed about even with the top of the foul circle and halfway between the center of the court and the sideline. However, these two players can be placed farther down court. If this is true, they both are usually stationed close to the sideline. The placing of the players away from the free throw area, as well as the number, will depend to some extent upon the rebounding ability of the remaining players stationed along the free throw lane. If the players stationed along the free throw lane are excellent rebounders, then two players can be positioned "out court" to receive the out pass and start the movement of the ball down court.

Special Plays Used from Missed Free Throws

The special plays which can be used from missed free throws presented in this chapter will be those in which the dribble is used, and others in which it is not used. The formations will include the *three-lane*, the *crossing* and the *long pass formations.*

THE THREE-LANE PATTERN USING THE DRIBBLE

The theory governing the use of the dribble in advancing the ball down court after gaining possession as a result of the missed free throw is the same as that governing the use of the fast break under similar circumstances. The reasoning behind the use of the dribble is that clearing the ball out to the side of the court to a point about 6 feet from the sideline and approximately parallel to the top of the free throw circle can be done without the danger of interception. If the ball is dribbled down the side of the court, the dribbler will encounter very little opposition and not have to contend with the congestion which exists in the middle of the court, especially in the area from the basket to the center circle. Usually the opposition will not try to defend against the player who is advancing the ball down the sideline. It is too busy back-pedaling and covering the middle of the court. The dribbler is able, therefore, to move the ball quickly to a position where it can be passed into the middle lane. The added time that it takes to dribble the ball instead of passing it will be offset by the advantage of having a clear path down the sideline. It will also be much easier for teammates to fill the center and the opposite side lane. The two players in the outside lanes should stay wide until they approach the basket. If the fast break is stopped, the middle man usually has the ball in the vicinity of the free throw lane. The two players in the outside lanes should stay wide until they approach the basket. The middle man who has the ball in the vicinity of the free throw line should be able to shoot or pass off to one of the side men.

The success of this type of maneuver will depend upon the ability of the players to start their movement down court in a systematic and organized fashion as soon as possible after they realize they have gained or are about to gain possession of the ball.

The fact that players can be stationed away from the basket can do much to enhance the success of the fast break type of play on the missed free throw. Certain principles should be adhered to. For instance, every effort should be made to free the three lanes at all times. The three lanes should not spread from sideline to sideline because of the great distance the ball will need to travel when passing. The outside players should be about one-third of the distance in from the sideline and about 2 yards ahead of the center man after the players have passed the center line of the court.

Parts of the Fast Break Type of Play Used After the Missed Free Throw

There are really three parts to the fast break type of play using the dribble, which can be employed after the free throw is missed. The first part is the outlet pass which is extremely important, because unless this is executed successfully the play cannot materialize. As soon as the rebound is won, the player in possession clears the ball to the side of the court before he returns to the floor, if possible. A few players may be able to rebound and hook the ball out before touching the floor. If the player cannot do this, he may fake and whirl for the pass-out, or he may fake and dribble out.

The second part of the play includes the team's attempt to move the ball down court into scoring position. After the ball is cleared from under the basket to the player on the side of the court, it is dribbled up the side of the court in a hard, fast-driving dribble until such time as it may be passed to the middle man. It should not be passed to him until he has reached the center circle area. The middle man keeps the ball all the way to the free throw line, unless he is closely guarded or has a chance for a pass to a free man for a lay-up.

The third or scoring part of the play has the middle man receiving the ball at the center circle and dribbling to the free throw circle. He then slows down to a controlled dribble to make one of the guards commit himself. He should not dribble beyond the free throw line unless he thinks he is able to drive all the way in for the lay-up. If he is not able to drive in, then he should always stop at the free throw circle area and wait for the opposing guard to commit himself. By doing this, he will not hurry the pass or shoot when he does not have a good percentage shot. By stopping at the free throw area, he makes it virtually impossible for one guard to cover two players, which can be done if the maneuver is hurried. By stopping, he forces one of the guards to commit himself to the dribbler. The wing man will then be open for a drive-in and a lay-up. The dribbler can also continue to the basket if he sees an opening. He can whip a quick pass off the dribble, or he can stop and take an easy shot from the free throw area. The dribbler also may drive to the free throw line, leave his feet in a jump shot fashion, fake a shot or a pass and flip a quick pass as he leaves his feet. If the dribbler, after receiving the ball at the center circle, is challenged by a defensive player, thus making it impossible for him to continue his dribble, he should pass the ball back to the sideline player. This series of plays will show the formations which can be used after a missed free throw in which the three-lane principle is used along with the dribble.

Diagram 8-1. This series of plays shows the player alignment with two players stationed "out court" during the free throw. This weakens the defensive rebounding but does enhance the success of the fast break type of play from the missed free throw. The out pass can now be made easily by either No. 1 or 2 should one of them obtain the rebound. It can easily be seen that by placing Nos. 4 and 5 in the positions shown in the diagrams, if the pass can be made to either of them quickly, they will have an excellent opportunity and be in a fine position to move the ball down court and into scoring position quickly. Of course, it must be remembered that the opposition will try and offset this advantage by withdrawing their players from the free throw lane area and placing them in defensive position against Nos. 4 and 5. The advantage will however still be in favor of Nos. 4 and 5 because they may execute their breaks in any direction and as a result confuse the defense. If the rebound goes to No. 1, as shown in the diagram, he will pass to No. 5 who has faked toward the basket and then moved out to the side of the court. With proper timing, he will be free to receive the pass from No. 1. No. 5 dribbles down the right side of the court and passes to No. 3 near the center circle. No. 3 has stepped in front of the free thrower and then moved down court. No. 4 moves down the left lane toward the basket. All three lanes are now filled, and advantage can be taken of the options which now exist.

Diagram 8-2. This play is similar to the previous one, except that the moves of Nos. 3 and 4 are different. The rebound is obtained by No. 1 and passed to No. 5. No. 3 steps in front of the free thrower to prevent the rebound from going to him. No. 3 holds

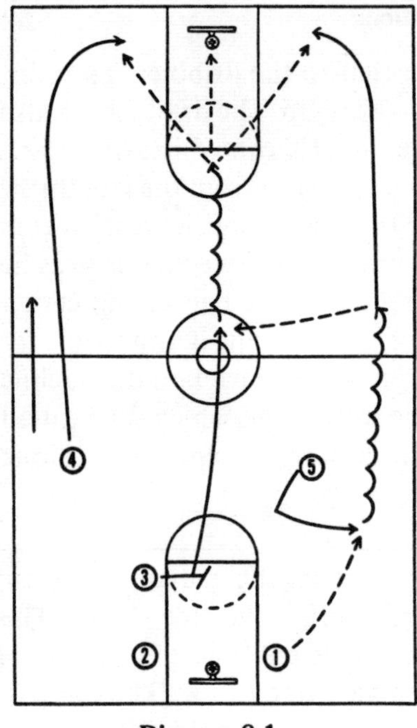

Diagram 8-1

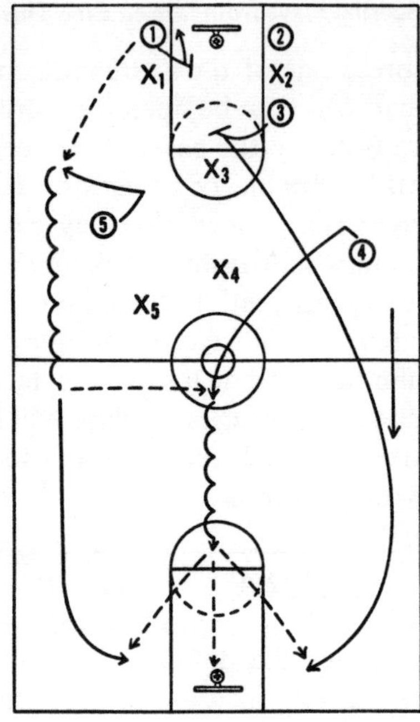

Diagram 8-2

this position until such time as No. 1 makes the pass to No. 5, as shown in the diagram. No. 4 moves across and toward the middle of the court. No. 3 now makes his move by driving toward the left side of the court and down the left lane. No. 5 dribbles hard down the right lane as soon as he receives the pass from No. 1. No. 4 cuts to his right, then left and down the center of the court as soon as he sees No. 5 start his dribble down the right lane. No. 5 passes the ball to No. 4 as soon as he is able to do so after No. 4 reaches the vicinity of the center circle. No. 4 dribbles to the free throw circle area, at which point he can shoot, drive in for a lay-up if the opportunity presents itself or pass off to No. 5 or 3, both of whom are approaching the basket from the outside lanes. Often when there is a crossing of players, the defensive players are unable to cope with this type of situation, and No. 4 will need to time his cut down the center of the court to coincide with the actions of No. 5.

Diagram 8-3. This diagram shows Nos. 4 and 5 stationed out court as the free throw is being attempted. No. 1 obtains the rebound and makes the out pass to No. 5 at the side of the court. No. 5 moves toward the free thrower, and then, as he sees No. 1 gain possession of the ball, he moves toward the side of the court to a

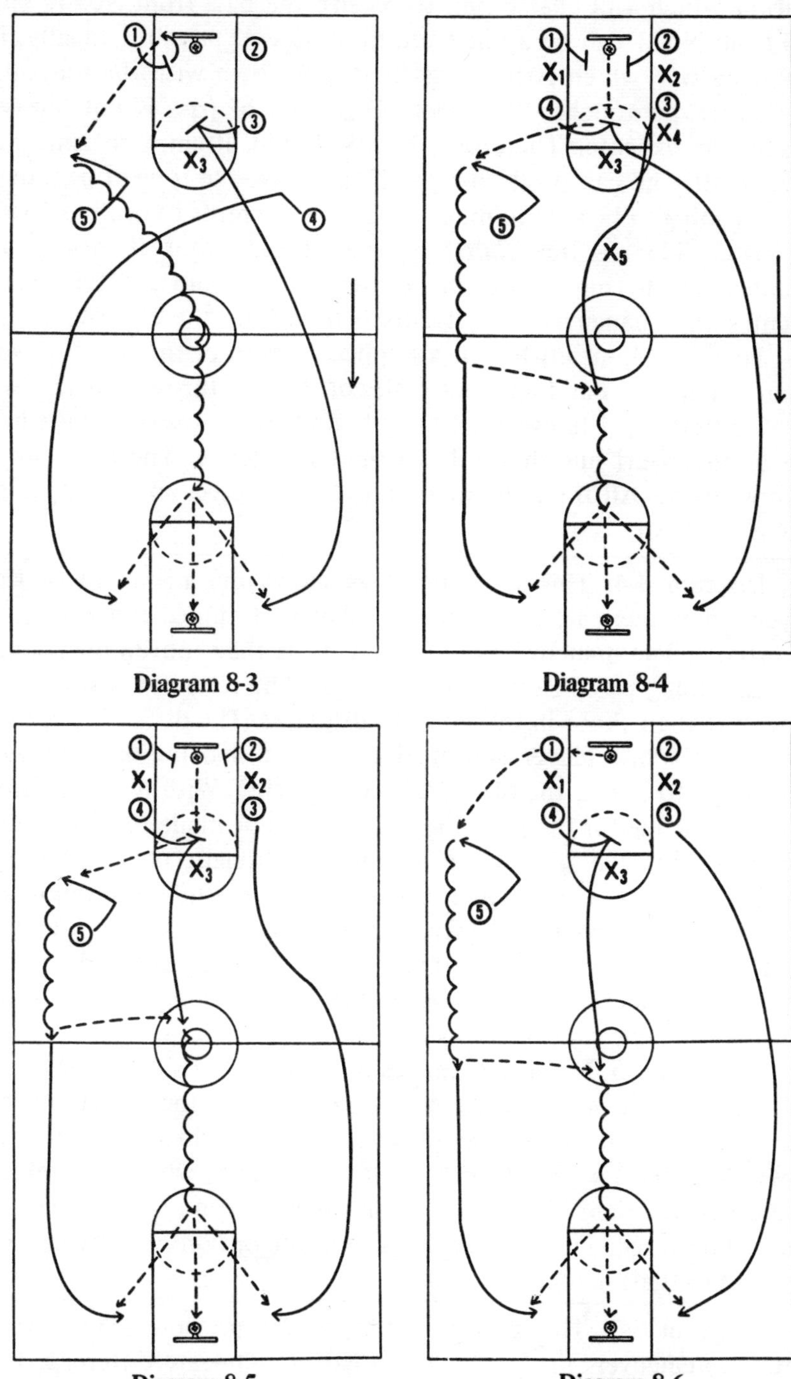

Diagram 8-3

Diagram 8-4

Diagram 8-5

Diagram 8-6

position which will enable him to receive the pass from No. 1. The pass from No. 1 can be a one-hand hook pass if possible. Ideally, it should be one which is made as he comes down with the rebound and before he touches the floor. This type of pass is not always possible to execute. Therefore, No. 5 should attempt to time his move so that he can position himself to receive the type of pass that No. 1 is going to be able to make. As No. 5 attempts to dribble down the right side of the court, he may decide that it would be advantageous to move into the center of the court. After No. 5 executes this maneuver, No. 4 cuts behind him, thereby filling the right lane. No. 3, meanwhile, has stepped in front of the free-thrower to cut off the rebounding possibilities of the free thrower. When No. 3 is sure that No. 1 has secured the rebound, he moves out to the left side of the court and drives down the left sideline. The three lanes are now filled. All three of these plays can be used on the opposite side of the floor.

Diagram 8-4. This series of plays shows the alignment of the players when there are four defensive players stationed along the free throw lane. The maneuvers of the players as they move down court after obtaining possession of the ball from the rebound is similar to some extent to those in the previous diagrams. The difference is that there is only one player stationed out court, and the out pass will need to go to him if the play is to begin quickly. With two out court players available for the pass, the out pass can be made to either side. Therefore, this play gives more rebounding strength, but it is limited in other respects. This diagram shows No. 4 obtaining the rebound, upon stepping in front of the free thrower after he has attempted the free throw. No. 4 moves the out pass to No. 5, who has faked a move toward the basket and then moved over to the sideline to a position which will enable him to receive the pass from No. 4. After making the pass to No. 5, No. 4 then moves toward the left side of the court and into the left outside lane. No. 3 moves down the middle of the court to a position at the center circle area, at which point he can expect to receive a pass if he is open from No. 5, who has dribbled hard down the right lane to a position where he can make the pass to No. 3. The three lanes are now filled, and the options may be carried out as the situation dictates.

Diagram 8-5. This play is similar to the previous play, except that the maneuvers made by players No. 3 and 4 are different. The ball is rebounded by No. 4 and the out pass is made to No. 5, who has faked a move toward the basket and then moved to the side of the court to position himself for the pass from No. 4. After making the pass to No. 5, No. 4 now moves down the center of the court, thereby filling the middle lane. As he approaches the center circle, he should expect a pass from No. 5, who, after he received the pass from No. 4, has dribbled quickly down the right side of the court to the position where he can make the pass to No. 4. No. 3 keeps his rebounding position until he is sure that No. 4 has possession of the ball. He then breaks down the left side of the court. Nos. 3 and 4 need to work cooperatively on this series of plays because the center and left lane will be occupied most of the time by either one of them. It is true, however, that No. 2 may at certain times be in a position to function in these lanes on this particular play. The determining factor which dictates the specific lanes the players will use for these plays is dependent upon the position in which they find themselves after the rebound is secured. No. 4, upon receiving the pass from No. 5, dribbles to the free throw circle area and executes one of the options previously mentioned.

Diagram 8-6. This series of plays shows four defensive players stationed along the free throw lane and only one player out court, with the rebound going to No. 1. The movements of players No. 3 and 4 are the same as in the previous diagram, except that No. 4 does not obtain the rebound. Instead, the rebound goes to No. 1, who makes the out pass to No. 5, as shown in the diagram. Here again, the importance of getting the out pass away quickly and accurately should be stressed, as this is a most important element in the success of this type of play from the missed free throw. No. 4 should not move out of the rebound area until he is sure that No. 1 has obtained the ball from the rebound and has made the pass to No. 5. Then, and only then, should No. 4 begin his move down court. The same is true regarding No. 3. He stays in rebounding position until such time as he is sure that No. 1 has not only controlled the rebound but also has successfully made the pass to No. 5. No. 3 then moves to the side of the court and breaks quickly down the left lane. All three lanes are now filled, and play should continue as in the previous diagrams until such time as the desired shot is obtained. It should be stressed here that it is entirely possible that in the process of rebounding, Nos. 2 and 3 may be in a position to change places. If this happens, it is conceivable that No. 2 may end up in the left lane instead of No. 3. This should not, however, affect the effectiveness of the play, because No. 2 can perform the same maneuvers as No. 3 would have been required to perform.

Diagram 8-7. This play is similar to the previous play, except that the maneuvers performed by Nos. 3 and 4 are different. The ball is rebounded by No. 1, and he in turn passes to No. 5, who has positioned himself to receive the out pass by faking toward the basket and then out toward the sideline. No. 4 steps in front of the free thrower as soon as it is legal to do so in order to cut off the rebounding possibilities, and also to enhance No. 4's chances of obtaining the rebound. As soon as No. 4 is certain that No. 5 has possession of the ball, he leaves his screen and moves toward the left side of the court and then down the left outside lane. No. 3 remains in his rebounding position until he is sure ball possession has been obtained. As he sees No. 4 breaking into the left lane, he immediately moves into the center lane and moves toward the center circle, at which point he may expect to receive the pass from No. 5, who is dribbling hard down the right outside lane. The three lanes are now filled and the play is carried out as in the previous diagram. This play again points out the fact that player positions at the time of the rebound will determine which players will be in the center and left outside lanes. All players should be observant of the situation and be ready at all times to adapt their movements to the requirements demanded by the play at any given time. This comes only with constant practice.

Diagram 8-8. In establishing any pattern which may be used in moving the ball swiftly down court after gaining possession from the missed free throw, it must be kept in mind that the defense will sometimes force a change in the pattern of movement of the offensive players. The players, therefore, should be alert to these changes and be ready to change the pattern as the situation dictates. This diagram illustrates this change. No. 4, having obtained possession of the ball on the rebound, executes the out pass to No. 5, who has positioned himself to receive the pass by breaking toward the rebound area and then out to the side of the court. After receiving the out pass from No. 4, No. 5 turns and attempts to dribble down the right side of the court, using the predetermined plan of attack.

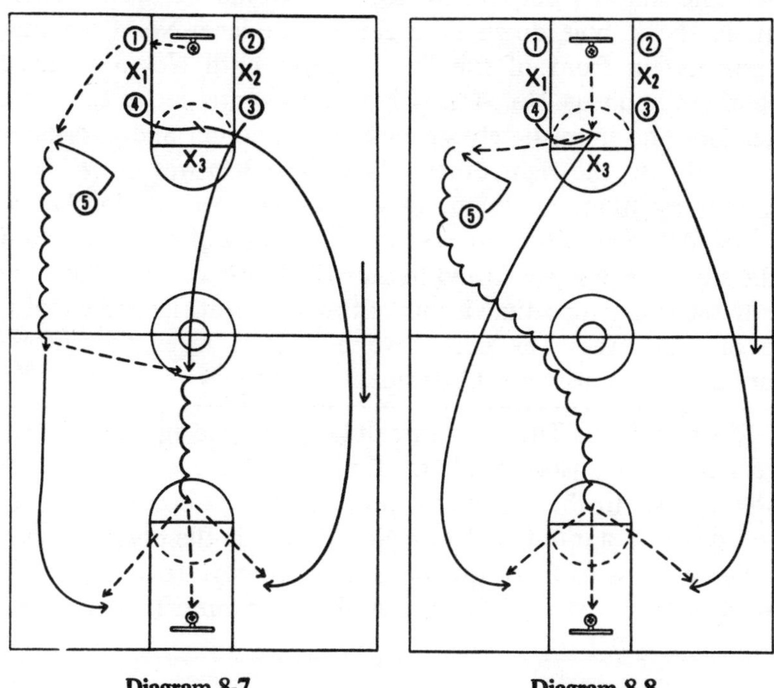

Diagram 8-7 Diagram 8-8

However, at this point, he sees that his path is blocked and his movement down the sideline is being contested by the defense. In order to continue the play, No. 5 dribbles into the center lane and continues the dribble, if he is able to do so, to the free throw circle area. As soon as No. 4 sees No. 5 move into the center lane, he in turn cuts behind No. 5 and into the right lane. No. 3 moves out to the left side of the court as soon as he is sure No. 5 has possession of the ball. No. 3 then moves down court using the left outside lane until he is in a position to receive the pass from No. 5, if he chooses to make the pass.

Diagram 8-9. This play is similar to the previous play, except that the rebound is obtained by No. 1 who makes the out pass to No. 5. Under ordinary conditions, No. 5 would dribble down the right outside lane. However, as in the previous diagram, No. 5 finds his progress blocked and is forced to move into the center lane, where he continues his dribble to the free throw circle, as shown in the diagram. It should be emphasized that No. 5 does not move into the center lane unless forced to do so, as it would be much easier to continue the dribble down the right outside lane. No. 4 remains in his position in front of the free thrower until No. 5 begins his dribble. As soon as No. 4 sees No. 5 make his move toward the center lane, he immediately changes his direction and cuts behind No. 5 and into the right outside lane. No. 3 moves down the left lane, thereby filling all three lanes. Excellent cooperation between Nos. 4 and 5 is absolutely necessary. The ability of all players to size up the situation at a glance and to move immediately into the correct lane at the opportune time is one of the secrets of the success of this type of maneuver. The ability to adjust to meet the different situations as they arise must be evident at all times.

Diagram 8-10. The next three plays describe the moves of the players after the unsuccessful free throw, with the out court players stationed close to the sidelines and on the center court line. One of the purposes of stationing players No. 4 and 5 in the positions shown in the diagram is to force the opposition to move two players away from the free throw area, thereby weakening their offensive rebound

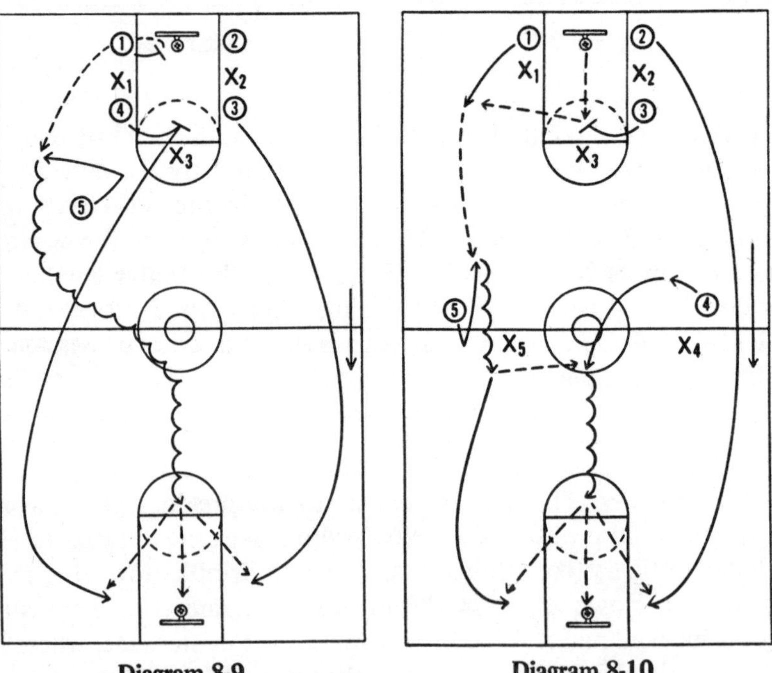

Diagram 8-9 Diagram 8-10

strength. This is especially true if the defensive rebounding is superior, and it usually will be because of the positioning of the two defensive rebounders next to the basket on either side of the free throw lane. The opposition is forced to have players guarding Nos. 4 and 5, because if they do not, either one or both of these players may move farther down court and be in a position to receive a long pass. In this play, No. 3 steps in front of the free thrower and obtains the rebound. He immediately passes to No. 1, who moves out to the sideline and positions himself to receive the out pass. No. 5 fakes toward the offensive basket, then breaks back toward No. 1 and receives the pass from him. No. 4, upon seeing No. 5 about to receive the pass, cuts toward the center of the court, thereby filling the center lane and making himself available for the pass from No. 5. No. 5 may dribble the ball toward the offensive basket a short distance as shown in the diagram, or he may make the pass to No. 4 immediately upon receiving the ball himself. No. 2 moves down the left outside lane. The three lanes are now filled. No. 4 dribbles toward the free throw circle and chooses the option he wishes to use to produce the best scoring opportunity.

Diagram 8-11. This play shows the players stationed in approximately the same positions as in the previous diagram. However, instead of the rebound going to No. 3, who is stationed in front of the free thrower, it goes to No. 1. No. 1 immediately makes the pass to No. 5. No. 1 attempts to make this out pass as quickly as possible by turning and making a one-handed baseball type of pass to No. 5. If he is able to do this while he is still in the air, after he obtains the rebound it will enhance the chances of the play being successful. If No. 1 is not able to make this type of pass, he dribbles toward the sideline to clear himself so that he is able to make the pass to No. 5. No. 5 fakes toward the offensive basket and then breaks back to receive the pass from No. 1. No. 3 steps in front of the free thrower, and, after he is sure that No. 1 has successfully obtained the rebound and made the pass to No. 5, he moves quickly down the center of the court. No. 4 moves toward the defensive basket until such time that he sees No. 5 receive the pass from No. 1. He then reverses his direction and moves down court in the left outside lane. No. 5 passes the ball to No. 3 and then cuts toward the basket as shown in the diagram. The three lanes are now filled. No. 3

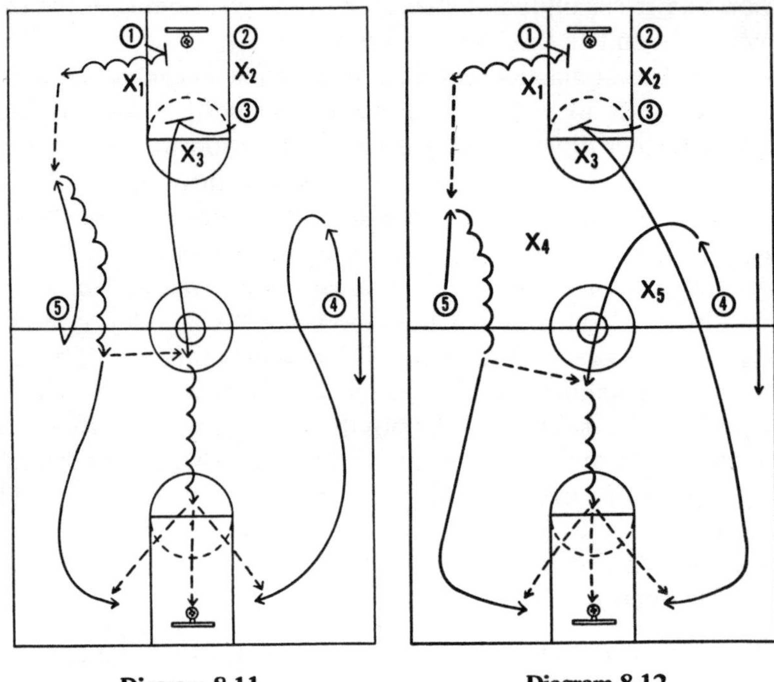

Diagram 8-11

Diagram 8-12

dribbles to the free throw circle where he may exercise the options that are available to him. He may shoot, drive in for the lay-up or pass to either No. 4 or 5, both of whom are driving for the basket.

Diagram 8-12. This play also is one in which two players are stationed near the sideline and on the center line. The player movement is the same as in the previous diagram, except those of Nos. 3 and 4. No. 1 obtains the rebound and makes the out pass to No. 5. No. 4, upon seeing No. 5 receive the pass, breaks to the center of the court after having moved toward the defensive basket. No. 3 steps in front of the free thrower and holds his position until he is sure that No. 5 has safely received the pass from No. 1. He then moves toward the left side of the court and the left outside lane. No. 5 passes to No. 4 whenever it is possible for him to do so. No. 4 dribbles to the free throw circle and exercises the options which present themselves. The success of this play depends upon the movements of Nos. 4 and 5. These players must put the pressure on the players guarding them. They should always be free to receive the pass from No. 1. They can do this only by proper faking and maneuvering to get themselves into a good position to receive the pass. The main purpose, however, of this type of play, is to spread the players over the court, so that the chances of moving the ball out of the back-court area as quickly as possible can be accomplished. This helps to prevent the defensive players from positioning themselves in such a manner as to make it difficult to advance the ball down court.

THE THREE-LANE PATTERN USING THE HALF-COURT DRIBBLE

Since the opposition will miss the free throw from 25 to 40% of the time, the team, as has been previously mentioned, should be prepared for this eventuality. It should be ready to move into an offensive pattern immediately if possession of the ball is obtained from the missed free throw. Actually, the defensive team has a terrific rebounding advantage. If it exploits this advantage and moves into protective blocking positions on both sides of the lane, the rebound from a missed free-throw should nearly always be obtained by the defensive team. This is especially true if all the players, who are legally allowed to do so, are positioned along the free throw lane, as shown in the following diagrams. With the use of proper pinching and blocking maneuvers performed by the defensive players, the defensive team should be able to screen out the offensive players and minimize the offensive team's rebounding efforts most of the time. How this can be accomplished will be shown in the following diagrams. Because the defensive team is able to gain possession of the ball from the rebound a large percentage of the time, it should be prepared to spread out and move into the fast break pattern quickly so that possible scoring situations can be taken advantage of. The rules give the defensive team an advantage, which in turn can also give them possession of the ball with a minimum of effort. This advantage should not be sloughed off, as it does play an important part in winning or losing. In fact, it can often be the difference between winning and losing. By using the scoring possibilities resulting from the plays which will be shown in the following diagrams, a team can gain "the winning edge."

Diagram 8-13. This diagram shows players No. 4 and 5 stationed in the inside lane spaces. When X1 shoots the free throw, they both block out X4 and X5, knowing, of course, that these players cannot penetrate the free throw lane boundary line until the ball touches the ring or backboard, or until the free throw ends. No. 1 has the assignment of blocking out X1 on the shot in case it is missed. No. 5 secures the ball from the missed free throw rebound. He immediately looks for the opportunity to make the outlet pass. No. 3 moves to the side of the court, as shown in the diagram, so that he may be in a position to receive the outlet pass from No. 5 as soon as he sees that No. 5 has gained possession of the ball. No. 1, after executing a screen on X1, also breaks down court for a possible outlet pass deep down and to the side of the court. He may also furnish the outlet pass for No. 5 if he is free to receive a long pass down the side of the court in this particular area. No. 2 breaks fast and hard down the left side of the court and in the outside lane. Meanwhile, No. 4 immediately breaks for the center court area, at which point he may either hook back for a possible outlet pass from No. 5 or continue on down the court in the center lane. This would set up a three-lane fast break pattern.

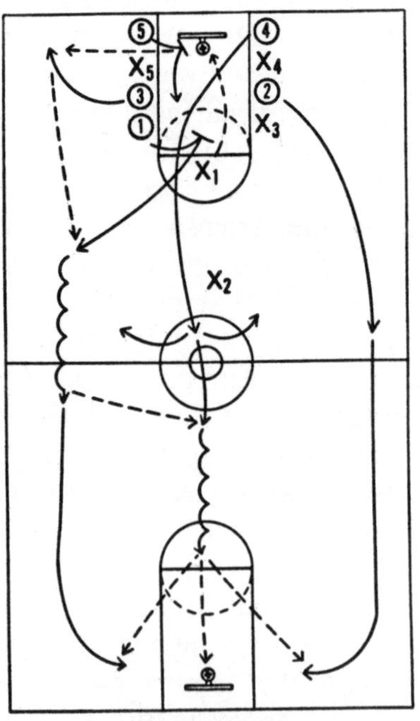

Diagram 8-13

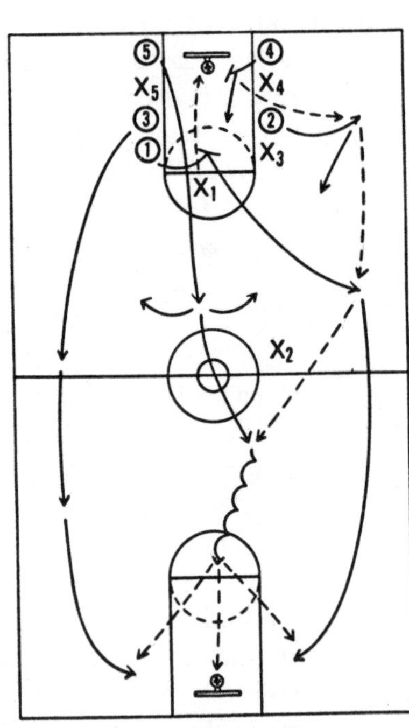

Diagram 8-14

Diagram 8-14. If No. 4 should secure the rebound from the free throw missed by X1, then the players would execute the movements as shown in Diagram 8-14. No. 2 moves to the side of the court in anticipation of receiving the outlet pass from No. 4. No. 1, after blocking out X1, then breaks wide down the court to receive the pass from No. 2. This means that No. 1 breaks to the left side of the court when the ball is rebounded on the same side. No. 3 breaks fast, hard and deep down the right side of the court. No. 5 breaks to the center of the court and either hooks back to help out with release passes if this move is needed, or continues on down the court on the fast break pattern if the ball has been passed to No. 1. Nos. 5, 3 and 1 are now positioned in a fast break pattern which develops into scoring opportunities. Nos. 2 and 4 follow the play.

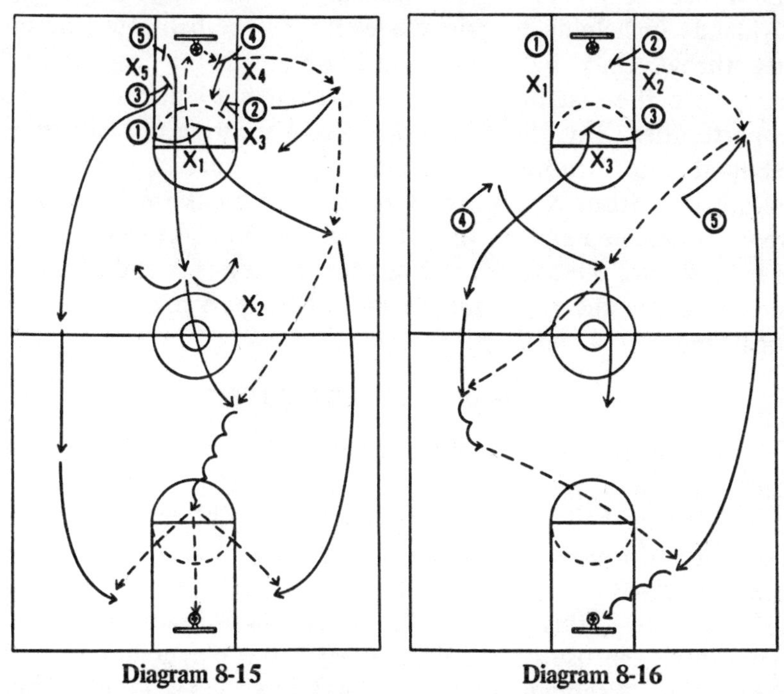

Diagram 8-15 Diagram 8-16

Diagram 8-15. To be more defensive minded, and to be sure of getting control of the ball, the defensive team should position all five of their players on the free throw lane when the opponents are at the free throw line. They take the positions shown in Diagram 8-15. By practicing this particular play, the players will become very proficient at blocking out their opponents along the free throw lane. The diagram shows Nos. 4 and 5 positioned in the lane spaces adjacent to the end line. The next spaces are occupied by X5 (the opponent's center) and X4, a forward. No. 1 is assigned to block out X1, the free thrower, after he has taken his shot. Nos. 5 and 3 concentrate on blocking out X5. To do this, No. 5, at the appropriate time, steps with his right foot at an angle across the lane so as to block out X5. As No. 5 executes this move, No. 3 steps with his left foot at a similar angle into the lane, so as to completely block out or sandwich in X5, so that he is ineffective in securing any rebound from the missed free throw. Across the lane, Nos. 4 and 2 perform the same kind of a maneuver against X4. This limits his effectiveness and removes him from the play. No. 2 should also be able to block out X3 if necessary. Practice on blocking out the opponents will pay dividends in helping to gain possession of the ball after the missed free throw. Once ball possession is obtained, the team must then move into the fast break pattern of play that will result in scoring opportunities. This diagram shows No. 4 securing the ball from the rebound. No. 2 moves to the side of the court so as to receive a release pass from No. 4. No. 1 releases his block on X1 and moves down court deep and on the left side. No. 5 breaks to the middle of the court. No. 3 cuts hard and fast for the opposite end of the court, moving down the right outside lane. Nos. 1, 5 and 3 lead the fast break and Nos. 4 and 2 trail the play.

THE CROSS-OVER PATTERN

The three-lane fast break type of play from the missed free throw, as stated previously, is by far the most popular method used in moving the ball quickly down court in present day basketball. The use of the dribble in this type of play, as well as in all phases of the game, is always controversial. Some coaches allow their players to dribble in using this type of play while others do not. Some coaches only allow the use of the dribble after the player has crossed the center line. Although most teams use three lanes in advancing the ball down the floor quickly after the missed free throw, the crossing type of play has recently gained favor. This type of maneuvering takes advantage of moving screens by having the players cross paths. The ball cannot be advanced as swiftly using this method of attack if one is to believe in the mathematical theory that the shortest distance between two points is a straight line. However, it does provide the advantage that accrues from screening, and the fact that the players are cutting across court instead of moving in a straight line makes it more difficult for the opposing players to guard them man-for-man. There is a tendency for the guards to "lose" the man they are guarding when the offensive player cuts behind a teammate. It is especially difficult for the defensive players to "cover them" when they are shorthanded, such as exists in a 2-on-1 or 3-on-2 situation. Many times in the guard's efforts to try and prevent a score on a 2-on-1 situation under the previously described circumstances, he may be forced into a situation where he may make a mistake, which will result in an easy lay-up for the opposition. As a result, he is forced to back-pedal, hoping in this way to force the opposition into attempting a shot from out court rather than giving them the easy lay-up.

The plays which are shown from this formation require very little dribbling, and the emphasis is placed on passing. Another important attribute that is absolutely necessary in determining the success of this type of play is timing. It is absolutely essential that each player be in the correct position at the proper time, so that there is no delay in passing the ball when the player in possession of it is ready to make the pass. This necessitates good teamwork on the part of each player as well as the ability to use good judgment and to think far enough ahead so that the play can be successful.

Diagram 8-16. This series shows a variety of plays whereby the ball is passed rather than dribbled, except when it may be necessary to do so. In some situations, it may be necessary to use the dribble to take advantage of a particular development that may come about as the result of a missed assignment, either defensively by the opposition or offensively by a teammate. In this play, No. 2 takes the rebound and passes immediately to No. 5. No. 2 attempts to make the pass while still in the air after taking the rebound (before his feet touch the floor). This is very difficult to accomplish but it will do much to make the play a success if it is done correctly. No. 5 fakes toward the basket and then moves out to the sideline and positions himself to receive the pass from No. 2. No. 4 also fakes toward the basket, but, as soon as he is sure that No. 2 has obtained possession of the ball from the rebound, he moves across the court to a position as shown in the diagram. No. 4 times his move so that he will be in this particular area at the time No. 5 is ready to make the pass to him. After receiving the pass from No. 5, No. 4 passes to No. 3, who is cutting down the right side of the court. No. 3 makes this move after having first stepped in front of the free thrower from his position along the free throw lane area. No. 3 now passes to No. 5, who, after having made the pass to No. 4, moves quickly down the left side of the court. No. 3 passes to No. 5 for the lay-up.

Diagram 8-17. This play shows the rebound being obtained by No. 1. By far the largest number of rebounds will be obtained by either No. 2 or 1 because of the advantageous position they have on either side of the free throw lane next to the basket, as provided for by the rules. The ball does not carom very far away from the basket on the missed free throw like it does on the missed basket attempt. The reason for this action taken by the ball is quite obvious. The ball is not coming from as great a distance most of the time on the attempted free throw as it is from the attempted shot from out court. As a consequence, the ball, after it strikes the rim, will fall to either side and close in to the basket, enabling the inside players to retrieve it. The ball is also thrown up at the basket when the free throw is being attempted with a softer touch, which in itself will be a big determining factor in how far out from the basket it will carom if the free throw is missed. This diagram shows No. 1 retrieving the rebound and passing quickly to No. 4, who has faked a move to the basket and then moved down court to a position where he can receive the pass. No. 5 moves quickly to a position near the center circle, at which point he receives a pass from No. 4. No. 2 moves out to the left side of the court as soon as he sees the pass being made to No. 4. He then moves quickly down the left side of the court toward the basket, where he receives the pass from No. 5 and goes in for the lay-up.

Diagram 8-18. Player No. 2 obtains the rebound in this play, which has four defensive players positioned along the free throw lane. Player No. 4 is stationed near the sideline and the center court line. No. 2 obtains the rebound and makes the out pass to No. 3 as quickly as possible. In order to receive the pass from No. 2, No. 3 moves out to the side of the court, as shown in the diagram. His position will depend upon how quickly No. 2 is able to pass the ball to him. If the pass from No. 2 is delayed, this may mean that he is able to move farther down court before the ball is passed to him.

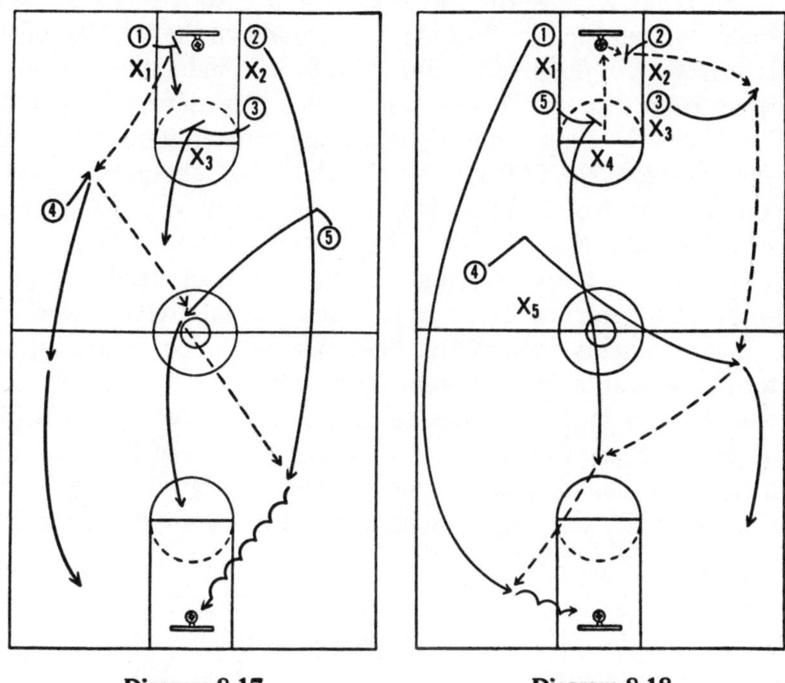

Diagram 8-17

Diagram 8-18

Upon seeing that No. 2 is about to make the pass to No. 3, No. 4 fakes toward the defensive basket and then cuts sharply across court to a position shown in the diagram. He must time his cut so that he arrives at this position at a time when No. 3 is ready to pass the ball to him. This also means that in the process of making this move, he must outmaneuver his guard so that this defensive player is not able to intercept the pass from No. 3. No. 5, who has stepped in front of the free thrower in the conventional manner to cut off the out rebound, breaks down the center of the court after No. 2 secures the rebound. At the same time, No. 1 cuts down the right side of the court. No. 4 passes the ball to No. 5 who can either go in for the lay-up, or if he is guarded, pass off to No. 1 breaking in from the right side.

Diagram 8-19. This play shows most of the player movements going to the right side of the court. The play then ends up with the pass, which results in the basket being made back to the left side of the court. The fact that the play is being concentrated to one side of the court will enable No. 2 to move swiftly down the left side of the court undetected. This will enable him to slip under the basket for the pass from No. 5. The success of this play depends upon the ability of No. 2 to move quickly down the court in time to be ready for the pass from No. 5. Player No. 1 obtains the rebound and makes the out pass to No. 4. This pass, as in all previous plays, must be executed quickly. No. 4 breaks toward the defensive basket to about midway between the center line and free throw circle and about 8 feet in from the sideline. No. 3 steps in front of the free thrower, and then breaks quickly toward the right side of the court to near the center line and about 6 feet from the sideline. No. 1 makes the pass to No. 4, who in turn passes to No. 3 at a point shown in the diagram. No. 5 moves over quickly to the right side of the court to a point midway between the center line and the top of the offensive free throw circle, and approximately 8 feet in from the sideline. No.

Diagram 8-19

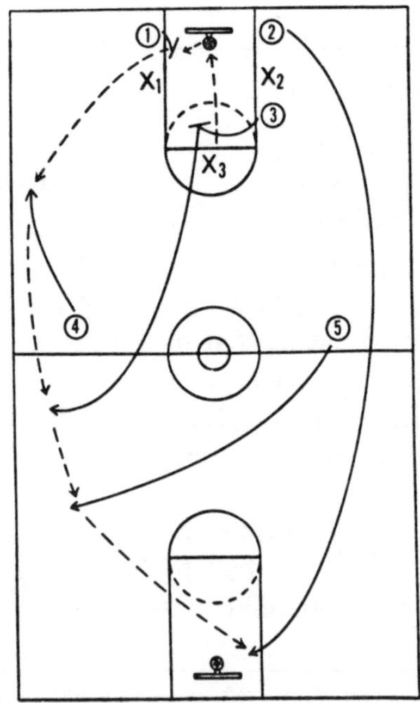

3 passes the ball to No. 5 at this point. No. 5 passes to No. 2, who by now should be in a position near the basket.

THE LONG PASS OR BUTTERFLY PATTERN

The long pass has always been an offensive weapon when used at the right time and under the proper circumstances. It cannot, however, be used constantly, because its success depends not only upon the element of surprise, but it must also be employed only under ideal conditions. When the play is successful, it almost always results in a sure basket. It therefore cannot be depended upon as a main offensive weapon. It can, however, be included in the team's repertoire of plays to be used for special situations, because if it is used correctly and at the right time, it will often provide the team with "the winning edge." An ideal time to use this type of play is after the missed free throw, particularly if the team attempting the free throw is behind and is attempting to gain possession of the ball by using pressing tactics. This type of situation presents an ideal opportunity for the use of the long pass type of play, because, after the missed free throw, every one of the defensive players is concentrating on getting the ball, thereby making it possible for an offensive player to slip unnoticed down court and station himself in a position to receive the long pass. The use of this play can be predetermined only to a certain extent, and, of course, it is the type of play that does not have to be carried out in its entirety if in the judgment of the passer it will not be successful. The passer, who in most cases is also the rebounder, should be able to determine at a glance whether or not it would be feasible to make the pass. If it is not, he should hold the ball and choose another method of advancing it down court and into the scoring area. This type of play can be used successfully several times during the game, and particularly near the end of the game. The play can be used from any of the aforementioned formations. The players responsible for making the decision as to its use will first of all be the out court player and second, the passer. These players must work together cooperatively or the play cannot succeed. The out court player must make the initial move down court, and there should be a predetermined agreement among all the players as to when this type of play is to be attempted and the circumstances and conditions which must exist before its use is contemplated.

Diagram 8-20. This series of plays shows different versions of how the long pass may be used to score the quick basket. It is very difficult, if not impossible, to predetermine the use of this type of play each time it is to be used. This diagram shows the usual player alignment for the free throw attempt. Player No. 1 obtains the rebound and makes the out pass to No. 4. In order to receive the pass, No. 4 breaks in toward the basket and then out toward the side of the court to position himself to receive the pass. No. 5 has already decided that, because of the position of the opponents, he can slip behind them and be in a good position to use the long pass play. No. 5 will be the player to make this decision, and the area in which he will receive the pass will depend on the position of the opponents at the time and No. 4's ability to make the pass successfully. In making the pass, No. 4 will need to use a baseball type of pass and lob the ball high enough so that it will clear the defensive players. No. 4 can, if he is not able to make the pass immediately, maneuver for a very brief period of time in order to free himsef to make the pass. If he does this, he will need to decide whether to make the pass based on the fact that No. 5 may not be open because of the delay. No. 5 may then move toward the sideline in order to be in a better position himself for the pass, and then attempt to outmaneuver the guard who is covering him on a 1-on-1 basis.

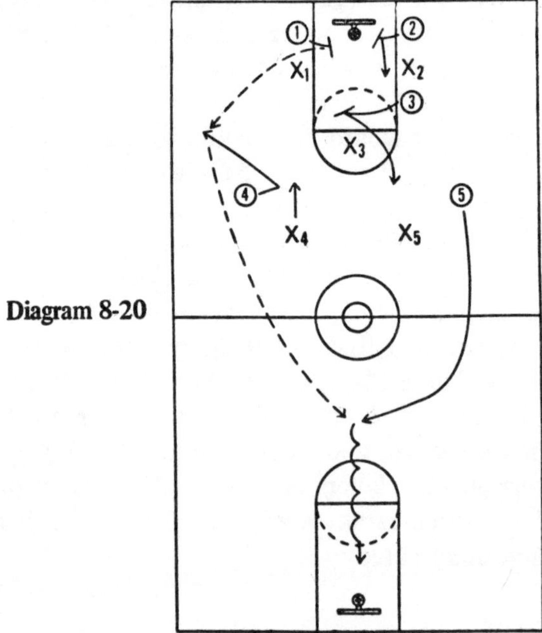

Diagram 8-20

Diagram 8-21. The alignment of the players in this play places four defensive players on the free throw lane, with player No. 5 stationed out court. It is a long pass play that will materialize only if conditions exist which are conducive to the use of such a play. These conditions will be determined at the time the play is to be used, and cannot be predetermined. Player No. 5 must decide whether he is going to be able to move down court quickly without being detected by the opposition. If the conditions are not conducive to the use of this play, it should not be used because the pass can easily be intercepted. On the other hand, if the pass can be made successfully, the play can result in a sure basket. Player No. 1 obtains the rebound and immediately looks down court for the long pass opportunity. If No. 1 is able to turn and make the long pass to No. 5 down court, he should do so. If he cannot make the pass immediately, he can dribble away from the congested area and still make the pass. No. 1 will need to size up the situation and make the decision as to whether he should or should not make the pass. The success of this play will depend upon whether the opposition is in a position where it is difficult to defend against the long pass. This often happens when the opposition is attempting to score and has all their players near the offensive basket. This play not only is a potential scoring threat

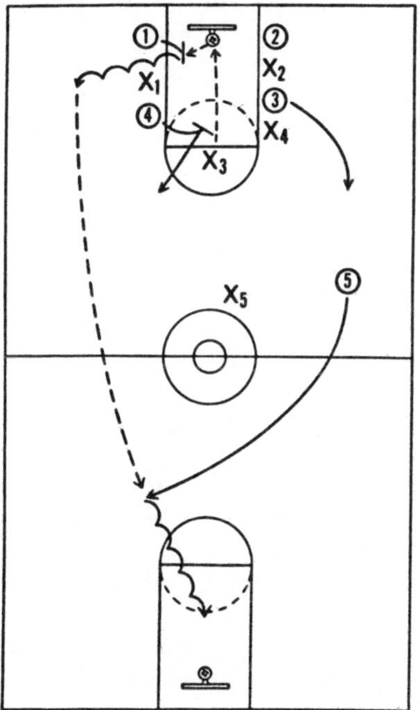

Diagram 8-21

but also it tends to make the opposition honest. They must keep players back on defense to guard against this type of play.

Diagram 8-22. This type of long pass play is somewhat different than the two previous plays, in that the pass is relayed down the floor instead of using the long pass. The ball can, however, be moved quickly down court using the method shown in the diagram, even though there may be a slight delay each time it is handled. Player No. 1 obtains the rebound and attempts to make the out pass while he is still in the air to No. 4. This is important because if the play is to accomplish its purpose, the out pass must be executed quickly. If there is too much of a delay, it will give the opposing guards an opportunity to get back on defense and thereby nullify the long pass attempt, which is the primary purpose of the play. No. 4 passes to No. 5 as soon as he is able to do so after receiving the pass from No. 1. No. 5 is stationed directly in the center of the court, where he can move in any direction. No. 5 times his move so that he will be in a

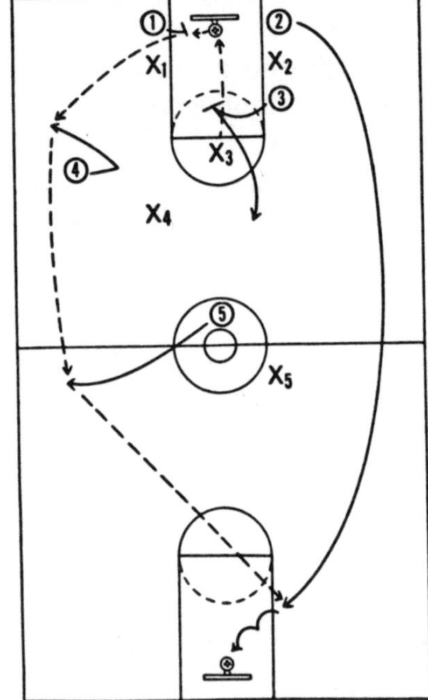

Diagram 8-22

position to receive the pass from No. 4 at the exact instant that No. 4 is ready to make the pass. No. 2 leaves his position as soon as he sees No. 1 obtain the rebound and breaks down the left sideline toward the offensive basket. No. 5 passes the ball to No. 2.

A Final Word from the Authors

Certainly, all the plays which can be used for special situations in basketball have not been discussed in this book. In fact, the book has just touched on the many that are available and in use today by basketball coaches throughout the country. It has, however, provided the reader with a wide variety of special situation plays that can be added to and applied to the many special situations that occur frequently in every basketball game that is played. The ones that have been discussed can serve as a basis and a nucleus for others that the coach himself can devise. These plays will be appropriate for use by his particular players and will be those which will exactly fit a particular situation and demand a specific plan of action. The coach, more than anyone else, knows the capabilities of his players and their individual abilities to adjust to changing situations. His own ability to use his knowledge to select, develop and apply these plays to a specific situation will be a determining factor in their success. However, it should always be remembered that in the last analysis, *players*—not *plays*—win the game.

Basketball has undergone many changes throughout the years. Perhaps one of the reasons the game has become so popular is because it has kept abreast of the times. These changes have been the result of the men associated with the game having great foresight and being willing to accept change. As a result basketball has had the benefit of both individual and group thinking, and this in itself has brought about improvements and changes over these many years. The men who have been most instrumental in making these changes have not always been the rulemakers, although in many cases this was and still is true. Many of the changes, however, have been brought about by coaches. Their study of the game has resulted in the use of techniques and strategy, the results of which forced changes in the rules in order to equalize offensive and defensive tactics, and to prevent unusual circumstances and conditions which would diminish spectator as well as player interest and appeal. Coaches have and still are striving to perfect these techniques of coaching so that their teams may reap the benefits of their knowledge and understanding of the game.

Basketball coaching no longer consists of throwing out the ball and choosing up sides for a scrimmage. Basketball is a scientific, complicated and demanding game, in which players who have had the advantage of receiving expert coaching and conditioning guidance from coaches who have studied and understand the game, are pitted against each other in competition in games throughout the world.

Modern day basketball demands an all out effort by both coaches and players if they are to be successful. The abilities of the top teams and coaches are so nearly equal that one successful play or strategic move can spell the difference between winning and losing. It is not only important and necessary but also absolutely imperative that teams be prepared to cope with every special situation which may occur during the course of the game. This can be accomplished by using special plays. The knowledge of and ability to know when and where to use these plays, provides the team with a distinct advantage in its efforts to obtain "the winning edge." The game of basketball has become so specialized in recent years that the coach and player who understand the game better than their opponents have a better chance to win, other things being equal.

While coaching clinics, schools and written material provide information which is easily assimilated by coaches and players alike, still the coach needs to apply this knowledge, keeping in mind the abilities of his players, in such a way that it will produce the desired results. If he is to be successful in the won and lost column and a leader in his field, he needs to do more than this. He not only needs to use the information at hand and immediately available, but also he needs to experiment with and research the possibilities which exist, the result of which will give his players the advantage needed to win.

The successful coach can no longer neglect or ignore the fact that he not only needs to teach his players the necessary fundamentals of the game and how to play it, but he also must teach them the strategy and "*know-how*" which will allow them to meet and defeat every effort of the opposition to confuse and bewilder them by the use of special situations and tactics. To do this, he must prepare and avail himself with the information and knowledge necessary to do the job. The coach who does not use his knowledge and ingenuity cannot expect to keep abreast of the game. As a result, he cannot compete on an equal basis with the coach who does. If he does not use and apply his knowledge of the game in an effort to bring about something new, innovative and useful, which in turn will provide his players with the know-how to meet these special situations successfully, he cannot be successful in terms of winning and losing.

While the material presented in this book is not all inclusive as far as presenting plays, strategies and tactics which meet every special situation in basketball, it is hoped that it will stimulate the thinking of coaches and players alike in their own efforts to provide their players with plays which will give them "the winning edge."

Index

P